The Hispanic Child

The Hispanic Child

Speech, Language, Culture and Education

Alejandro E. Brice

University of Central Florida

Allyn and Bacon

Boston • *London* • *Toronto* • *Sydney* • *Tokyo* • *Singapore*

Executive Editor and Publisher: *Stephen D. Dragin*
Editorial Assistant: *Barbara Strickland*
Production Administrator: *Gordon Laws*
Editorial-Production Service: *Modern Graphics*
Composition Buyer: *Linda Cox*
Manufacturing Buyer: *Chris Marson*
Cover Administrator: *Kristina Mose-Libon*

Library of Congress Cataloging-in-Publication Data

Brice, Alejandro E.
    The Hispanic child : speech, language, culture, and education / Alejandro
E. Brice.
        p. cm.
    Includes bibliographical references and index.
    ISBN 0-205-29530-4
    1. Hispanic American children—Education. 2. Language arts—United
States. 3. Hispanic American children—Social conditions. 4. Education,
Bilingual—United States.
    I. Title.
    LC2672.4 .B75 2002
    371.829'68073—dc21
                             2001035533

05 04 03 02 01   10 9 8 7 6 5 4 3 2 1

Dedication
This book is dedicated to my parents, Arturo and Ofelia Brice, who believed in my ability to succeed and gave me the confidence and self-esteem in order to do so. Without their love and support I would not have been able to reach the professional heights I have and been able to give back to Latino children. Thank you for being the wonderful parents you have been. Con cariño siempre, Su hijo, Alejandro.

Contents

Preface

This book has been a three-year project with a lifetime history behind it. I, personally, experienced the "sink or swim" method of bilingual education. In 1965, there were no bilingual education programs in place for young, Spanish–English learning, Cuban American children. I was able to survive schooling and go on to complete a Ph.D. However, there were many struggles along the way. There continue to be struggles for myself and for young Hispanic and Latino children in schools today. Other multicultural books or books dealing with Hispanic issues do not address issues of school-age children specifically. Hence, the birth of this book. One of the reviewers for this book graciously stated that this book is a comprehensive volume, including information not addressed elsewhere. I and the contributing authors (Raquel Anderson, Carolyn Conway Madding, and Celeste Roseberry-McKibbin) have attempted to include information that is applicable in the form of Best Practice suggestions and through real experiences. In addition, we have attempted to include current information and content-rich information.

Chapter 1 includes information on demographic changes, access to health care, attitudes of Hispanics in the United States, and school and classroom needs of Hispanic students. It sets the tone for classroom issues. Although this book is geared towards speech–language pathologists, it is also readable by English as second language teachers, special educators, general classroom teachers, and school psychologists.

Chapter 2 addresses immigration issues and legislation and litigation issues that have impacted the way we deliver services to children in school, i.e., bilingual and monolingual students seen for speech and language services. Chapter 3 discusses the Spanish language. Although Hispanics are united by a common language, there exist many dialects of Spanish and many cultural differences among all Hispanics and Latinos in the United States. Issues of religion and family values affect the Spanish language. Language considerations for SLPs are given in a review of Spanish phonetics, phonology, morphology, and syntax. Chapter 4 reviews some second language acquisition issues. Myths about bilingual students along with a talk about similarities and differences in first and second language acquisition are given.

Chapter 5 offers information on distinguishing a difference from a disorder, a common dilemma facing many SLPs in schools today. Chapter 6, "Socialization Practices of Latinos," is a contributed chapter from Carolyn Conway Madding.

Chapter 7 delves into the clinician becoming a qualitative researcher. The issues of why research is needed and how it can be implemented are covered.

Chapter 8 provides the SLP with information regarding the importance of classroom pragmatics to academic success. Student and teacher pragmatics for bilingual Latino students are covered. Chapter 9 continues with this theme and looks at pragmatics from a summative research paradigm, that is, a meta approach to ethnography.

Chapter 10 is a contributed chapter from Raquel Anderson that deals with practical assessment strategies with Hispanic students. She illustrates this discussion with two case studies. Chapter 11 reviews use of the World Wide Web and lists 39 practical and applied sites. Chapter 12, the final chapter, is a contributed chapter from Celeste Roseberry-McKibbin, "Principles and Strategies in Intervention."

In sum, this book is meant to be comprehensive, yet not all-inclusive. We know that we have only briefly touched on the many topics affecting bilingual Hispanic children in U.S. schools. As we enter the new century, we hope that all clinicians will understand their bilingual caseload, provide appropriate services, and approach all their interactions with their bilingual students in an informed and compassionate manner.

I would like to acknowledge the hard work and contributions from the authors, Dr. Raquel Anderson, Dr. Carolyn Conway Madding, and Dr. Celeste Roseberry-McKibbin. I sincerely believe that their chapters truly make this work and book much richer and beneficial for all speech and language clinicians. I also acknowledge the following reviewers for their comments and suggestions: Raquel Anderson, Indiana University—Bloomington; Aquiles Iglesias, Temple University; Carolyn Conway Madding, California State University—Long Beach; Elizabeth Peña, University of Texas—Austin; Rosemary Quinn, San José State University; Terry I. Saenz, California State University—Fullerton. Thank you.

Introduction

As the Hispanic population of the United States continues to increase dramatically, speech–language pathologists (SLPs) repeatedly face the challenge of how best to provide educational services for those whose primary language is Spanish. As of 1999, thirty-two million individuals identified themselves as being Hispanic (U.S. Bureau of the Census, 1999). Communication is a major barrier for many Hispanic students. For culturally and linguistically diverse (CLD) Hispanic school-aged students, the problems with communication are acute due to the language and contextual demands placed on them by the school and academic environment. By the time children reach school, they should exhibit a wide range of language abilities that are critical to their school success. In this book, I and the other authors will discuss factors that should be considered in making programmatic decisions for Hispanic students. Although the focus of this book is on Hispanic students, the fastest-growing non-English-speaking population in the United States, the information presented here is relevant to other culturally and linguistically diverse students whose first language is not English.

Demographic Changes

A multicultural group that is becoming the largest in the United States is the Hispanic or Latino population. Both *Hispanic* and *Latino* will be used here to refer to all native Spanish-speaking and Spanish-descent individuals who reside in the United States. According to the 1990 census, Hispanics comprise twenty-eight million people, or over 10% of the U.S. population. The 1990 census data (Current Population Reports,1990), states that 12.1% of the U.S. population defines itself as African American, 9.0% as Hispanic, and 7.7% as another cultural background. Campbell (1996) stated:

> The Hispanic origin population is projected to increase rapidly over the 1995 to 2025 projection period, accounting for 44 percent of the growth in the Nation's population (32 million Hispanics out of a total of 72 million persons added to the Nation's population). The Hispanic origin population is the second fastest-growing population, after Asians, in every region over the 30 year period (p. 2).

Campbell (1996) also stated that, in 1995, 74% of Hispanics resided in the following five states: California, Texas, New York, Florida, and Illinois. California, with 9 million Hispanics, has the largest share of the Hispanic population, followed by Texas, New York, Florida, and Illinois. California's Hispanic population should double over the 1995 to 2025 period (21 million, which should represent 36% of the total Hispanic population in the year 2025). Texas will remain in second place with 17% of the Hispanic population in 2025; New York is expected to decline from 9 to 6%. Florida is expected to switch from fourth to third place. Illinois will remain the same, in fifth place.

Overall, 87% of the Hispanic population in the United States is concentrated in 10 states: California (34.4%), Texas (19.4%), New York (9.9%), Florida (7%), Illinois (4%), New Jersey (3.3%), Arizona (3.1%), New Mexico (2.6%), Colorado (1.9%), and Massachusetts (1.3%).

Access to Health Care

There are numerous implications, for speech–language pathologists, regarding inadequate provision of health care, although it is important not to overgeneralize these findings to all Hispanic cultures, students, or families. Hispanic children who are frequently sick and don't get medical care are absent from school more, thus missing academic information. As of 1997, only 71.4% of Hispanics had health insurance coverage compared to 85% of the general U.S. population (U.S. Bureau of the Census, 1997). When they do attend school, these Hispanic children may be unable to fully concentrate and participate in school activities. Second, children who do not see doctors frequently have ear infections that go untreated. This can be of great detriment to auditory discrimination and overall auditory processing skills, language development, and articulatory–phonological skills as well as general attention skills. Finally, children who do not get dental care may have dental/orthodontic conditions that preclude successful speech therapy.

Hispanic women from low Socioeconomic Status backgrounds tend to get woefully inadequate prenatal care. Low SES women from multicultural backgrounds are particularly vulnerable. For example, excluding Cubans, only 60% of Hispanic women have prenatal care in the first trimester as opposed to 80% of European Americans (Council Report on Scientific Affairs, 1991). Not only are pregnant low-income women malnourished, their children tend to grow up malnourished. According to Brown and Pollitt (1996), it is estimated that 12 million American children have diets that are significantly below the recommended allowances of nutrients established by the National Academy of Sciences. Malnutrition and disrupted cognitive performance are now being linked; Brown and Pollitt state that childhood malnutrition produces permanent, structural damage to the brain. Between birth and two years of age, the brain grows to approximately 80% of its adult size; malnutrition during this period is especially devastating to cognitive growth. This devastation occurs partially because malnourished small children frequently crawl and walk slightly later than average, which limits their exploration of their social and physical environments. Negative effects are also due to illness, inadequate brain growth and delayed intellectual development, and lethargy and withdrawal (Brown & Pollitt, 1996).

Thus, the quality of health care is affected by the socioeconomic status of the individuals. Of particular interest is their level of educational achievement, occupational achievement, and income (Ginzberg, 1991; Kirkman-Liff & Mondragón, 1991). Kirkman-Liff and Mondragón (1991) state that "the most dominant contextual variables for health, level of income and *education* [emphasis mine] are lowest in the nation [for Hispanics]" (p. 1399). Kirkman-Liff and Mondragón (1991) also found that 34% of the variance in wages between Mexican-descent men in Arizona and other non-Hispanic men was attributed to levels of education.

Access to health care is directly related to educational achievement; therefore, its discussion here is relevant to the school achievement of Hispanic students (Kirkman-Liff & Mondragón, 1991; Roseberry-McKibbin & Brice, 1998). There is a large gap between the level of educational achievement of Hispanics in the United States and that of non-Hispanics (i.e., European Americans). For example, 9% of Mexican Americans are still employed in farming (Ginzberg, 1991). Unfortunately, a large percentage of Hispanics and other minorities are still employed in low-wage sectors where employers fail to provide health insurance benefits. Becerra and Shaw (1984) indicated that Hispanics (other than Cubans) have a younger age profile than the at-large population, which translates into an increased need and reduced use of health care. The younger population is more susceptible to poor pregnancy outcomes, poor growth and development of children, drug use, and HIV/AIDS and other infectious diseases (Roseberry-McKibbin, 1995). A large percentage of resources is directed toward use of emergency hospital admissions. Continuity of care is typically low. The high birthrate of Mexican Americans indicates a greater need for prenatal and postnatal care for women and children. Another health problem facing Mexican American and Puerto Rican populations is a higher incidence of type II diabetes as compared to other population groups (Council Report on Scientific Affairs, 1991; Schur, Bernstein, & Berk, 1987).

Access to adequate health care is also hampered by the lack of health care professionals who are minorities. Deal-Williams (personal communication, December 7, 1999) stated that the American Speech-Language-Hearing Association has numbers for Hispanics and numbers for bilingual individuals but not for both. As of June, 1999, there were 1,507 Hispanic certified SLPs and 16 who were dual certified in audiology within the American Speech-Language-Hearing Association, a professional association of more than 90,000 members. Equally disturbing, less than 5% of U.S. physicians and students are Hispanic (Council Report on Scientific Affairs, 1991). Byrd and Thomas (1993) stated that "the nursing profession needs to set as a priority the goal of attracting an increased number of minorities to the profession" (p. 26). Thus, it is apparent that there is a lack of qualified Hispanic health care professionals, in particular speech–language pathologists. The training of culturally diverse health care professionals is a priority in order to serve the growing, culturally diverse Hispanic population in the United States.

As of 1990, 17 million persons spoke Spanish in the home (U.S. Bureau of the Census, 1990). Language can be a barrier to access for many Hispanic patients; Hispanic patients who speak English are more likely to have a regular source of medical care compared to those who just speak Spanish (Kirkman-Liff & Mondragón, 1991). Kirkman-Liff and Mondragón (1991) found in a survey that "Hispanics who were interviewed in Spanish have lower health status" and worse access to care than Hispanics who were interviewed in English" (p. 1401). This same conclusion also applies to the children of parents who speak only Spanish and those who also speak English. Language also exacerbates difficulties associated with adapting to life in the United States in old age because Hispanics are less likely to know about and use health and social programs for the elderly (Szapocznik, Scopetta, Kurtines, & Arnalde, 1978). Thus, not speaking English can and does impact upon receipt of health care for all family members.

Access to health care by Hispanics is also affected by perceived health care needs and insurance status as well as culture, language, and other factors (Council Report on Scientific Affairs, 1991). Mexican Americans have the least insurance and visit physicians least often. Puerto Ricans have the highest physician-visit rates. Only 60% of Hispanics (excluding Cubans) initiate prenatal care in the first trimester compared with 80% of European Americans (Council Report on Scientific Affairs, 1991).

Of the three major subgroups of Hispanics, Puerto Ricans have the worst health care status (worse than Mexican Americans and Cuban Amer-

TABLE 1.1 *Hispanics Aged 45 to 74 with Diabetes*

Puerto Ricans	26.1%
Mexican Americans	23.9%
Cuban Americans	15.8%

TABLE 1.2 *Hispanics Who Smoke*

Mexican Americans	43.6%
Cuban Americans	41.8%
Puerto Ricans	41.3%

icans). Compared with European Americans, Hispanics have three times the risk of diabetes (obesity and diet are highly correlated to diabetes) (Council Report on Scientific Affairs, 1991). Table 1.1 lists the percent of those Hispanics by cultural group with diabetes. Almost half of the Puerto Rican survey respondents had hypertension yet were unaware of it (Council Report on Scientific Affairs, 1991) (see Table 1.2). Smoking is known to contribute to hypertension.

Hispanics in general are about as likely as the overall general U.S. population to identify a place they go to for medical care. Hispanics are, however, less likely to identify a physician's office as their primary care site. Puerto Ricans (49%) are least likely to identify the physician's office as their primary care site or usual medical care facility (Council Report on Scientific Affairs, 1991). Figure 1.1 shows the percentage of health insurance and Medicaid coverage among African Americans and Hispanics (Council Report on Scientific Affairs, 1991).

Attitudes of Hispanics in the United States

Mexican Americans are taught that enduring sickness is a sign of strength (Schur et al., 1988). Mexican Americans also tend to rely on home remedies and care by other family members. Cultural values are reflected in health care, and the implications for speech–language pathologists are unavoidable, yet, at times, not obvious. Table 1.3 offers values and implications for working with Hispanic clients with particular cultural values that may differ from those of the speech–language clinician (Ponchilla, 1993).

Schooling and Hispanic Students

Levine and Padilla (1980) indicated that Hispanics generally find a lack of understanding of their values and culture by the school counselor. This finding is most likely applicable to Hispanics and speech and language services provided in schools. Awareness of some Hispanic values may assist SLPs, teachers, or other educational professionals, and the following are some general guidelines. One should use caution with these guidelines, however, and not overgeneralize.

1. Some Hispanics may prefer to organize into extended family support systems.
2. Some Hispanics may tend to be more present-oriented. Immediate reinforcement may have to be built into individualized education plans.
3. Some Hispanics may come to seek help only when they perceive the situation to be in a crisis. Control over the immediate environment may not be perceived as strongly (i.e., an external locus of control is displayed) as with European Americans (Levine & Padilla, 1980; Queralt, 1984).
4. Use of the Spanish language is an important social tool (Garcia & Lega, 1979).
5. To be *simpático* (charming) is important as is the use of *tener sentido de humor* (to be humorous) (Queralt, 1984). To be judged *pesado* (disagreeable) is a cultural sin (Queralt, 1984).

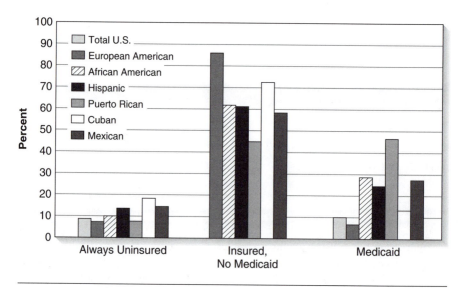

FIGURE 1.1   *Insurance and Medicaid Coverage among European Americans, African Americans, and Hispanics*

TABLE 1.3   *Cultural Values and Implications for Health Care and Educational Professionals in Serving Hispanics*

Values	Implications
Respect elders, experts, those with curing powers (e.g., *curanderos, santeros*).	Recognize elders, greet the family and community elders.
Circularness, wholeness.	Work with the student and her/his family in a team effort.
Silence is valued.	Listen. Wait for answers. Do not offer immediate answers; ponder before responding. Be comfortable with silence.
Privacy for personal matters.	Do not start to ask questions; tell why you are asking and why the information is important.
Congeniality, graciousness is cherished.	When food and drink are offered accept the hospitality.
Accept what is. Health problems are the result of past behaviors.	Preventative health care is not seen as important; the value of prevention may take time to teach.
Modesty and reluctance to show pain, suffering, signs of illness.	A heightened awareness of comfort levels for students is indicated.
Illness is supernatural.	Give anatomic and physical descriptions for illnesses; work with traditional practies.
Negative thoughts or actions may cause it to occur.	Cautionary statements should be stated in the positive.
Time is viewed differently.	Family events take precedence over appointments with SLPs, teachers. Appointments need to be flexible.
Belief in traditional healers, *curanderos, santeros,* folk medicines.	Incorporate traditional beliefs whenever possible.
Healers give tangible objects.	Leave something at the end of a meeting—for example, a pamphlet, a small toy for motor and cognitive stimulation.

6. Hispanics may fall into more of a "being" orientation, that is, giving more importance to activities involving spontaneity than European Americans. European Americans fit more into a "doing" orientation, where the primary emphasis is on work, competition, and achievement (Queralt, 1984). Queralt maintained that "it should be understood, however, that 'doing' or 'being' orientations have little to do with activity level..." (Queralt, 1984, p. 118).

7. Hispanic males may tend to display *machismo* or display very traditional role manners of interaction. Traditionally, Hispanic males may perceive their role in the household as one of provider and disciplinarian. The sharing of roles and flexibility in roles is definitively not *machismo*. It should be noted that the Hispanic mother's devotion to her children is compensatory, not dysfunctional. Because the mothers may get less attention from their husbands, they may focus or concentrate more of their energies on their children. Child-rearing practices are thus influenced by *machismo* and the particular structure of Hispanic families.

Needs of Hispanic Students

The emotional and social needs of the Hispanic student may vary depending on the degree of Latino identity that the student holds. However, most parents and students will be compliant with the education system. Parent participation may vary. Active participation of the parents assisting with homework lessons varies with the degree of understanding of the U.S. school system and the English language.

Education will be supported by most families because most Hispanics believe in the value of education as a means of advancing oneself (Ogbu & Matute-Bianchi, 1986). Speech–language pathologists, teachers, and educational professionals may expect that their Hispanic students will display varying degrees of English-language proficiency, which will depend on the degree that English fluency is valued in the home. Some first- and second-generation students may display some limited English skills because of limited exposure to and practice of English in school and in the home.

Classroom Implications

Generally speaking, one can assume that most Hispanics will initially benefit from activities that involve the group rather than the individual. Also, most Hispanics will use Spanish as another language. The parents are likely to speak Spanish in the home. Because language is a reflection of culture, it would be advisable to maintain the home language as a means of maintaining active communication with the parents and as a means of keeping the Latino culture alive. As a consequence, attempts to maintain the Spanish language will be a benefit to the child's educational success. The following points for making learning an additive process have been adapted from Hamayan (1992) and Wong-Fillmore (1992):

1. SLPs and teachers should make learning English in the classroom and in social contexts a positive experience in which both Spanish and English are valued. This may be accomplished by infusing cultural in-

formation at different levels. At the first level, surface cultural features may be introduced, e.g., holidays. At the next level teachers may add cultural themes to the classwork. Infusion of cultural bits of information across all lessons may be the next stage. This is followed by changing the way lessons are provided; for example, making the lesson more group-oriented, which is typical of how many Hispanic students problem solve. High-level thinking should be involved in most tasks. The children should be encouraged to participate in problem-solving tasks. SLPs should verbalize how they solve problems to provide a cognitive model.

2. Bilingualism should be promoted in both the home and school. Children should be allowed to speak Spanish when it facilitates their communication (Brice & Perkins, 1997). The children's comfort level for using English should be allowed to mature and not be a forced issue.

3. Children should have well-developed Spanish skills before learning English.

4. Opportunities for reading and writing in both Spanish and English should be provided. Parents should be encouraged to read to their children in Spanish. Preliteracy skills, knowing about the written word and books, are generalizable across languages. An appreciation of books is not specific to English or North America.

5. Ample opportunities to interact with native Spanish speakers—that is, other Hispanics—should be provided.

6. The children should receive appropriate instruction in English. Learning English should reflect natural language usage.

7. The children should be allowed to make errors in English. They should also be allowed to demonstrate their knowledge in nonverbal ways, as is typical of many second-language learners.

Conclusions

Hispanics in the United States consist of many different Hispanic subcultures—Mexican American, Puerto Rican, Cuban American, Central American, and South American. Although most Hispanics may share Spanish as a common language, each nationality has its own distinct customs, dialect, and ways of interacting. Among the Hispanics in the United States, Mexican Americans are the largest Hispanic group, followed by Puerto Ricans and Cuban Americans (U.S. Bureau of the Census, 1992). Hispanics primarily reside in California, Texas, New York, Florida, and Illinois. Most Hispanics will continue to speak Spanish as a tie to the Latino culture and are proud to be Hispanic. Although their means of learning will be different, SLPs, teachers, and others will find working with Hispanics to be an enriching experience.

Focus of This Book

The central theme of this book is to discuss language and school issues of Hispanic students for speech–language pathologists, including issues for monolingual and bilingual (i.e., Spanish–English-speaking) clinicians. These issues will be highlighted and accentuated through case studies and best practices for school-based speech–language pathologists. Topics to be covered include the following: (a) changes in U.S. schools, (b) heterogeneity of the Hispanic/Latino populations, (c) second-language acquisition, (d) distinguishing a difference from a disorder, (e) socialization practices of Latinos, (f) qualitative research, (g) pragmatics research from bilingual classrooms, (h) a meta-ethnography of qualitative research, (i) practical assessment strategies with Latino students, and (j) use of the World Wide Web for professional education appropriate for bilingual students.

References

Becerra, R., & Shaw, D. (1984). *The Hispanic elderly.* Lanham, MD: University Press of America.

Brice, A., & Perkins, C. (1997). What is required for transition from the ESL classroom to the general education classroom? A case study of two classrooms. *Journal of Children's Communication Development, 19*(1), 13–22.

Brown, J. L., & Pollitt, E. (1996). Malnutrition, poverty, and intellectual development. *Scientific American, 96*(2), 38–44.

Byrd, C., & Thomas, M. J. (1993). Minorities in nursing. *Journal of College Admissions, 141,* 26–28.

Campbell, P. R. (1996). *Population Projections for States by Age, Sex, Race, and Hispanic Origin: 1995 to 2025.* Washington, DC: U.S. Bureau of the Census, Population Division, PPL-47.

Canfield, D. L. (1981). *Spanish pronunciation in the Americas.* Chicago, IL: The University of Chicago Press.

Council Report on Scientific Affairs, American Medical Association (1991). Hispanic health in the United States. *Journal of the American Medical Association, 265*(2), 248–252.

Current Population Reports. (1990). *The Hispanic population in the United States: March 1990.* Washington, DC: Bureau of the Census.

Garcia, M., & Lega, L. (1979). Development of a Cuban ethnic identity questionnaire. *Hispanic Journal of Behavioral Sciences 1*(3), 247–261.

Ginzberg, E. (1991). Access to health care for Hispanics. *JAMA, 265*(2), 238–241.

Hamayan, E. (1992). *Meeting the challenge of cultural and linguistic diversity in the schools: Best practices in language intervention.* Paper presented at the Broward County Exceptional Student Education Inservice, Ft. Lauderdale, FL.

Kayser, H. (1995). *Bilingual speech-language pathology. An Hispanic focus.* San Diego, CA: Singular Publishing.

Kirkman-Liff, B., & Mondragón, D. (1991). Language of interview: Relevance for research of southwest Hispanics. *American Journal of Public Health, 81*(11), 1399–1404.

Levine, E., & Padilla, A. (1980). *Crossing cultures in therapy: Pluralistic counseling for the Hispanic.* Monterey, CA: Brooks/Cole Publishing Company.

Ogbu, J., & Matute-Bianchi, M. (1986). Sociocultural contexts of language development. *Beyond language: Social and cultural factors in schooling language minority students.* Los Angeles, CA: Evaluation, Dissemination, and Assessment Center.

Ponchillia, S. V. (1993). The effect of cultural beliefs on the treatment of native peoples with diabetes and visual impairment. *Journal of Visual Impairment and Blindness, 87*(9), 333–335.

Queralt, M. (1984). Understanding Cuban immigrants: A cultural perspective. *Social Work Journal, 29,* 115–121.

Roseberry-McKibbin, C., & Brice, A. (1998, November). *Service delivery issues. Serving clients from low income backgrounds.* Paper presented at the American Speech-Language-Hearing Association Annual Convention, San Antonio, TX.

Roseberry-McKibbin, C. (1995). *Multicultural students with special language needs.* Oceanside, CA: Academic Communication Associates.

Schur, C., Bernstein, A., & Berk, M. (1987). The importance of distinguishing Hispanic sub-populations in the use of medical care. *Medical Care, 25,* 627–641.

Szapocznik, J., Falleti, M., & Scopetta, M., (1977). *Psychological social issues of Cuban elders in Miami.* Miami, FL: Spanish Family Guidance Clinic and Institute for the Study of Aging.

Szapocznik, J., Scopetta, M., Kurtines, W., & Arnalde, M. (1978). Theory and measurement of acculturation. *InterAmerican Journal of Psychology, 12,* 113–130.

U.S. Bureau of the Census. (1999). *Population estimates program. Population division.* Washington, DC: Author.

U.S. Bureau of the Census. (1997). *Health insurance coverage: 1997. Population division.* Washington, DC: Author.

U.S. Bureau of the Census. (1990). *Education and social stratification branch. Population division.* Washington, DC: Author.

Wong-Fillmore, L.W. (1992). *When does 1+1 =<2?* Paper presented at Bilingualism/bilingüismo: A clinical forum, Miami, FL.

Changes in U.S. Schools

Immigration/Migration

There are multiple reasons that Hispanics continue to come to the United States, such as increased economic possibilities or the seeking of sanctuary for political reasons. Immigrants, by definition, migrate to another country for economic and social reasons, while refugees are typically viewed as political or social exiles or expatriates. The reason that Hispanics and Latinos come to this country may have to do with political ideology or to do with the poor economic situations in their home countries. This book will not delve into the reasons behind migration to the United States. However, a brief overview of the different types of immigration waves as they apply to political refugees (e.g., Cuban Americans and some Central Americans) will assist speech–language pathologists in working with some bilingual Hispanic children.

Immigration Waves

According to Stein (1981), the push-pull theory states that persons are pushed from an area because of negative factors and pulled to another area due to positive influences. The wave theory (as first applied by Stein, 1981) stated that people leaving their country at different times may have different characteristics. High-level government and military officials, the educated, and the urban elite are usually those who emigrate first (thus being first-wave immigrants). The second wave includes lower-level officials from the government and military, less-educated merchants, and those wishing to be reunited with those from the first wave. Third-wave immigrants include rural poor farmers and the least educated of the immigrants. These least-educated immigrants may have low levels of literacy in their own language and may be ill-equipped for formal schooling in an urban environment.

It is reported by Becerra and Shaw (1984) that "many Mexican Americans and Puerto Ricans return to their homelands in their late years while many Cuban Americans are political refugees and remain in the U.S." (p. 2). Refugees leave their homeland for political reasons and are usually not able to return.

Demographic Changes in U.S. Schools

According to the National Association of Bilingual Education (NABE) (as reported in Taylor, 1999), the number of bilingual students has grown at more than four times the rate for the overall school population. Enrollment of students in the United States from culturally and linguistically diverse backgrounds, particularly Hispanic students, has significantly increased over the last few years (Baca & Harris, 1988; Cole & Deal, 1989). In the United States, there were 21 million Hispanic students enrolled in school (U.S. Bureau of the Census, 1999). In California, it was reported in 1997 that 36% of all K–12 students come from a non-English-speaking home language environment (Taylor, 1999). Spanish is the third most widely spoken world language after all the dialects of Chinese and English (Crystal, 1997), and the United States has the fifth-largest Spanish-speaking population in the world (Grimes, 1996). Therefore, it is not surprising that 8% of the U.S. population is Spanish speaking (Bedore, 1999).

The number of Spanish-speaking school children grew from 2.5 million to 3.6 million between 1979 and 1989, with many of these children exhibiting difficulties in oral English (MacArthur, 1993). The education patterns of these students varies along the entire education continuum. De Leon Siantz (1996) stated:

> only 28.7% of 3- and 4-year-old Hispanic children were enrolled in preschool programs of any kind compared to 3% Blacks and 43% of Whites . . . . Nearly 30% of Hispanic children in grades 1–4 are enrolled below grade level . . . . The Hispanic dropout rate increased to 35.7% in 1988 from 28.6% in 1980 (p. 15).

These students exhibit various levels of functioning within the context of the European American school culture. They are acculturating to the predominant culture of the school system, but at different rates and at different levels. Some students from families and community backgrounds with different cultural perspectives may have had little experience with the values, activities, and other components of life in the United States (Brice, 1992).

Ginzberg (1992) stated that "a particular disadvantage of the Hispanic population, many of whom are first generation, is the large gap between their level of educational achievement and that of the white majority"

(p. 23). Marshall (1992) stated that "only about 25 percent of the Hispanic high school graduates in recent years have taken courses that qualify them for college work" (p. 49). Thus, many Hispanic students do not receive the education that they deserve. The nationwide high school graduation rate is 9.2% for Hispanics, yet the rate for non-Hispanics is 21.2% (Branch, 1993). It should be noted that Florida Hispanics are better educated than their counterparts around the nation, with their college graduation at 14.2%. However, this is still below the national average for non-Hispanics.

At-risk Factors

MacArthur (1993) found that persons who spoke languages other than English were at least twice as likely to drop out of school prior to completing high school than English-only speakers. Other at-risk factors include low family incomes and low parental educational attainment (MacArthur, 1993). MacArthur (1993) also reported that among foreign-born Spanish speakers, those who had immigrated after 1980 had higher dropout rates than those born in the United States. Thus, adolescent Hispanic students enrolled in school today face a difficult and often abbreviated school career when compared to their English-only speaking peers. It therefore seems that knowledge of English plays a significant role in educational attainment for many Hispanic students.

Civil Rights Legislation

The Civil Rights Act of 1964 (P.L. 88-352), and the subsequent court cases, was a considerable victory for the civil rights movement. It also served as a precedent for legislation concerning equal education. The Civil Rights Act mandated that school districts receiving federal funds were not to discriminate on the basis of race, religion, or national creed.

On May 25, 1970, a memorandum issued by the director of the Office for Civil Rights to all school districts with more than 5% culturally and linguistically diverse students informed the districts that they had to take affirmative action to support students in overcoming English language deficiencies. According to the directive, school districts could no longer assign students to classes for the developmentally delayed based on English language assessments. Thus, a precedent was set that evaluation for placement could not be based on a single skill (i.e., English language). The Equal Educational Opportunities Act of 1974 (P.L. 93-380) continued the efforts begun in earlier civil rights legislation. It strengthened the guarantee that culturally and linguistically diverse students had equal educational rights, even where school districts were not receiving federal funds. Thus, an argument for equal education for all students was formed through civil rights legislation. The Civil Rights Act established nondiscrimination in the schools as a policy, while the May 25th memorandum set forth a directive that school districts had to assist students in overcoming their English language deficiencies. It also established that students could not be placed in programs for the developmentally delayed solely on the basis of English language deficiency. The Equal Opportunities Act carried civil rights guarantees to school districts not receiving federal funds; thus, schools had to conform although they were not directly receiving assistance.

Civil Rights Litigation

Litigation is and probably will be the primary means for culturally and linguistically diverse populations (e.g., Hispanics) to establish equity within the school education system. Early court cases that became pivotal for future legislation and litigation included *Brown v. the Board of Education of Topeka* (1954), *Meyer v. Nebraska* (1923), and *Lau v. Nichols* (1974). In *Brown v. the Board of Education,* the Supreme Court decided that separate educational facilities based on race could not be equal. This decision was based on the judgment that separate facilities could not be equal because such facilities deprived learners of equal protection under the law as guaranteed by the 14th Amendment. Since the *Brown* decision, equal protection under the 14th Amendment has been interpreted to include the educational rights of culturally and linguistically diverse and handicapped students. In *Meyer v. Nebraska,* regulations that prohibited elementary instruction in non-English languages were struck down. The Supreme Court's final verdict was that proficiency in a non-English language was an acceptable endeavor and was therefore not injurious to the health, morals, or understanding of students. Thus, a precedent for non-English instruction was set. *Lau v. Nichols* was a class action suit brought before the Supreme Court on behalf of 1,800 Chinese students. The Court stated "that there was no equality of treatment merely by providing students with the same facilities, textbooks, teachers, and curriculum, for students who do not understand English are effectively foreclosed from any meaningful education." The Court further stated that special language programs were necessary if schools were to provide students with an equal educational opportunity. Therefore litigation has provided students with equal access to facilities, the ability to receive instruction in a non-English language, and special language programs if necessary.

Special Education Legislation and Litigation

In 1970, Congress enacted new legislation in response to concerns and opinions voiced by certain advocacy groups. The Education of the Handicapped Act (P.L. 91-230) established that handicapped students merited close attention of federal and state education agencies. The Education for All Handicapped Children Act (P.L. 94-142) was enacted in 1975. This legislation encouraged school systems to place and move handicapped students into general education classrooms.

The Individuals with Disabilities Education Act (I.D.E.A.) (*Federal Register,* 1986) embodied all the former aspects of P.L. 94-142 (the Education for Handicapped Children Act) and added two new disabling conditions not found under P.L. 94-142, i.e., traumatic brain injury and autism. The Education of the Handicapped Act Amendments of 1986, P.L. 99-457 (*Federal Register,* 1986) for infants and preschoolers was also embodied in the regulations under I.D.E.A.

The major contributions of P.L. 94-142 to culturally and linguistically diverse (CLD) students were in the areas of assessment and placement. Section 612 (5) (C) specified that all testing and evaluation materials and procedures were to be selected and administered so that there would be no racial or cultural biases present. All materials and procedures must be provided in the child's native language or primary mode of communication unless it is clearly not feasible to do so. Also, the assessment and placement process could not rely solely on one criterion. Section 615 provided a series of safeguards protecting the civil rights of handicapped students and their parents or guardians: "Both P.L. 94-142 and the Equal Opportunity Act require that school districts take affirmative action to locate students in need of special education services. School districts are charged with the responsibility for using culturally and linguistically appropriate methods to locate students with handicapping conditions" (Fradd & Vega, 1986, p. 63).

The concept of a right to an education appropriate for handicapping conditions comes from two court decisions. The cases are *Pennsylvania Association for Retarded Children v. Commonwealth of Pennsylvania* (1972) and *Mills v. the Board of Education of District of Columbia* (1972). The case of the Pennsylvania Association for Retarded Children (PARC) ended in a consent agreement and was not fully litigated. However, *Mills* did go to trial and the decision established the constitutional right of handicapped children to a public education commensurate with their ability to learn.

Of importance to this discussion is the case of *Lora v. the Board of Education* (1978). This class action suit involved the disproportionate classification and assignment of African American students to special schools for emotionally disturbed children in New York. "These placements were premised in part on the use of standardized tests that were assailed as being socioeconomically and culturally biased" (Galagan, 1985, p. 292). *Larry P. v. Riles* (1979) was the first class action suit that addressed the issue of proof. In this case, the allegations involved the notion that a disproportionate number of African American students were being classified and placed in developmentally delayed classes throughout the state of California based upon the use of socially and culturally biased IQ tests. "The trial court ruled that the discriminatory effects of IQ testing (i.e., disproportionate number of Black children placed in EMR classes) was sufficient to establish a prima facie case of racial and cultural discrimination" (Galagan, 1985, p. 292). The cases of *José P. v. Ambach* (1978) and *Drycia v. the Board of Education of the City of New York* (1979) both asserted that timely evaluations and placement procedures were necessary for handicapped learners.

Through legislation and litigation it has been established that handicapped students were deserving of an appropriate education commensurate with their needs, were entitled to nondiscriminatory testing and placement, and were entitled to classification not based on any one criterion or instrument. Students were also entitled to assessment in their native language or primary mode of communication. Through P.L. 94-142 (and later I.D.E.A.) and P.L. 91-230, funding for services was provided for the school districts to meet the needs of handicapped learners.

Bilingual Legislation and Litigation

The federal government became involved with bilingual education with the passage on January 2, 1968, of the Bilingual Education Act (P.L. 90-247), also known as Title VII of the Elementary and Secondary Education Act (1965). The primary purpose of this law was to assist students in developing competence in English language skills. However, bilingual programs were transitional in nature and native language instruction was limited to providing quick transition to all-English instruction. It was the first time that the federal government acknowledged the lack of English language skills as a blockade to equal educational opportunities.

The 1968 act was limited, and therefore was amended in 1974 by the passage of P.L. 93-380. In this act the requirement that a Limited English Speaking Ability (LESA) child be from a low income was removed. This lifted the ceiling for students who could be served under this legislation. Also, means of assessing the bilingual program were added to the 1974 amendment. The Bilingual Education Act was further amended in 1978 with P.L. 95-561, which changed the definition of the target population from LESA (Limited English Speaking Ability) to LEP (Limited English Proficiency). This expanded the population being served by allowing students with limited English reading, writing, speaking, and understanding to be included in the program. The use of the native language was maintained in this version of the amendment, although it was subordinated to a stronger English language emphasis. In 1984, the Bilingual Education Act (P.L. 98-511) was again amended. While bilingual education is still viewed as compensatory, CLD students are now viewed as a national linguistic resource.

The case of *Aspira v. the Board of Education of the City of New York* (1974) established the need to use proficiency tests in determining eligibility of bilingual students for bilingual programs. In the case of *Casteneda v. Pickard* (1981), the court asserted that proof of intent was not necessary in order for the plaintiffs to experience discrimination as detailed in the Equal Educational Opportunity Act of 1974. The school district in the *Casteneda* decision had not provided teachers with the appropriate tests to measure student progress. Hence, the issue of proper assessment was readdressed.

In summary, equal educational opportunities rest upon correct placement of students into programs. The passage of the Civil Rights Act, the Education for all Handicapped Children Act of 1975 (P.L. 94-142.), the Individuals with Disabilities Education Act (I.D.E.A.), the May 25th memorandum, the Bilingual Education Acts of 1968, 1974, 1978, and 1984 and the numerous class action suits brought forward made imperative the proper assessment and placement of Hispanic students.

Best Practices

The "Best Practices" for this section come primarily from the many court cases and laws that have been passed to serve culturally and linguistically diverse special needs students. Five major points are summarized:

1. Affirmative action is needed to support Hispanic students in overcoming their English language deficiencies. Knowledge of English plays a substantial role in Hispanic students' school success.
2. Evaluation of students cannot be based on a single skill—knowledge of English or testing through English only. Testing must be done in Spanish and under a variety of conditions.
3. The *Lau v. Nichols* (1974) decision stated that "students who do not understand English are effectively foreclosed from any meaningful education." Therefore, instruction and therapy must me conducted in Spanish as much as possible to ensure understanding.
4. All racial and cultural biases must be removed from assessment (P.L. 94-142, *Federal Register,* 1977). Assessment decisions cannot rest on he basis of a sole criterion.
5. The transition to a general education classroom should not be quick. Maintenance of the native language, Spanish, is encouraged as a national resource, according to the Bilingual Education Act of 1984 (P.L. 98-511).

In summary, not only must educators deal with identifying handicapping aspects, they must also do this without letting the social, cultural, and linguistic factors concerning CLD students interfere with their educational decisions. Speech–language pathologists, general education classroom teachers, special educators, psychologists, and bilingual teachers are the ones to whom this responsibility has been delegated.

References

Aspira v. Board of Education of the City of New York, 58 FRD 62 S.D.N.Y. (1973).

Baca, L., & Harris, K. (1988). Teaching migrant exceptional children. *Teaching Exceptional Children, 20*(4), 32–35.

Becerra, R., & Shaw, D. (1984). *The Hispanic elderly.* Lanham, MD: University Press of America.

Bedore, L. (1999). The acquisition of Spanish. In O. Taylor & L. Leonard (Eds.), *Language acquisition across North America* (pp. 157–207). San Diego, CA: Singular.

Bilingual Education Act, P.L. 90–247, 81 Stat. 783 816 (Jan. 2, 1968).

Brice, A. (1992). The Adolescent Pragmatics Screening Scale: Rationale and development. *Howard Journal of Communications, 3,* 177–193.

Brown v. the Board of Education of Topeka, Kansas, 347 U.S. 483, 74 S.Ct. 686 (1954); 349 U.S. 294, 75 S.Ct. 853 (1955).

Castaneda v. Pickard, 648 F. 2d 989, 5th Cir. (1981).

Cole, L., & Deal, V. (1989). New CCCs require multicultural literacy. *Perspectives: The ASHA Office of Minority Concerns Newsletter.* (Available from Office of Minority Concerns: American Speech-Language-Hearing Association, 10801 Rockville, MD 20852).

Crystal, D. (1997). *The Cambridge encyclopedia of language* (2nd ed.). Cambridge, UK: Cambridge University Press.

de Leon Siantz, M. L. (1996). Profile of the Hispanic child. In S. Torres (Ed.), *Hispanic voices: Hispanic health educators speak out.* New York, NY: NLN Press.

Drycia v. Board of Education, 79 C. 2562 E.D.N.Y. (1979).

Federal Register. (1986). *Education of the Handicapped Act Amendments of 1986,* Part H for infants and toddlers with disabilities and the preschool grant program, P.L. 99-457.

Federal Register. (1977). *Education for All Handicapped Children Act, P.L. 94-142 Regulations, 42*(163), Sec. 121a 303. Vol. No. 163 42, Washington, DC: U.S. Government Printing Office.

Ginzberg, E. (1996). Access to health care for Hispanics. In A. Furino (Ed.), *Health policy and the Hispanic* (pp. 22–31). Boulder, CO: Westview Press.

Grimes, B. (Ed.). (1996). *Ethnologue: Languages of the world* (13th ed.). Dallas, TX: Summer Institute of Linguistics. Available URL: http://www.sil.org/ethnologue.

José P. v. Ambach, 3 EHLR 551:245, 27 E.D.N.Y. (1979); 669 F. 2d 865 2d Cir. (1982); 557 F. Supp. 11230 E.D.N.Y. (1983).

Larry P. v. Riles, 495 F. Supp. 926 (N.D. Cal 1979) aff'd, 83-84 EHLR 555:304 (CA9 1984).

Lau v. Nichols, 414 U.S. 563 (1974).

Lora et al. v. Board of Education of City of New York et al., 74 F.R.D. 565 E.D.N.Y. (1977); 456 F. Supp 1121 E.D.N.Y. (1978); Final order, 1979; Remanded 623 F.2d Cir (1980); Amended and supplemental orders (1980); Final order, 587 F. Supp. 1572 E.D.N.Y. (1984).

MacArthur, E.K. (1993). *Language characteristics and schooling in the United States, a changing picture: 1979 and 1989.* Washington, DC: National Center for Education Statistics.

Marshall, R. (1992). Education, productivity, and the nation's future. In A. Furino (Ed.), *Health policy and the Hispanic* (pp. 48–54). Boulder, CO: Westview Press.

Meyer v. Nebraska, 262 U.S. 390 (1923).

Mills v. the Board of Education of District of Columbia, 348 F. Supp. 866 D.D.C. (1972).

Pennsylvania Association For Retarded Children v. Commonwealth of Pennsylvania, 334 F. Supp. 1257 (1972); 343 F. Supp. 279 (1972).

Stein, B. (1981). Understanding the refugee experience: Foundations for a better resettlement system. *Journal of Refugee Resettlement, 1*(4) 1–10.

Taylor, O. (1999). Cultural issues and language acquisition. In O. Taylor & L. Leonard (Eds.), *Language acquisition across North America* (pp. 21–37). San Diego, CA: Singular.

U. S. Bureau of the Census. (1998). *Educational attainment in the United States: March 1998.* Washington, DC: Author.

The Spanish Language

Heterogeneity of Hispanics

Hispanics in the United States are not a homogeneous group. In 2000, it was reported that there were 32 million Hispanics in the United States (U.S. Bureau of the Census, 2000b). Population reports indicate that the largest Hispanic groups in the United States are Mexicans (58%), followed by Puerto Ricans (13%) and Cubans (6%). Therefore, this chapter shall report on these Hispanic subgroups, who make up 77% of the entire Hispanic population in the United States.

The linguistic and language considerations of the diverse Hispanic subgroups (i.e., Mexican, Puerto Rican, and Cuban) need to be considered according to each group's needs. Some of the considerations that need to be accounted for when serving these diverse Hispanic and Latino populations include the following: cultural influences, family system and obligations, and the variety of Spanish spoken by each subgroup.

Cultural Influences

Cultural influences include such sociological variables as the average age of the group and subgroup, family size and income, the education level attained, and occupations. Other variables such as religion, family values, and the various varieties of Spanish as spoken by Mexicans, Puerto Ricans, and Cubans will be discussed.

The Hispanic population of the United States tends to be younger than the overall non-Hispanic U.S. population. The median age of Hispanics is 26.5 years and the mean age is 28.8 years, while the median white, non-Hispanic U.S. population age is 38.1 years and the mean age is 38.5 years (U.S. Bureau of the Census, 2000a). Mexicans have the youngest average age (24 years), while Cubans have the oldest (39 years). Puerto Ricans and

Central and South Americans have an average age of 27 and 28, respectively. The majority of Cubans in the United States are within the age range of 15 to 44 years (463,000, or 43.9%). This is followed by the 45 to 64 age group (287,000, or 27.2%) (U.S. Bureau of the Census, 1992).

Only 12% of the elder Hispanic population is over 65, while the overall non-Hispanic U.S. population tends to have more elder adults (approximately 19%). Cubans tend to have more elder Hispanic adults than all the other Hispanic subgroups (14%) (Current Population Reports, 1990; U.S. Bureau of the Census, 1998a). As a group, the percent of young children (0–18 years of age) for Hispanics and non-Hispanics is not similar (35% versus 55%). Among Mexicans and Puerto Ricans this group makes up 30% of each subgroup, while it is less for Cubans (16%) (U.S. Bureau of the Census, 1998a; Current Population Reports, 1992).

Hispanic families are, on average, larger than the overall non-Hispanic U.S. population (2.19 children versus 1.85 children) (U.S. Bureau of the Census, 1998a). The average for Mexicans is the largest among Hispanics, being 4.1 children (Valdivieso & Davis, 1988). Related to family size is family composition, that is, who composes the Hispanic family. The 1998 census population survey indicates that 5.5% of non-Hispanic U.S. households are headed by women, while 34% of Hispanic households are headed by women.

Income and Educational Attainment

More Hispanics live in poverty than those in the non-Hispanic U.S. population (22.8% versus 7.7% for white non-Hispanics) (U.S. Bureau of the Census, 2000b). As of 1990, 33% of Puerto Ricans and 28% of Mexicans were living in poverty, while only 15% of Cubans lived in poverty (more closely resembling the 1990 U.S. average of 12%).

The lack of opportunity for education adds to the issue of poverty. The 2000 Census Population Reports indicate that 51.7% of all Hispanics have attained a high school education compared to 77.6% of all races in the U.S. population. Cubans more closely approximate the non-Hispanic U.S. population (Langdon & Cheng 1992). Becerra and Shaw (1984) stated that "within the Hispanic population older Cubans had a significantly higher level of education than did older Puerto Ricans or Mexican Americans" (p. 3). Only 11% of all Hispanics complete four years of a college education, while 25% of the white U.S. population completes a four-year college program (U.S. Bureau of the Census, 1998b). It should be noted that Cubans more closely approximate the non-Hispanic population, with a 20% college graduation rate (Current Population Reports, 1990).

Hispanics hold different jobs according to their specific subgroup (i.e., Mexican, Puerto Rican, Cuban). Mexican men have been employed in farming, forestry, and fishing jobs more than other Hispanic subgroups. Cubans have been more inclined to be employed in managerial and professional positions. Cubans and Puerto Ricans tend not to be employed in farming, forestry, or fishing types of jobs (Langdon & Cheng, 1992).

Religion

Mexicans are almost universally Roman Catholic (97%); 3% are Protestant (World Atlas, 1991). In addition, the majority of Mexicans are of Mestizo descent (i.e., Indian and Spanish heritage) (60%); 30% are Indian, 9% are of white European ancestry, and 1% are other. Mexicans may cling to a variety of folk and religious beliefs about illness and disability (Kayser, 1998). One such belief is *mal ojo* (or "evil eye"), an evil gaze cast by a jealous person who stares at a pregnant woman. This evil gaze may cause the child to be handicapped. When a pregnant woman does not satisfy her *antojos* ("cravings"), it is believed to result in a defect to the child. A scare or *susto* is also thought to cause defects in a child. One should not overgeneralize some of these folk beliefs to all Mexicans or all Hispanics, as they are believed by only a small portion of the population. However, the SLP should be aware that these beliefs exist.

Puerto Ricans are also predominantly Roman Catholic (85%); 15% are Protestant and other denominations. Puerto Ricans, like Cubans, come from European and African ancestry.

Cubans were predominantly (85%) Roman Catholic before Fidel Castro (the current dictator in Cuba today) assumed power. There are an unknown number of practitioners of Santería, although it is believed to be widespread in Cuba and among recent refugees to the United States (Brice, 1993). Santería is a combination of Roman Catholicism and African religion. It is not known how many Cubans practice Santería. It is probably most prevalent with those living under the Castro era. Those who came in the first and second wave of immigration (1960 to 1979) are probably Roman Catholic practitioners. The Santería cults have been entrenched since the eighteenth century when African slaves began them on Cuba's sugar plantations. Three major Afro-Cuban cults exist: the Yoruba, the Bantu Palo Monte, and the Abakuá secret societies. The priests are known as Babalaos (Oppenheimer, 1992).

Family Values[1]

Mexican American families are significantly larger than all other ethnic and Hispanic families. Mexican families average 4.1 individuals; other Hispanic families average 3.45 and non-Hispanic families average 2.49 (Becerra, 1998). Marriage patterns are similar to those of other Latino groups. The

---

[1]For a further discussion of family values of other Hispanics and Latinos please refer to Chapter 6, "Socialization Practices of Latinos" and Chapter 12, "Principles and Strategies in Intervention."

Mexican family is a blend of traditional and new values. The rituals relating to birth, marriage, and death remain an integral part of the Mexican culture (Becerra, 1998). The continuous flow of Mexicans to this country reinforces these values.

Puerto Ricans are American citizens, yet are still Hispanic and Latino. This interaction of cultures was a result of the 1898 Spanish-American War in which the United States claimed Puerto Rico as a possession (Sánchez-Ayéndez, 1998). A large Puerto Rican migration to the United States began in the 1920s and has increased significantly over the last 80 years (Sánchez-Ayéndez, 1998). The Puerto Rican family today resembles the modified extended family predominant on the island, with childrearing vested in the nuclear family. It is expected that extended families also predominate in the United States but with a smaller number of *abuelos* (grandparents), *tías,* and *tíos* (aunts and uncles). Decisions regarding childrearing are made predominantly by mothers (Sánchez-Ayéndez, 1998), and Puerto Rican grandparents continue to assist with childrearing (Sánchez-Ayéndez, 1994). Adult children are expected to provide and care for their elderly parents. Puerto Rican families are like many other Latino families, yet the factors of migration and re-migration to the United States do influence these families more so than other Latinos. This impact of migration and re-migration needs to be further investigated as it affects SLP service delivery.

Cubans "value highly family ties and their family units, which extend in many cases to include grandparents, cousins, aunts, and uncles" (Klovern, Madera, & Nardone, 1974, p. 255). Cubans value the family as a unit. Therefore, a priority for many Cuban fathers is to accommodate their work situation so that the family is unified and enhanced as a family unit (Greco & McDavis, 1978). Escovar and Escovar (1981) report that "Cuban-American parents are perceived as using more contingent reinforcement than Anglo parents but the differences are not statistically significant" (p. 16). Escovar and Escovar (1982) also reported in a study of Latinos, particularly Cubans, that "Hispanic and Latin parents may make more use of threats but are less likely to follow them with actual punishment, thus appearing to use less physical punishment" (p. 15). In terms of discipline, Escovar and Escovar (1981) reported:

> Notably Cuban-American mothers use the same disciplinary mechanism (i.e., affective punishment, deprivation of privileges, and physical punishment) as Anglo mothers. Interestingly Cuban-American mothers are perceived as being the most protective and using the highest level of achievement pressure (pp. 17–18).

Brice (1993) reported that Cuban children are not allowed to explore their environment as freely as their American peers. Thus, activities such as crossing the street, going to the store alone, or going to school alone may not be permitted in certain Cuban families. Pampering, overprotection, and babying of children are common practices among mothers and fathers of Cuban American children (Queralt, 1984). Older sons in the traditional Cuban American family are seen as the next heir to family responsibilities, whereas older daughters in traditional Cuban American families have the responsibility of taking care of and assisting with the children.

Language Considerations for SLPs

Spanish is the most widely spoken Latin language. Castilian or an American Spanish ("American" refers to New World Spanish spoken in South, Central, and North America) is spoken by more than two hundred million persons. It is estimated that by the year 2000 there were approximately four hundred million Spanish speakers worldwide (Canfield, 1981).

Spanish is the primary language of Mexicans, Puerto Ricans, and Cubans. In Mexico, there also exist 52 different Indian languages, and approximately 4 million Mexicans in Mexico speak an Indian language (Langdon & Cheng, 1992). Because Puerto Ricans are also U.S. citizens, Spanish and English are used in Puerto Rico. One out every two Hispanics in the United States speaks Spanish in the home. This figure rises to 72% among Puerto Ricans and 87% among Cubans (Szapocznik et al., 1978). Virtually all older Cubans in the Miami, Florida, area use Spanish and almost none use English (Szapocznik et al., 1978).

Spanish Versus English Phonetics

Stockwell and Bowen (1965) classify Spanish as having a simpler consonantal system than English. Spanish has 19 consonants, which include two semivowels, while English has 24 consonants, including two semivowels. In English, all syllables must have a vowel with the exception of syllabic consonants (Cook, 1996). Spanish consists of 42 phonemes with 19 consonant phonemes (Navarro, 1968). English has about 45 phonemes. The number of phonemes depends on the dialect and accent used (Cook, 1996). Spanish does not contain the following sounds in the final position of words: /p, b, f, v, tʃ, m/. Spanish words tend to end with: /r, s, d, n, l, z/ and vowels. Spanish contains certain voiced fricative phonemes that are allophones of their respective voiced stop consonants, e.g., /b, ß/, /d, ∂/, /g, v/.

The vowel system of Spanish is considered less complex than that of English. Vowels do not significantly vary from one position to another as occurs in English, and Spanish contains only five monothong vowels, while English contains 13 monothong vowels (MacKay, 1987). Spanish vowels occur in stressed and unstressed positions; in English only one vowel occurs in an unstressed position, the schwa / ∂/. Vowels in English may be preceded or followed by one or more consonants. Differences in unstressed English vowels do not distinguish one word from another as they do in Spanish (Hadlich, Holton, & Montes, 1968). Spanish stress has only two stress positions: primary and weak or absent. English can be said to have four stress positions: primary, secondary, tertiary, and weak or nonstress (Dalbor, 1969). Spanish stress is louder than English stress and corresponds more to the English tertiary stress.

The Spanish phonemes /t,d,n,l/ are more anteriorly placed than in English, approximating dental or interdental positions (Navarro, 1968). A Spanish speaker saying the word *nadar* will produce the /d/ consonant interdentally and be perceived by English speakers and listeners to be producing a medial "th" although, in fact, he or she is producing a Spanish /d/.

TABLE 3.1 *Frequency of Occurrence of Spanish vs. English Sounds (based on Hammond, 1989; Nash, 1977)*

Spanish		English	
Sound	Frequency	Sound	Frequency
/s/	17.08%	/t/	12.77%
/n/	12.27%	/n/	11.46%
/r/ tap	9.95%	/r/	8.32%
/t/	8.30%	/l/	7.69%
/k/	8.3%	/s/	7.47%
/l/	6.72%	/z/	4.90%
/m/	6.53%	/m/	4.74%
/j/	5.97%	/ð/	4.61%
/b/	4.99%	/k/	4.30%
/p/	4.02%	/w/	3.67%
/w/	2.18%	/b/	3.48%
/g/	1.24%	/h/	3.26%
/r/ trill	0.93%	/v/	3.17%
/f/	0.90%	/f/	2.86%
/h/	0.64%	/p/	2.35%
/ʧ/	0.56%	/ŋ/ "ing"	2.20%
/ñ/	0.53%	/j/	2.01%
		/g/	1.57%
		/ø/	0.97%
		/ʃ/	0.63%
		/ʤ/ "judge"	0.88%
		/ʧ/	0.63%
		/ʒ/ "rouge"	0.16%

The Spanish /r/ consists of a tap (sometimes referred to as a "flap," which approximates a stop in occlusive features) and the trill is a vibrant (i.e., the tongue vibrates). The American Spanish /s/ (as opposed to the Castilian /s/ of Spain) is quite similar to the American English /s/; however, the American Spanish /s/ can be aspirated. This is quite common in many American Spanish dialects, e.g., *mas* —> /mah/.

Spanish Versus English Phonology

Children will most likely show the same kinds of process development in learning to speak their different languages (Cook, 1996). Natural processes do capture some general truths about development; e.g., that fricatives are harder than nasals or stops for children to acquire, consonants in syllable onsets are easier than syllable codas, etc. (Stampe, 1979). However, the forms of these processes differ from language to language and the differences are determined by the language itself. Certain aspects of the development and use of English and Spanish phonology also differ. English dialects are primarily affected by vowel differences; some Spanish dialects (e.g., Mexican, Puerto Rican versus Cuban) are noted for consonantal changes seen in fricatives, liquids, and nasals (Goldstein & Iglesias, 1996).

The length of syllables is relatively constant in Spanish. Bowen and Stockwell (1960) stated that "all syllables are either one or two units long . . ." (p. 25). Thus, intervocalic consonants in Spanish may be very important (Hammond, 1989). Hammond (1989) discusses this issue further. Spanish may also have many more assimilation processes (Hammond, 1989). In Spanish, assimilation is particularly evident in nasal phonemes (Hadlich, Holton, & Montes, 1960; Harris, 1969). Terrel (1989) argued that "consonants may be articulatorily weakened, resulting in various sorts of substitutions and assimilations" (pp. 205–206).

English may place more focus on stress and timing; Spanish may be more syllable focused. Hadlich, Holton, and Montes (1968) stated that "Spanish is said to have syllable-timed rhythm. Languages like English, which has syllables of unequal length dependent largely on the number and placement of stresses, are said to have stress-timed rhythm" (p. 202). Terrel (1989) stated that "Spanish syllables tend to be almost equal in length and Spanish speakers never use an uh sound" (p. 210). Thus, Spanish avoids the uneven rhythm and heavy stress of English. Spanish also tends to produce tense sounds at the beginning of syllables and lax sounds at the end of syllables, hence syllable initial sounds are salient while syllable final sounds are less salient (Bjarkman, 1989; Hammond, 1989; Hooper, 1976). Tense sounds are produced with considerable muscular force and tension. For example, *busque* may become *buque* in the Cuban Spanish dialect. Bjarkman (1989) noted that the entire coronal series /t, d, ð, n, s/ is weakest for Spanish and is strongest for English. Hence, the coronal sounds in some dialects of Spanish will tend to be deleted in syllable-final or word-final positions.

Most English words and syllables end with consonants, while Spanish syllables and words tend to end with vowels (e.g., *zapato*-"shoe," *lampara*-"lamp," *acabó*-"finished"). Eblen (1982) stated that "in Spanish [i.e., American Spanish], /s/ and its allophone [z] are the only fricatives allowed in word-final position" (p. 210). The sounds of /x/ and /ð/ may also occur in some Spanish dialects in the final position. The few Spanish words that end with nonfricative consonants tend to be nasals, /r/ and /s/. English has 24 consonants that may end in the syllable-final position (Nash, 1977). In English, the voiced "th", /ð/, tends to occur with high frequency, as evidenced in demonstrative and article function words (*the, this, that, there, those*), while the Spanish /s/ occurs with high frequency in single syllables and function words (e.g., *los, las, ellos, ellas, estos, estas*) (Nash, 1977).

English has many true consonant clusters while Spanish does not. The consonants that are contiguous are consonant sequences; however, they typically occur at intersyllabic boundaries (Stockwell & Bowen, 1965). For example in the Spanish word *estampa,* the consonant sequence of "st" is not a consonant cluster (*es/tam/pa*). A deletion of the /s/ would be a postvocalic omission and not a consonant cluster reduction.

Some phonemes occur in Spanish that do not occur in English. For example, Spanish has the tap /r/ and trill /rr/ phonemes (e.g., *para, decir, tronco*). The tap /r/ is a fricative, while the trill /rr/ (e.g., *parra, rapido*) is a vibrant (Canfield, 1981). Neither the trill /rr/ nor the /x/ (a velar voiceless fricative) occur in English. Spanish contains certain voiced fricative phonemes that are allophones of their respective voiced stop consonants, e.g., /b, ß/, /d, ð/, /g, v/ (Bjarkman & Hammond, 1989).

Dialects of Spanish

Eblen (1982) revealed that some variations in adult Mexican Spanish phonology models can be attributed to dialectal differences. These variations are not disorders of phonology when the adult model also displays the phonological process. For example, in Mexican Spanish the syllable final /s/ may be deleted. Deletion of the syllable final /s/ has been noted as characteristic of Spanish in the Caribbean (Eblen, 1982; Hammond, 1989). Eblen (1982) concluded from his study of six Mexican Spanish children that substitution of /tʃ/ for /s/ made up 34% of all substitutions, /s/ deletion accounted for 28% of the total, and substitutions of stops for fricatives (stopping) accounted for 28%. Eblen (1982) stated that "children learning a particular language are constrained by the dialectal allophones of their community, exhibit some patterns documented for many languages, yet show individual patterns in their attempts to produce adult forms of phonemes in their language" (p. 217). Thus, children normally copy the adult phonological variations of a language (expressed as a dialect), yet children can be apt to show true phonological errors.

Hammond (1989) noted certain phonological variations of Caribbean Spanish. The well-documented phonological processes taken from Hammond included (1) syllable-final and word-final aspiration or deletion of /s/; (2) /r/ and /l/ substitutions, which can occur in syllable-final and word-final positions; (3) general word-final consonant deletion; (4) word-final /n/ velarization; (5) vocalization of word-final liquids; and (6) phonetic alteration of /tʃ/ and /ʃ/. Lesser-known processes of Caribbean Spanish include (1) vowel nasalization following nasal consonant deletion (perhaps related to vowel elongation following consonant deletion as noted by Hammond, 1989); (2) flapping (trilling) of intervocalic /d/, that is, /d/ —> trill /rr/; (3) sonorant devoicing; (4) word-final vowel devoicing; and (5) consonantal gemination (doubling of consonantal sounds).

Hammond (1989) stated that in "Cuban Spanish any syllable-final or word-final /s/ may optionally be deleted. In syllable-final environments within a word, however, whenever /s/ is deleted an obligatory phonological rule of compensatory vowel lengthening must also occur . . ." (p. 140). Hammond (1989) also stated that "in all Caribbean dialects of Spanish, it has long been known that the phoneme /s/ may optionally be aspirated or deleted in syllable-final position within a word or in word-final position" (p. 38). The feature of deletion does apply to other sounds. Bjarkman (1989) stated that the /d/ phoneme is the most commonly deleted sound in rapid, intervocalic speech. He supports this by stating, "Final /d/ in Spanish (*usted, edad, verdad, Madrid,* etc.) has weakened inaudibility for most dialects; *pasao* for *pasado* 'past' and *soldao* for *soldado* 'soldier' are not uncommon for most Spanish speakers" (p. 124).

Spanish Morphological and Syntactic Development

Some studies have reported the acquisition of Spanish morphology. However, these studies have intermixed the use of age and mean length of utterance to determine developmental levels. Hence, it is difficult to make comparisons and establish an overall developmental chart. The information available from Gonzalez (1983), Kvaal, Shipstead-Cox, Nevitt, Hodson and Launer (1988), and Radford and Ploenig-Pacheco (cited in Bedore, 1999) is compiled and presented in Tables 3.2 and 3.3.

Best Practices

The following strategies were developed to continue the flow of language and communication in the general education classroom and therapy room (Brice & Perkins, 1997). Using them should help keep the flow of language

TABLE 3.2 *Spanish Morphological Development*

Morpheme	MLU Productivity (Correct use of form in at least three obligatory contexts)	MLU Achievement (Correct use of form in 80% of obligatory contexts)	Approximate Age (Observed/ Acquired)
Demonstrative *esa,ese* (that) *esas,esos* (those) *esta,este* (this) *estas,estos* (these)	2.6	2.6	
Nongendered *eso* (that one) *esos* (those) *esto* (this one) *estos* (those)			
Articles *Definite Article la, las, el, los* *Indefinite Article una, uno, unas, unos*	2.6	2.6	
Copulas *(ser, estar)*	2.6	2.6	
Regular *Present Indicative* <u>Son</u> *pollos* "They <u>are</u> chickens"	2.6	2.7	2.6 years/4.6
Irregular *Present Indicative Pido* "I ask"	2.6	2.8	
Regular Past *Preterit Indicative agarr<u>ó</u>* "He grabb<u>ed</u>"	2.6–3.2	2.8–3.2	2.6 years/4.6
Present Progressive *Est<u>oy</u> pint<u>ando</u>*			2.6 years/4.6

TABLE 3.2 *Continued*

Morpheme	MLU Productivity (Correct use of form in at least three obligatory contexts)	MLU Achievement (Correct use of form in 80% of obligatory contexts)	Approximate Age (Observed/Acquired)
"I <u>am</u> paint<u>ing</u>" **Periphrastic Future** <u>Van a</u> tom<u>ar</u> "They <u>are</u> go<u>ing</u> <u>to</u> <u>drink</u>"			2.6 years/4.6
Plurals	2.8	3.2	
Imperfect Camin<u>aba</u> "I <u>used to walk</u>"			3.0 years/4.6
Present Subjunctive Acab<u>emos</u> "<u>That we finish</u>"			3.0 years/4.6
Possessive /de/	3.2	3.2	
Periphrastic Past <u>iba a</u> peg<u>ar</u> "<u>was going to</u> <u>spank</u>"			3.0 years/4.6
Periphrastic Future Progressive <u>Voy a</u> est<u>ar</u> v<u>iendo</u> "<u>I am going to</u> <u>see</u>"			3.0 years/4.6
Preposition /en/ /in/	4.2–4.5	4.2–4.5	
Irregular Preterite	4.2	4.6	
Past Subjunctive Hic<u>ieras</u> "<u>That I do</u>"			?/4.6 years

TABLE 3.3 *Spanish Syntactic Development*

Syntactic Structure	Approximate Age
Simple Imperative Command *Tom<u>alo</u>* "<u>Take it</u>"	2.0 years
Third Person Singular *No vien<u>e</u>* "He do<u>es</u> not come"	2 years
Indirect Object *Me está pintando <u>los zapatos</u>* "He is shining <u>my shoes</u> (for me)"	2.6 years
Direct Object *<u>La</u> agarró esta muchacha* "This girl took <u>it</u>"	2.6 years
Yes/No Questions	2.6 years
Information Questions *Qué* ("What") *Dónde* ("Where") *Para qué* ("What for") *Cuándo* ("When") *Quién* ("Who") *Por qué* ("Why") *Cómo* ("How")	2.6 years
Gerund	2.6–3.0 years
Full Sentence Negation	2.6 years
Subject-Verb-Object Position Changes *S-V-DO* *Yo tengo zapatitos* "I have little shoes" *V-S-DO* *Comí yo huevos* "I ate eggs" *V-DO-S* *Perdío las gomas el autobus* "The bus lost its tires"	2.9 years

TABLE 3.3 *Continued*

Syntactic Structure	Approximate Age
Imperatives *Verb + Indirect Object Pronoun + Direct Object Pronoun* *Dámela* "Give it to me" *Verb + Reflexive Pronoun + Direct Object Pronoun* *Tómatelo tu* "You drink it"	3.0 years
Compound Sentences with Use of *y* ("and")	3.0 years
Locative Verb Clauses *Allá dondé esta la casa* "Over there where the house is"	3.0 years
Conditional Clause with Use of <u>*si*</u> ("if") *Si no el me pretas atencíon, le voy a castegar* "If he does not pay attention to me, I am going to punish him"	3.0 years
Tag Questions with Use of <u>*verdad*</u> ("right/correct") *Este niño se porta bien, verdad?* "This boy behaves well, right?"	3.3 years
Comparative <u>*mas*</u> ("more" or "er- comparative")	3.3 years
Compound Sentences with Use of <u>*pero*</u> ("but")	4.6 years
Comparison of Equalities with Use of <u>*como*</u> ("like")	4.6 years

continuous and thus increase the phonological, morphological, syntactic, and pragmatic growth of Spanish-English speaking students.

1. *Native language appreciation.* The use of the child's native language also conveys an unsaid appreciation of the student's language and culture. Even instances of using a few words of the student's native language will indicate that the home language is valued and equal to English.
2. *Spontaneous language use.* The SLP should allow the children to freely engage in conversation. Children who spontaneously use language have more opportunities to practice their existing language skills.

3. *Acceptance of the message.* The SLP should accept the child's communicative intent and not directly correct the utterance. The SLP should provide a correct model of incorrect productions.

References

Becerra, R. (1998). The Mexican-American family. In. C. H. Mindel, R. W. Habenstein, & R. Wright (Eds.), *Ethnic families in America* (4th ed.) (pp. 153–171). Upper Saddle River, NJ: Prentice-Hall.

Becerra, R., & Shaw, D. (1984). *The Hispanic elderly.* Lanham, MD: University Press of America.

Bedore, L. M. (1999). The acquisition of Spanish. In O. L. Taylor & L. B. Leonard (Eds.), *Language acquisition across North America* (pp. 157–204). San Diego, CA: Singular.

Bjarkman, P. C. (1989). Abstract and concrete approaches to phonological strength and weakening chains: Implications for Spanish syllable structure. In P. C. Bjarkman & R. H. Hammond (Eds.), *American Spanish pronunciation* (pp. 106–136). Washington, DC: Georgetown University Press.

Bjarkman, P. C., & Hammond, R. H. (1989). (Eds). *American Spanish pronunciation.* Washington, DC: Georgetown University Press.

Bowen, J. D., & Stockwell, R. P. (1960). *Patterns of Spanish pronunciation. A drillbook.* Chicago, IL: The University of Chicago Press.

Brice, A. (1993). *Understanding the Cuban refugees.* San Diego, CA: Los Amigos Research Associates.

Brice, A., & Perkins, C. (1977). What is required for transition from the ESL classroom to the general education classroom? A case study of two classrooms. *Journal of Children's Communication Development, 19*(1), 13–22.

Canfield, D. L. (1981). *Spanish pronunciation in the Americas.* Chicago, IL: The University of Chicago Press.

Cobb, C. E., Jr. (1992). Miami. *National Geographic, 181*(1), 86–113.

Cook, V. (1996). *Second language learning and language teaching* (2nd ed). New York, NY: Arnold.

Current Population Reports. (1990). *The Hispanic population in the United States: March 1990.* Washington, DC: Bureau of the Census.

Dalbor, J. B. (1969). *Spanish pronunciation: Theory and practice.* New York: Holt, Rinehart, and Winston.

Eblen, R. E. (1982). A study of the acquisition of fricatives by three-year-old children learning Mexican Spanish. *Language and Speech, 25*(3), 201–220.

Escovar, L., & Escovar, P. (1981, Fall). *Comparison of childrearing practices of Anglos, Cuban-Americans, and Latin Americans.* Paper presented at the Florida Atlantic University Public Forum.

Faltis, C. J. (1989). Code-switching and bilingual schooling: An examination of Jacobson's new concurrent approach. *Journal of Multilingual and Multicultural Development, 10*(2), 117–127.

Goldstein, B., & Iglesias, A. (1996). Phonological patterns in normally developing Spanish-speaking 3- and 4-year-olds of Puerto Rican descent. *Language, Speech, and Hearing Services in Schools, 27,* 82–89.

Gonzalez, G. (1983). Morphology and syntax. In J. P. Gelatt & M. P. Anderson (Eds.), *Bilingual language learning system.* Available from American Speech-Language-Hearing Association, 10801 Rockville Pike, Rockville, MD 20852.

Greco, M. E., & McDavis, R. J. (1978). Cuban-American college students: Needs, cultural attitudes, and vocational development program suggestions. *Journal of College Student Personnel, 19*(3), 254–258.

Hadlich, R. L., Holton, J. S., & Montes, M. (1968). *A drillbook of Spanish pronunciation.* New York: Harper and Row Publishers.

Hammond, R. M. (1989). American Spanish dialectology and phonology from current theoretical perspectives. In P. C. Bjarkman & R. H. Hammond (Eds). *American Spanish pronunciation* (pp. 137–169). Washington, DC: Georgetown University Press.

Harris, J. W. (1969). *Spanish phonology.* Cambridge, MA: The M.I.T. Press.

Hooper, J. G. (1976). *An introduction to natural generative phonology.* New York, NY: Academic Press.

Kayser, H. (1998). *Assessment and intervention resources for Hispanic children.* San Diego: Singular Publishing Group.

Klovern, M., Madera, M., & Nardone, S. (1974). Counseling the Cuban child. *Elementary School Guidance and Counseling, 8*(4), 255–260.

Kvaal, J., Shipstead-Cox, N., Nevitt, S., Hodson, B., & Launer, P. (1988). The acquisition of 10 Spanish morphemes by Spanish-speaking children. *Language, Speech, and Hearing Services in Schools, 19*, 384–394.

Langdon, H., & Cheng, L. (1992). *Hispanic children and adults with communication disorders.* Gaithersburg, MD; Aspen.

Lanier, M. (1974). *Children are the revolution: Day care in Cuba.* New York: Viking Press.

MacKay, I. (1987). *Phonetics: The science of speech production* (2nd ed.). Boston, MA: College Hill.

McCoy, C., & Gonzalez, D. (1986). *Hispanics in Florida and the United States. Cuban immigrants in Florida and the United States: Implications for immigration policy,* (Monograph Number 3). Gainesville, FL: Bureau of Economic and Business Research.

Nash, R. (1977). *Comparing English and Spanish: Patterns in phonology and orthography.* New York: Regents Publishing Company.

Navarro, T. (1968). *Studies in Spanish phonology.* Coral Gables, FL: University of Miami Press.

Oppenheimer, A. (1992). *Castro's final hour.* New York: Simon & Schuster.

Queralt, M. (1984). Understanding Cuban immigrants: A cultural perspective. *Social Work Journal, 29,*115–121.

Sánchez-Ayéndez, M. (1998). The Peurto Rican family. In C. H. Mindel, R. W. Habenstein, & R. Wright (Eds.), *Ethnic families in America*(4th ed.) (pp. 199–222). Upper Saddle River, NJ: Prentice-Hall.

Sánchez-Ayéndez, M. (1994). Puerto Rican elderly women. In M. Sotomayor (Ed.), *Triple jeopardy: Aged Hispanic women: Insights and experiences.* Washington, DC: National Hispanic Council on Aging.

Sandoval, M. (1979). Santería as a mental health care system: An historical overview. *Social Science and Medicine, 13B,* 137–151.

Stampe, D. (1979). *A dissertation on natural phonology.* New York, NY: Garland.

State of Florida. (1981). *A resource manual for the development and evaluation of special programs for exceptional programs for exceptional students: Volume III-B, evaluating the non-English speaking handicapped.* Tallahassee, FL: State of Florida Department of Education.

Stockwell, R. P., & Bowen, J. D. (1965). *The sounds of English and Spanish.* Chicago, IL: The University of Chicago Press.

Szapocznik, J., Falleti, M., & Scopetta, M. (1977). *Psychological social issues of Cuban elders in Miami.* Miami, FL: Spanish Family Guidance Clinic and Institute for the Study of Aging.

Szapocznik, J., Scopetta, M., Kurtines, W., & Arnalde, M. (1978). Theory and measurement of acculturation. *InterAmerican Journal of Psychology, 12*, 113–130.

Terrel, T. D. (1989). Teaching Spanish pronunciation in a communicative approach. In P. C. Bjarkman & R. H. Hammond (Eds). *American Spanish Pronunciation* (pp. 196–214). Washington, DC: Georgetown University Press.

U.S. Bureau of the Census. (2000a). *Population estimates program.* Washington, DC: Author.

U.S. Bureau of the Census. (2000b). *Current population survey.* Washington, DC: Author.

U.S. Bureau of the Census. (1998a). *Current population survey.* Washington, DC: Author.

U.S. Bureau of the Census. (1998b). *Educational attainment in the United States.* Washington, DC: Author.

U.S. Bureau of the Census. (1992). *Population projections program.* Washington, D.C.: Author.

Valdivieso, R., & Davis, C. (1988). *U.S. Hispanics: Challenging issues for the 1990s.* Washington, D.C.: Population Reference Bureau.

Whitfield, M. (1993, January). Cuba soap rations whittled down. *Miami Herald, 24A.*

World Atlas, (1991). [Computer program]. Novato, CA: The Software Toolworks.

Second Language Acquisition

As the Hispanic population of the United States continues to increase dramatically, SLPs face the continuing dilemma of how to provide therapy or instruction. The problem is compounded when SLPs must provide services to students from bilingual or monolingual Spanish-speaking homes. In this chapter, second language acquisition factors are reviewed that must be considered when making instructional decisions.

Normal Processes of Second Language Acquisition

Before a discussion of linguistic factors proceeds, it is necessary to define some key components affecting bilingual language acquisition and development. These components include (a) bilingualism, (b) language proficiency, (c) language transference and interference, (d) fossilization, (e) interlanguage, (f) the silent period, (g) code switching (and code mixing and borrowing of words), and (h) language gains and language attrition.

Bilingualism

Students who possess fluency in more than one language may show proficiency levels from minimum ability to complete fluency in both languages (Gutierrez-Clellen, 1999). Language is more than its oral component, that is, speaking. Professionals in fields outside of speech–language pathology think of language according to the domains of speaking, listening, reading, and writing (Brice & Rivero, 1996). Hence, bilingualism, as defined here, is the ability to speak, listen, read, and/or write in more than one language with varying degrees of proficiency.

Definition of Language Proficiency

Language proficiency can be categorized at multiple levels (Skutnabb-Kangas, 1981). A shift in thinking has occurred in the profession of bilingualism, as measuring a child's dominant language proficiency has lost favor. This practice has been universally questioned by experts in the field (Döpke, 1992; Miller, 1988). However, measuring proficiency in each of the child's languages (e.g., Spanish and English) seems to be a better indicator of ability.

A student may exhibit one of five degrees of proficiency (we are not limited to five; however, these seem to be the most basic levels). A Native Dominant speaker shows proficiency in Spanish yet little proficiency in English. This corresponds to someone performing at a novice level in English [on the Educational Testing Service (ETS) Oral Proficiency rating or the American Council of Teachers of Foreign Language Scale (ACTFL) or a 0 on the Foreign Services Institute (FSI) scale of oral proficiency]. Refer to Figure 4.1 for an illustration of these oral proficiency scales. A more current oral proficiency rating scale has been developed and widely used internationally by Wylie & Ingram, 1999.) An English Dominant speaker shows the opposite, with proficiency in English but not in Spanish. A Balanced Bilingual shows a high degree of proficiency in both English and Spanish. The level of proficiency is at the level of Advanced on the ETS/ACTFL scale, 3 on the FSI, or 3 on the ISLPR (Wylie & Ingram, 1999). A Mixed Bilingual shows limited proficiency in both languages (Intermediate on the ETS/ACTFL, 2 on the FSI or ISLPR), whereas a Low Bilingual shows minimal proficiency in both Spanish and English. This speaker demonstrates Novice or Novice to Low abilities (ETS/ACTFL) or 0 to 0+ abilities on the ISLPR (Wylie & Ingram, 1999) or on the FSI scale. This speaker may appear to be language disordered to the SLP or teacher. The student's low ability may or may not be the result of a language disorder in both languages. This determination must be made through exhaustive language testing. Table 4.1 illustrates some levels of bilingual proficiency.

Language Transfer and Interference

Language transference is the ability or inability to transport information from the native language to the second language. Brice and Rivero (1996) stated that "language transfer is the cross-linguistic influence two or more languages may have on each other. It is not simply language interference or reliance on native language abilities" (p.2). Hence, language transfer is the ability to ferry and transport language knowledge from Spanish to English;

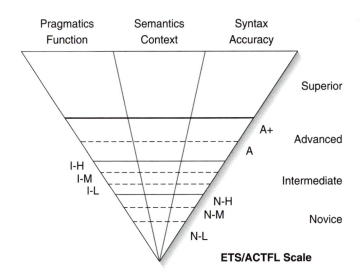

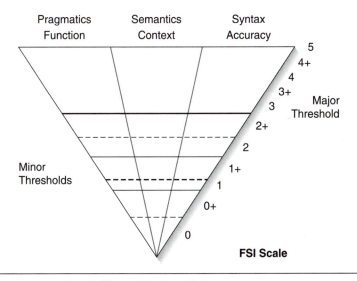

FIGURE 4.1 *Levels of Bilingual Oral Proficiency**

Oral Language: Proficiency Scales; Educational Testing Service/American Council on the Teaching of a Foreign language, Foreign Service Institute

interference occurs when Spanish intrudes on learning English. Spanish syntax may be superimposed onto English (e.g., "The ball red is mine.") This superimposition may occur at any language level (i.e., phonologically, morphologically, semantically, or pragmatically). Examples of language interference are found in Table 4.2.

TABLE 4.1 *Types of Bilingual Proficiency Exhibited by Students*

	Spanish Proficiency	English Proficiency
Native Dominant	Yes	No
English Dominant	No	Yes
Balanced Bilingual	Yes	Yes
Mixed Bilingual	Partial	Partial
Low Bilingual	No	No

Fossilization

Roseberry-McKibbin (1995) stated that "fossilization occurs when specific second language 'errors' remain firmly entrenched despite good proficiency in the second language (Pica, 1994) (p. 132)." Fossilized items can be idiosyncratic to a child or be common practice within a child's language community. An example in Spanish would be *El gobierno reducio el impuesto/* "The government reduced the taxes" (the correct grammatical form would be *El gobierno redujo el impuesto*). An example in English would be, "I seen you playing at the ball game last night." Thus, fossilized forms are resistant to change.

Interlanguage

Brice (1994) stated that "interlanguages (IL) are approximations of the target language (L2) [i.e., English; clarification mine] while it is still being learned. Children who have not quite developed a proficiency in the second language may still be using an interlanguage system (Selinker, 1991) (p.137)." Hence interlanguages are combinations of English and Spanish that are developmentally appropriate. They are an approximation of English as the child is acquiring English with varying dosages of Spanish rules imposed.

Silent Period

Roseberry-McKibbin (1995) described the silent period this way:

> Some students when learning a second language, go through a silent period in which there is much listening/comprehension and little output (Krashen, 1992; Duran & Chong, 1994). It is believed that students are learning the rules of the language during this silent period; the silent period can last anywhere from three to six months, although estimates vary (p. 132).

TABLE 4.2. *Examples of Language Interference (Brice & Montgomery, 1998; Dulay & Burt, 1974)*

Type of Error	Construction	Examples
Interference	Possessive pronoun + agreement. Not allowed in English; obligatory in Spanish.	Now she's putting hers clothes on. (*Ahora ella se está poniendo su ropa.*)
	Omission of obligatory "how" in English; obligatory in Spanish	I know to do all that. (*Yo sé qué hacer todo eso.*)
	Use of infinitive for gerund. Not allowed in English; obligatory in Spanish.	I finish to watch tv when it's four o'clock. (*Yo termino de ver la tv cuando es la cuatro.*)
	Do-subject agreement missing.	Where the spiders go.
	Object pronoun missing.	My mother can fix.
	Trouble with irregular past tense and prepositions.	Yesterday, we go see my grandma. (*Ayer, nosotros fuimos a ver mi abuela.*) We went to. I calling to you later. Last week we seeing some good movie.
	Trouble with future tense marker.	I will called you.
	Copula "be" and possessive "s" marker.	This is the car of my mother. (*Ésto es el carro de mi madre.*)
	Trouble conjugating the "to be" verb.	When we beauty the room it pretty. (*Cuando arreglamos el cuarto está bonito.*)
	Trouble with negation forms.	In my country not we eat pork. (*En mi país no comemos puerco.*)
	Trouble with negation and singular possession.	This house no is my. (*Esta casa no es mía.*)
	Trouble with "s" markers and articles.	This three boy is playing on basketball team.
	Trouble with verb-subject forms; past tense inversion; wh-questions.	For why you asking me this question before? (*Por qué me estás preguntando esta pregunta antes?*)
	Wrong "no" placement; "no-not" distinction; "do" missing.	It no cause too trouble. (*Éso no me causa mucha problema.*)

(continued)

TABLE 4.2 *Continued*

Type of Error	Construction	Examples
	Use of noun for possessive pronoun.	She name is Maria. (*Su nombre es María.*)
	Overuse of "do."	We do got no more book. (*Nosotros no tenemos mas libros.*)
	"-ing" with modal.	Now we will talking about. (*Ahora nosotros estamos hablamos de éso.*)
Developmental Errors	Irregular treated as regular form.	She took her teeths off.
	Two verbal words tensed where only one is required.	I didn't weared my any hat.
	Accusative pronoun with nominative.	Me needs crayons now.

It is noted in the literature (Wong-Fillmore, 1992) that some students may not initially speak and may prefer to remain silent. These silent children may be attempting to gain internal proficiency before speaking or may still have difficulties processing English. It is estimated that silent periods may last from three to six months or even longer (perhaps up to a period of one year) (Roseberry-McKibbin, 1995).

Code Switching, Code Mixing, Borrowed Words

Code switching and code mixing is language alternation or switching between two or more codes, that is, languages. It can structurally be divided into code switching (CS) and code mixing (CM). Code switching is the alternation of English and Spanish across sentence boundaries; hence it is an intersentential alternation. In code switching the teacher may say, "*Ya, se acabó* ("It is over"). *Siéntate* ("Sit down"). The time is up." The alternation is between the sentences of "*Siéntate*" and "The time is up." Another example is the child saying, "*Ahora es buena hora para dormir* ("It is now a good time to sleep"). Turn off the lights." Code mixing is the alternation within a sentence, at the word, or within a word level. It is an intrasentential alternation. A code-mixed example is the teacher saying, "Each book *es uno.*" Another example is the child incorporating words or phrases into her or his Spanish from English: "*La voy a poner en un* frying pan ("I am going to put it into a frying pan")." Code switching or code mixing appear along the entire continuum of language proficiency.

In some instances it may be due to lack of appropriate lexicons or words in the second language (i.e., the student may have word-finding difficulties), yet, at other times it may be sophisticated language use with sound cognitive, social/pragmatic, and linguistic functioning. Pennington (1995) spoke of a bilingual teacher "who used Cantonese almost as much as English, [he] did not seem to do so out of any language deficit but rather exhibited a *form of highly skilled bilingual behavior* [emphasis added] akin to simultaneous interpretation" (p. 95).

Language alternation allows the bilingual speaker to combine the pragmatic, syntactic, and morphological dimensions of both languages. Indicators of possible deficiencies in code switching (Brice, 2000; Brice, Roseberry-McKibbin, & Kayser, 1997) may consist of

1. Long pauses indicating word searching and retrieval difficulties,
2. Inability to switch and mix between the two languages with ease,
3. An overpreponderance of one language.

Poplack (1980) identified four characteristics of successful code switching. Hence, the opposite of these may also indicate deficiencies with code switching and code mixing:

1. Rough transition between languages with false starts,
2. Marked awareness of the alternation between the languages,
3. Alternations or switches at the nouns or word level only, and
4. Alternations used for communicating untranslatable items.

Borrowing, the third language alternation phenomenon, entails integration of the word or phrase from one language into the other. The borrowed word or phrase therefore becomes a part of the other language and is assimilated into the second language. Borrowed words and phrases take on their own phonological, morphological, and semantic characteristics (Gumperz, 1982; Kamwangamalu, 1992). For example, a case of phonological borrowing is the word *sagüesera* borrowed from the English "southwest." *Sagüesera* has come to denote a specific Latin Cuban section of town in Miami, Florida. Not only has the pronunciation changed but also the meaning of the word "southwest" has changed and become specific to mean the "southwest" section of Miami.

Language Gains and Attrition (Loss)

Brice (1994) stated that "additive bilingualism is when another language (L2) is added to the native language (L1) and neither is in jeopardy of being lost, so that the second language is added onto the first" (p.137). Hence, English is added to Spanish and both are maintained.

Brice (1994) also noted that "subtractive bilingualism occurs when at some stage in development of the native language (L1), it is replaced by the more prestigious dominant language (L2)" (p.137). In subtractive bilingualism, the native language, in this case Spanish, is lost at the cost of gaining English. Language loss can affect the semantic, syntactic, and pragmatic aspects of language (Anderson, 1997).

Some common language loss patterns may be seen in deficient code switching and code mixing. For example, certain words have been incorporated into the Puerto Rican Spanish of individuals living in New York (Gumperz, 1982). Many changes observed have been attributed to deficient language transference. These include:

1. Borrowing of English words for Spanish words (e.g., *el roofo/* "the roof," *leakiando/*"leaking"). In many instances these words have been borrowed and used within the community; hence language loss in the community may be occurring.
2. Borrowing of a translation. An idiomatic expression is borrowed from the second language and may consist of a direct translation. It is typically ungrammatical in the second language (e.g., *Te llamo para atras/*"I will call you back." The correct form is, *Te devuelvo la llamada* or *Te llamaré*).

Myths About Bilingual Students

Speech–language pathologists (SLPs), English as a second language (ESL) teachers, school psychologists, general education teachers, and counselors all need to be aware of the language functioning of Hispanic students in order to better serve them in school. Certain myths about second language acquisition persist and faulty decision making is sometimes based on the myths that are perpetuated. This section will attempt to dispel some of those myths and provide the research basis for a more appropriate truth (refer to Table 4.3).

Similarities and Differences in First and Second Language Acquisition

Acquisition of a second language is not entirely a new process for children. Some similarities and differences exist in first and second language acquisition (Dulay & Burt, 1974). Regarding similarities, in first language acquisition there is a silent period. In second language acquisition, the child listens and does not speak right away. Generally, rules of acquisition are the same when a person is acquiring English or Spanish. Developmental similarities include:

TABLE 4.3 *Myths About Bilingual Students*

Myth(s):	Truth(s):
1. Learning a second language takes little time and effort.	Studies have shown that learning English as a second language may take from 2–3 years for oral language skills and 5–7 years for higher-level, cognitive and academic language skills (Collier, 1987; Hakuta, 1986).
2. First and second language learners encounter the critical stage at puberty where learning is severely reduced (Lenneberg hypothesis).	Early versus late learning is dependent on two main variables: Age Upon Arrival (AOA) and length of residence (LOR) in the United States. Second language learning is primarily linear, inversely related to age where there is no cutoff age at which learning severely drops (Flege, 1992).
3. All language skills (listening, speaking, reading, writing) readily transfer from L1 to English (L2).	Reading is the skill that transfers most readily (Brice & Rivero, 1996; Carson, Carrell, Silberstein, Kroll, & Kruehn, 1990; Hakuta 1986; Major, 1992; Pica, 1994).
4. Code switching is an automatic indication of a language disorder.	CS may indicate high-level language skills in both L1 and L2 (Brice, 2000; Brice, Mastin, & Perkins, 1997b; Cheng & Butler, 1989; Reyes, 1995).
5. All bilinguals are balanced bilinguals and exert little effort in maintaining their balance.	Balanced bilinguals are the exception, rather than the norm, and it takes great effort to maintain high levels in both languages (Hakuta, 1986; Skutnabb-Kangas, 1981).
6. Children do not lose their first language.	Loss of the L1 and an underdeveloped L2 represent cognitive problems associated with language for normal L2 learners (Wong-Fillmore, 1992).
7. Exposure to English is sufficient for L2 learning.	Conditions for language learning include: need to communicate; access to speakers from that language (English); interaction, support, and feedback from speakers of that language; and time (Wong-Fillmore, 1992).
8. In order for students to better learn English, their parents should speak only English at home.	Conditions under which English is likely to be an additive process include: learning both L1 and L2 in the social context (both are valued and used in various contexts); bilingualism is promoted at home; a well-developed L1 before learning English; ample opportunities to interact with English speakers; the English speakers know the language well enough; learners receive appropriate instruction (Wong-Fillmore, 1992).

(continued)

Myth(s):	*Truth(s):*
9. Reading in the native language is detrimental to reading in English.	Children who live in literacy-rich home environments, regardless of whether it is in L1 or L2, develop the necessary prereading skills and literacy orientation skills that result in successful reading (Hamayan & Damico, 1991).
10. SLPs can test only in English to determine a language disorder in a bilingual child.	Children must be tested in both L1 and L2 (Brice & Montgomery, 1996; Hamayan &

1. Easier sound forms and words are acquired before more complex forms.
2. Labels are acquired first.
3. It is common for errors to occur in learning L1 and L2.

However, some differences have been noted in L1 and L2 acquisition. The following characteristics are not as prevalent in first language acquisition:

1. Avoidance of topics, tenses, words, situations. Children learning a first language do not avoid certain syntactic tenses, morphological constructions, or word choices. For example, some children in learning English will use the simple present tense "I sit" versus present progressive tense " I am sitting."
2. Spanish-English-speaking children may also use social and cognitive strategies not typically used by monolingual children. For example, repeating to oneself and starting and stopping a sentence several times is seen with bilingual children.
3. Children learning a second language can often experience certain psychological barriers such as fatigue. ·
4. If Spanish is not maintained while English is being acquired, then Spanish may atrophy and be lost.

Separate Versus Single Language Systems

Debate exists as to whether children acquiring a second language initially develop two separate language systems or a single system (including semantics and syntax). Do the children separate out the two systems or use a single (mixed) undifferentiated system (Döpke, 1992; Grosjean, 1982; Lanza, 1992; Volterra & Taeschner, 1978)?

Single Systems. An early view of simultaneous acquisition was characterized by Volterra and Taeschner (1978) and Grosjean (1982). They stated that two lexical systems appeared in the young bilingual child that were combined in a mixed, single system. The child at a later stage of development was able to separate, differentiate, and use the two systems. Vocabulary words rarely overlapped. Fantini (1985) stated that phonological differentiation began at around 24–30 months. Volterra and Taeschner (1978) stated that the child applied the same syntactic rules to both lexicons. Each word was tied to the particular context in which it was used. At a later stage, the child was able to correctly produce lexical and syntactic structures from both languages. Interference was confined to the syntactic level. To decrease interference, the child may have tried to keep the two languages as separate as possible—by, for example, associating one language with one parent. Eventually the child was able to separate out the two systems and not have interference between the two languages. Support for this model has declined over the last decade.

Separate Systems. Contrarily, Lanza (1992) claimed in her case study that her subject (who was 2.1 to 2.7 years of age) was able to differentiate language use in "contextually sensitive ways" at an early age and used separate systems initially in her development. Lanza stated that her subject was able to keep both languages separate with each parent and was able to code mix when appropriate. Thus, she was able to keep the languages separate or mix them, depending on the context of language use (i.e., which parent she spoke to). Thus, the use of a single syntactic system model is questioned.

Pearson, Fernandez, and Oller (1993) compared the simultaneous language and word development of 25 bilingual children and 35 monolingual children between the ages of 8 and 30 months of age. A parent report form (the MacArthur Communicative Development Inventory) was used to assess the child's receptive and expressive vocabulary in Spanish-English and English. They measured sound-meaning pairings (e.g., "ba" for "ball," labelled as Total Vocabulary), total lexicalized concepts (Total Conceptual Vocabulary), and translation equivalents or doublets (two sound-meaning pairings for a single lexical concept). Their conclusions were that the bilingual children were not slower to develop vocabulary than the monolingual children. The comparison and close relationship of the bilingual group's vocabulary growth to the monolingual group's vocabulary growth suggest that measurement of bilingual children's growth should be based on their knowledge of both languages.

Pearson, Fernandez, and Oller (1995) also recorded the vocabulary development of bilingual children using the MacArthur CDI. The two language systems of the 27 bilingual children, aged from 8 months to 2 years 6 months, were contrasted and compared. They investigated the number of pairs of translation equivalents for each child at different ages. Translation equivalents were noted for 30% of all words at early and later development and vocabulary stages. Thus, the claims by Volterra and Taeschner (1978) that bilingual children do not have corresponding words in the other language were not supported.

Genesee, Nicoladis, and Paradis (1995) examined the language differentiation of five bilingual children ranging in age from 1 year 1 month to 2 years 2 months of age. Language samples and observations from parents revealed that the children code mixed their languages (i.e., French and English) and were able to differentiate between their two language systems. The authors concluded that the child code mixing was not due to parental input but that language dominance seemed to play some role in the code mixing.

Conclusions regarding whether a bilingual child uses one lexical and syntactic system or is able to differentiate the systems at an early age are still under investigation and so the data are inconclusive. However, if doublets or use of translation equivalent pairs is one indication that the bilingual child processes both languages simultaneously and separates words into two different lexicons, then the existing evidence seems to favor this latter view. Further empirical research is needed.

Best Practices

School-based SLPs face major challenges as they provide services to bilingual students and try to identify those in need of speech–language services. Information on assessment of bilingual students is growing (Brice, 2000; Brice & Montgomery, 1996; Cheng, 1996; Crago, Eriks-Brophy, Pesco, & McAlpine, 1997; Gutierrez-Clellen, 1996; Hamayan & Damico, 1991; Kayser, 1996; Kayser, 1995; Langdon & Saenz, 1996; Quinn, 1995; Roseberry-McKibbin, 1997; Westby, 1997). Brice, Roseberry-McKibbin, and Kayser (1997) have provided some best-practice considerations to use when assessing bilingual children.

1. It is not possible for a child to have a language disorder only in one language (Brice, Roseberry-McKibbin, & Kayser, 1997).
2. The bilingual child needs to be compared, performance wise, to other children who come from a similar cultural, linguistic, and economic background. Home, school, and community data need to be examined.
3. It should not be assumed that all bilingual children have the same language experiences.
4. Children from bilingual backgrounds often have had fewer opportunities to hear and use English. It is normal for these second-language users to demonstrate a lower level of English proficiency. Even if the

child is exposed to a monolingual or predominantly English background, the English usage may not be the same as that other children have been exposed to or the English of the school.

5. Grammatical errors in the second language that are similar to those of first-language users are to be expected and must not be viewed as evidence of a disorder (Dulay & Burt, 1974). Some interference of the Spanish (mapping of L1 onto L2) on English is normal. However, most errors in English are developmental.

6. Language loss is a normal phenomenon when opportunities to hear and use the first language are withdrawn and minimized. When one language is favored, the favored language usually becomes dominant. English-language-learning children who experience language loss in the L1 may display scores that are similar to those of bilingual children with true language disorders.

7. Shifting from one language (code switching) to another within an utterance or across utterances is not indicative of a language problem. It is a normal behavior of proficient bilinguals.

SLPs are serving and will continue to serve bilingual populations, and a need still exists for information about serving bilingual students in therapy. The number of bilingual speech–language pathologists in the United States is currently inadequate to serve the growing bilingual school population (Kayser, 1995). Deal-Williams (personal communication, December 7, 1999) stated that the American Speech-Language-Hearing Association has numbers for Hispanics and numbers for bilingual individuals but not for both. As of June, 1999, there were 1,507 Hispanic-certified SLPs and 16 who were dual-certified in audiology. Fifteen hundred and seven bilingual (Spanish-English) SLPs is an insufficient number to meet the needs of the speech–language-disordered cohorts of the approximately 32 million Hispanics currently residing in the United States. It is hoped that this chapter has enabled current SLPs to become better informed about some second-language-acquisition variables so that they can better serve Hispanic students.

References

Aguirre, A. (1988). Code switching, intuitive knowledge, and the bilingual classroom. In H. Garcia, & R. Chavez (Eds.), *Ethnolinguistic issues in education* (pp. 28–38). Lubbock, TX: Texas Tech University.

Anderson, R. (1997). (1997, February). Examining language loss in bilingual children. *Communication Disorders and Sciences in Culturally and Linguistically Diverse Populations Newsletter, 3*(1), 2–5.

Blount, B., & Padgug, E. (1977). Prosodic, paralinguistic, and interactional features in parent-child speech: English and Spanish. *Journal of Child Language, 4,* 67–86.

Brice, A. (2000). Code switching and code mixing in the ESL classroom: A study of pragmatic and syntactic features. *Advances in Speech Language Pathology. Journal of the Speech Pathology Association of Australia, 20*(1),19–28.

Brice, A. (1994). Spanish or English for language impaired Hispanic children? In D. Ripich & N. Creaghead (Eds.), *School discourse problems* (2nd ed.). San Diego, CA: Singular Publishing.

Brice, A., Mastin, M., & Perkins, C. (1997a). Bilingual classroom discourse skills: An ethnographic study. *Florida Journal of Communication Disorders, 17,* 11–19.

Brice, A., Mastin, M., & Perkins, C. (1997b). English, Spanish, and code switching use in the ESL classroom: An ethnographic study. *Journal of Children's Communication Development,19*(2), 11–20.

Brice, A., & Montgomery, J. (1998, July). *Assessment of bilingual/bicultural school age students for possible language disorders.* Workshop presented at the Australian Linguistics Institute, Brisbane, Australia.

Brice, A., & Montgomery, J. (1996). Adolescent pragmatic skills: A comparison of Latino students in ESL and speech and language programs. *Language, Speech, and Hearing Services in Schools, 27,* 68–81.

Brice, A. & Rivero, Y. (1996) Language transfer: First (L1) and second (L2) proficiency of bilingual adolescent students. *Per Linguam. The Journal for Language Teaching and Learning, 12*(2) 1–16.

Brice, A., Roseberry-McKibbin, C., & Kayser, H. (1997, November). *Special language needs of linguistically and culturally diverse students.* Paper presented for the American Speech-Language-Hearing Association Annual Convention, Boston, MA.

Campbell, P. R. (1996). *Population Projections for States by Age, Sex, Race, and Hispanic Origin: 1995 to 2025.* Washington, DC: U.S. Bureau of the Census, Population Division, PPL-47.

Canagarajah, A. S. (1995). Functions of codeswitching in ESL classrooms: Socialising bilingualism in Jaffna. *Journal of Multilingual and Multicultural Development, 6*(3), 173–195.

Canale, M., & Swain, M. (1980). Theoretical bases of communicative approaches to second language teaching and testing. *Applied Linguistics, 1,* 1–47.

Carson, J. E., Carrell, P. L., Silberstein, S., Kroll, B., & Kuehn, P. A. (1990). Reading-writing relationships in first and second language. *TESOL Quarterly, 24,* 245–265.

Cheng, L. (1996). Enhancing communication: Toward optimal language learning for the limited English proficient students. *Language, Speech, and Hearing Services in Schools, 27*(4), 347–354.

Cheng, L., R., & Butler, K. (1989). Code switching: A natural phenomenon versus language deficiency. *World Englishes, 8,* 293–309.

Collier, V. (1987). Age and rate of acquisition of second language for academic purposes. *TESOL Quarterly, 21*(4), 617–641.

Crago, M., Eriks-Brophy, A., Pesco, D., & McAlpine, L. (1987). Culturally based miscommunication in the classroom. *Language, Speech, and Hearing Services in Schools, 28*(3), 245–254.

Döpke, S. (1992). *One parent, one language. An interactional approach.* Amsterdam: Benjamins.

Dulay, H., & Burt, M. (1974). Errors and strategies in child second language acquisition. *TESOL Quarterly, 7*(2) 129–36.

Eisenberg, A. (1986). Teasing: Verbal play in two Mexicano homes. In B. Schieffelin & E. Ochs (Eds.), *Language socialization across cultures* (pp. 182–198). Cambridge, UK: Cambridge University Press.

Faltis, C. J. (1989). Code-switching and bilingual schooling: An examination of Jacobson's new concurrent approach. *Journal of Multilingual and Multicultural Development, 10*(2), 117–127.

Fantini, A. (1985). *Language acquisition of a bilingual child.* Boston, MA: College-Hill.

Field, T., & Widemayer, S. (1981). Mother-infant interactions among lower SES Black, Cuban, Puerto Rican and South American immigrants. In T. Field, A. Sostek, P. Vietze, & P. Leoderman (Eds.), *Culture and early interactions* (pp. 182–198). Cambridge, UK: Cambridge University Press.

Flege, J. (1992). Speech learning in a second language. In C. Ferguson, L. Menn, & C. Stoel-Gammon (Eds.), *Phonological development: Models, research, and application* (pp. 565–604). Timonium, MD: York Press.

Genesee, F., Nicoladis, E., & Paradis, J. (1995). Language differentiation in early bilingual development. *Journal of Child Language, 22,* 611–631.

Grosjean, F. (1982). *Life with two languages. An introduction to bilingualism.* Cambridge, MA: Harvard University Press.

Gumperz, J. (1982). *Discourse strategies.* New York: Cambridge University Press.

Gutierrez-Clellen, V. (1999). Language choice in intervention with bilingual children. *American Journal of Speech-Language Pathology, 8*(4), 291–302.

Gutierrez-Clellen, V. (1996). Language diversity: Implications for assessment. In K. Cole, P. Dale, & D. Thal (Eds.), *Advances in assessment of communication and language* (pp. 29–56). Baltimore, MD: Brookes Publishing.

Gutierrez-Clellen, V. (1995). Narrative development and disorders in Spanish-speaking children: Implications for the bilingual interventionist. In H. Kayser (Ed.), *Bilingual speech-language pathology: An Hispanic focus* (pp. 97–127). San Diego, CA: Singular.

Hakuta, K. (1986). *Mirror of language. The debate on bilingualism.* New York: Basic Books.

Halliday, M. (1978). *Language as social semiotic.* Baltimore, MD: Edward Arnold.

Hamayan, E., & Damico, J. (Eds). (1991). *Limiting bias in the assessment of bilingual students.* Austin, TX: Pro-Ed.

Jacobson, R. (1982). The implementation of a new bilingual instructional model. The new concurrent approach. In R. Padilla (Ed.), *Ethnoperspectives in bilingual education research,* Vol. III: *Bilingual education technology.* Ypsilanti, MI: Eastern Michigan University.

Kayser, H. (1996). Cultural/linguistic variation in the United States and its implications for assessment and intervention in speech-language pathology: An epilogue. *Language, Speech, and Hearing Services in Schools, 27*(4), 385–386.

Kayser, H. (Ed.). (1995). *Bilingual speech-language pathology. An Hispanic focus.* San Diego, CA: Singular Publishing.

Kamwangamalu, N. M. (1992). Mixers and mixing. English across cultures. *World Englishes, 11*(2/3), 173–181.

Langdon, H., & Saenz, T. (Eds.). (1996). *Language assessment and intervention with multicultural students.* Oceanside, CA: Academic Communication Associates.

Lanza, E. (1997). *Language mixing in infant bilingualism.* Oxford, UK: Clarendon Press.

Lanza, E. (1992). Can bilingual two-year-olds code-switch? *Journal of Child Language, 19,* 633–658.

Leopold, W. F. (1939a). *Speech development of a bilingual child: A linguist's record.* Vol. 1: *Vocabulary growth in the first two years.* Evanston, IL: Northwestern University Press.

Leopold, W. F. (1939b). *Speech development of a bilingual child: A linguist's record.* Vol. 2: *Sound learning in the first two years.* Evanston, IL: Northwestern University Press.

Leopold, W. F. (1939c). *Speech development of a bilingual child: A linguist's record.* Vol. 3: *Grammar and general problems.* Evanston, IL: Northwestern University Press.

Leopold, W. F. (1939d). *Speech development of a bilingual child: A linguist's record.* Vol. 4: *Diary from age two.* Evanston, IL: Northwestern University Press.

Loasa, L. (1980). Maternal teaching styles in Chicano and Anglo-American families: The influence of culture and education on maternal behaviors. *Child Development, 51,* 759–765.

Major, R. C. (1992). Losing English as a first language. *Modern Language Journal, 76,* 190–208.

Mattes, L., & Omark, D. (1991). *Speech and language assessment for the bilingual handicapped* (2nd ed.). Oceanside, CA: Academic Communication Associates.

Meisel, J. M. (1989). Early differentiation of languages in bilingual children. In K. Hyltenstam & L. K. Obler (Eds.), *Bilingualism across the lifespan: Aspects of acquisition maturity and loss.* Cambridge, UK: Cambridge University Press.

Merritt, M., Cleghorn, A., Abagi, J. O., & Bunyi, G. (1992). Socialising multilingualism: Determinants of code switching in Kenyan primary classrooms. *Journal of Multilingual and Multicultural Development, 13* (1–2), 103–121.

Miller, N. (1988). Language dominance in bilingual children. In M. J. Ball (Ed.), *Theoretical linguistics and disordered language* (pp. 235–256). San Diego, CA: College-Hill Press.

Pearson, B. A. , Fernandez, S., & Oller, D. K. (1995). Lexical development in bilingual infants and toddlers: Comparison to monolingual norms. *Language Learning, 43*(1), 93–120.

Pearson, B. A. , Fernandez, S., & Oller, D. K. (1993). Cross-language synonyms in the lexicons of bilingual infants: One language or two. *Journal of Child Language, 22,* 345–368.

Pennington, M. C. (1995). Eight case studies of classroom discourse in the Hong Kong secondary English class. *Research Report Number 42.* Hong Kong Department of English. City University of Hong Kong.

Pfaff, C. W. (1979). Constraints on language mixing: Intrasentential code switching and borrowing in Spanish/English. *Language, 55,* 291–318.

Pica, T. (1994). Questions from the language classroom: Research perspectives. *TESOL Quarterly, 28* (1), 49–79.

Planos, R., Zayas, L., & Busch-Rossnagel, N. (1995). Acculturation and teaching behaviors of Dominican and Puerto Rican mothers. *Hispanic Journal of Behavioral Sciences, 17,* 225–236.

Poplack, S. (1980). Sometimes I'll start a sentence in Spanish y termino en español: Toward a typology of code-switching. *Linguistics, 18,* 581–618.

Quay, S. (1995). The bilingual lexicon: Implications for studies of language choice. *Journal of Child Language, 22,* 369–387.

Quinn, R. (1995). Early intervention? Qué quiere decir éso . . . What does that mean? In H. Kayser (Ed.), *Bilingual speech-language pathology. An Hispanic focus* (pp. 75–96). San Diego, CA: Singular.

Reyes, B. A. (1995). Considerations in the assessment and treatment of neurogenic disorders in bilingual adults. In H. Kayser (Ed.), *Bilingual speech language pathology. An Hispanic Focus* (pp. 153–182). San Diego, CA: Singular Publishing.

Roseberry-McKibbin, C. (1997). Understanding Filipino families: A foundation for effective service delivery. *American Journal of Speech-Language Pathology, 6*(3), 5–14.

Roseberry-McKibbin, C. (1995). *Multicultural students with special language needs.* Oceanside, CA: Academic Communication Associates.

Skutnabb-Kangas, T. (1981). *Bilingualism or not. The education of minorities.* Clevedon, England: Multilingual Matters.

Taylor, O. (1999). Cultural issues and language acquisition. In O. Taylor & L. Leonard (Eds.), *Language acquisition across North America* (pp. 21–38). San Diego, CA: Singular.

Tenenbaum, H., & Leaper, C. (1997). Mothers' and fathers' questions to their children in Mexican-descent families: Moderators of cognitive demand during play. *Hispanic Journal of Behavioral Sciences, 19,* 318–332.

van Kleeck, A. (1994). Potential bias in training parents as conversational partners with their children who have delays in language development. *American Journal of Speech-Language Pathology, 3,* 67–78.

Volterra, V., & Taeschner, T. (1978). The acquisition and development of language by bilingual children. *Journal of Child Language, 5,* 311–326.

Westby, C. (1997). There's more to passing than knowing the answers. *Language, Speech, and Hearing Services in Schools, 28*(3), 274–287.

Wong-Fillmore, L. W. (1992). *When does 1 + 1 = <2?* Paper presented at Bilingualism/Bilingüismo: A Clinical Forum, Miami, FL.

Wylie, E., & Ingram, D. E. (1999). *International second language proficiency ratings.* Brisbane, Australia: Griffith University.

Zentella, A. C. (1997). *Growing up Bilingual.* New York: Blackwell.

Zukow, P. (1987). Siblings as effective socializing agents: Evidence from central Mexico. In P. Zukow (Ed.), *Sibling interaction across cultures: Theoretical and methodological considerations* (pp. 79–105). New York: Springer-Verlag.

Distinguishing a Difference from a Disorder

Contextual Information

Functional use of language (pragmatics) must be examined and may be a determining factor in making a decision about a language difference versus a language disorder (Brice & Montgomery, 1996; Damico & Oller, 1980; Damico, Oller, & Storey, 1983; Guthrie & Guthrie, 1987; Hymes, 1972; Prutting & Kirchner, 1987). According to Haslett (1987), "pragmatics has emerged as a serious research area in several disciplines" and "an adequate understanding of language itself will rely heavily on pragmatics" (p. 3). Pragmatics is defined as the ability to use language in specific contexts and for specific purposes. According to Prutting and Kirchner (1987), pragmatics

> are concerned with the relationship between linguistic knowledge and the principles governing language use. Pragmatics must, therefore, account for two divergent aspects of communicative competence: those aligned with structure [formalism] and those that operate apart from the structural properties of utterances [functionalism] (p. 105).

It seems clear, then, that language learners are faced with two different types of tasks in acquiring communicative competence: the comparatively well-known one of becoming proficient in the use of language form (formalism) and the less well-understood one of learning how to use those forms in specific contexts in order to achieve desired actions (functionalism).

Hymes (1972) stated that

> Those brought together in classrooms, even though having the language of the classroom in common, *may not be wholly members of the same speech commu-*

nity [emphasis added]. They may share a speech situation but bring to it different modes of using its language and of interpreting the speech that goes on there. (p. xxxviii)

Guthrie and Guthrie (1987) found

How teachers and students use language, *rather than particular linguistic aspects of speech, may have more to do with the way children learn* [emphasis added] and the miscommunication, misunderstanding, and educational difficulty students encounter (p. 206).

A strong relationship seems to exist between language proficiency and academic achievement (Brice & Montgomery, 1996; Cazden, 1988; Cummins, 1984; Hymes, 1972; 1980; Simon, 1985). Because pragmatics concerns language usage, it follows that a significant relationship between proficiency in pragmatics and academic achievement exists and that proficiency in pragmatics may play a more serious role in school success than other aspects of language proficiency (i.e., morphology, sematics, syntax). The role that pragmatics plays in differentiating a difference versus a disorder in Hispanic students will be discussed here along with other aspects of language (morphology, sematics, syntax) and what role they play in distinguishing a difference from a disorder.

Research addressing pragmatics or functional language of any kind in culturally and linguistically diverse populations is sparse compared with the wealth of information that has been generated for students of other ages and for other aspects of language. Ellis (1992) studied the illocutionary act of requests in an ESL classroom with two English language learners. His study revealed that the students developed only a limited ability to vary their choice of request strategies in accordance with classroom demands and contextual factors. Ellis concluded that

. . . even with more time the classroom environment is insufficient to guarantee the development of full target language norms, possibly because the kind of 'communicative need' that learners experienced was insufficient to ensure development of the full range of request types and strategies (p. 20).

Fraser, Rintell, and Walters (1980) compared native speakers of Spanish and native speakers of English and found that the Spanish speakers showed more deference to other speakers and that this deference increased with the other person's age. In addition, more deference was shown with speakers of the opposite sex.

Wolfson (1989) found in a study of non-native English speakers from the middle class and other social classes that men and women of different ages, from a variety of occupational and educational backgrounds and from various cultural and linguistic backgrounds, exhibited difficulties in initiating and maintaining conversations. Wolfson did not specify what cultural and linguistic background her subjects were from; however, she did note that some speakers were from Israel. The non-native English speakers failed to appreciate the function of compliments as social lubricants in the dominant European American culture, especially as a means of initiating conversations.

Brice (1992) indicated that Spanish-speaking students enrolled in ESL classes displayed difficulties in making requests of others and in listening to a speaker. He concluded that these difficulties may pose problems and place the ESL students at risk for failure in cooperative learning situations in the classroom. Rice, Sell, and Hadley (1991) noted that ESL preschool children initiated fewer interactions than "speech-impaired" or normally developing children. Thus, normally developing ESL children experience pragmatic difficulties that may be associated with learning a second language.

Research concerning the pragmatic difficulties of Hispanic students with language disorders has been sparse, especially in terms of language disorders concerning pragmatics. Brice and Montgomery (1996) found that Hispanic bilingual students receiving speech–language therapy also experienced pragmatic difficulties in the secondary (middle) school environment, and these difficulties were of a more severe nature than those of monolingual students receiving speech–language therapy. Their difficulties included an inability to express themselves in the classroom, to initiate and finish classroom discussions, to listen to classroom discourse and follow teacher directions, and to cue others about the course of classroom discussions. Hence, the bilingual students enrolled in speech and language therapy experienced general difficulties in expressing themselves.

Teacher Pragmatics

Brice, Mastin, & Perkins (1997) studied an ESL classroom to determine teacher and student functional uses of language, particularly language involving Spanish and English language alternations, that is, code switching and code mixing. The following were the results: (a) questioning occurred with the highest frequency in the ESL classroom (28.17%), followed by (b) the use of commands (16.99%), (c) giving information (14.33%), (d) giving feedback (13.90%), and (e) answering and responding (9.50%).

To summarize the ESL literature, educational professionals may misinterpret and misperceive culturally different behaviors as being indicative of abnormal language difficulties associated with language disorders. The students may not be ready for the pragmatics of the classroom, and a mismatch may occur between teacher uses of language and student pragmatics that are Hispanic in nature. This possible misunderstanding of pragmatic norms of culturally and linguistically diverse students may result in inappropriate teaching or lack of intervention to address the difficulties. Worse yet, these misunderstandings may lead to inappropriate referrals for speech and language testing. Thus, the ability to use language appropriately becomes an issue for students from culturally and linguistically diverse backgrounds.

Observation

Getting information from different sources (i.e., ethnographic or naturalistic observations), locations, and interactions with different individuals may lead to more culturally valid information than use of norm-referenced tests (Roseberry-McKibbin, 1995). Information can be gathered from an environment where the language problem is not noticeable. What are the communication expectations in environments where the child is experiencing problems and in environments where the child is not experiencing problems? Interactional data can be collected (pragmatics) about the student and a hypothesis developed after the first round of interaction. The hypothesis can be tested in different sessions (second observation round) and integrated for decision making. Such data (pragmatics) can be collected from teachers and staff (Brice & Montgomery, 1996). The factors to consider in gathering this data include

1. Speaker's rate of speech
2. Tone of voice
3. Length of directions
4. Complexity of directions
5. Level of vocabulary, word choice
6. Organization of ideas
7. Ease of listening to
8. Who starts and ends conversations
9. Maintaining topics
10. Taking turns
11. Allowing for acceptable wait times before responding
12. Eye contact, body language
13. Active listening
14. Conveying information in an acceptable manner, appropriate for the culture of the student

Environmental Influences

With children under age three, use of familiar conversational partners of Hispanic background is recommended when gathering data because these children respond poorly to strangers. In general, parents of handicapped children may need special instruction because of the parents' need to have their children perform. Typically, parents overuse questions and directive speech (Owens, 1995; Reed, 1994).

Older Hispanic children may also respond poorly to strangers. Their response depends on the amount of cultural exposure to Anglo American expectations that they have (Brice, Roseberry-McKibbin, & Kayser, 1997; Roseberry-McKibbin, 1995).

Working with Hispanic Parents and Children: General Characteristics

Religious holidays may take precedence over school attendance, particularly for Cuban Americans and Puerto Rican Americans. Religion pervades language and attitudes toward education, government, and politics (e.g., *adios* literally means "to God"). References to religion in conversation may be common (Brice, Roseberry-McKibbin, & Kayser, 1997).

The exact nature of a handicap may not be truly understood by family members. Traditional Hispanic families seem to have a broader definition of normal and a narrower concept of what defines a handicap. Children with handicaps may be seen as a punishment from God to the parents (external locus of control) or may be seen as a gift to become better parents. Professionals working with clients/students from the family are highly revered. Teachers for students are seen as authority figures. This may pose a problem in trying to encourage family members to become involved, because the professionals may be expected to do everything since they are the experts (Madding, 1999; Roseberry-McKibbin, 1995).

Hispanic families in general tend to be more enmeshed. Social and task orientations co-exist versus an Anglo American tendency to separate the two. There may be several conversations going on at the same time instead of only one speaker at a time. Group interactions and group work (field dependent) serve as the focus for working rather than individual work (field independent). Problem solving (especially with younger children) is group-oriented, collectivistic, and (more intermental processing versus intramental processing) individualistic (Brice & Campbell, 1999). Children are spoken to rather than being initiators of conversation. Conversational boundaries are not as rigid; that is, interruptions are not seen as being negative. Gaining attention in a conversation is done by speaking louder. Hissing to gain someone's initial attention is also seen. Getting to the point in an initial discourse is spiral rather than direct linear (Brice, Roseberry-McKibbin, & Kayser, 1997; Burnette, 1997; Franco et al., 1996; Madding, 1999; Mindel, Habenstein & Wright, 1998).

Modifying Assessment Procedures

Several considerations may be applied when testing bilingual Hispanic students in order to differentiate a language disorder from a language difference. These may take the form of modifying existing tests, using nonstandard procedures (i.e., language samples), taking steps to minimize bias in testing Hispanic students, examining examiner characteristics, examining student characteristics, examining the content items of the test(s) used, and using interventions prior to testing (Brice, Roseberry-McKibbin & Kayser, 1997; Mattes & Omark, 1991; Roseberry-McKibbin, 1995).

Modifying Tests

Tests can be adapted by modifying existing tasks, by reviewing content items, by modifying content, and by modifying scoring procedures. Norm-referenced scores should not be used when a test is modified. Ortiz (1990) stated that norms should not be used at all with culturally and linguistically diverse children. Table 5.1 lists the major types of test modifications.

An example of double scoring is seen with A, a 7–10-year-old female evaluated for possible language disorders. Items that were identical on the Spanish and English items are compared. If the student scored correctly on either version (Spanish or English), then the item was deemed correct and added to the total raw combined score. The Test for Auditory Comprehension of Language (TACL) was administered in both English and Spanish. A's test results are reported for English, Spanish, and Combined scores in Table 5.2. Her overall accuracy on the TACL was 67% when administered in Spanish and 82% when administered in English. The TACL subsections address specific parts of speech such as verb tense, plurality, number agreement, complexity of sentences, pronouns, and prepositions.

A scored better in English on 53% (10/19) of the syntactical features, while only scoring better in Spanish on 10% (2/19) of these features. She scored equally well in either language on 37% (7/19) of the syntactical features. Hence, A showed a marked prefence for better understanding in English. On three items (highlighted in bold in Table 5.2)—overall vocabulary, adjectives, and pronouns—a combined score (Spanish and English) resulted in a better score than individually in either language.

Nonstandardized Approaches to Assessment

The use of natural communication or language samples when evaluating English language learners has been documented in the literature (Gutierrez-Clellen, 1999; Langdon & Saenz, 1996; Mattes & Omark, 1991; Roseberry-McKibbin, 1995). More information on the use of nonstandard

TABLE 5.1 *Test Modifications*

Modification	Procedure
Modify the task.	Develop more practice items for each task.
	Demonstrate the nature of the desired response (e.g., pointing, repeating words, drawing, rapid versus slow responses, etc.) and give examples of responses that would give maximum vs. minimal credit.
	Instructions may have to be reworded.
	Students should be given ample time to respond (to allow for linguistic and cultural differences in processing spoken English and responding especially if the tasks are performed in English).
	Continue testing beyond the ceiling.
	Repeat the stimuli more than what is specified in the test manual.
	Repeat the item more than what is specified in the test manual.
Modify content.	On picture recognition tests have the child name the picture in addition to pointing to the item to ascertain appropriateness of the labels given by the test.
	Have the child explain why certain incorrect answers were given.
Modify scoring.	Double-score items for English and Spanish. Add up all correct responses in English and Spanish. Look at the English scores, Spanish scores, and combined scores.
	Analyze performance on individual test items (look beyond the scores to determine why the student is missing particular items and to determine patterns of responses).
	Do not report test scores, i.e., standard scores, if the test is not normed on your student (i.e., particular Spanish dialect that he/she speaks, SES, and geographic region should be considered).

approaches to assessment is provided in Chapter 10. Much developmental information for ELL students is not available, and thus some assessment specialists argue that use of language samples is therefore inappropriate. However, Mattes and Omark (1991) counter this argument by saying that language samples do allow clinicians to make a distinction between normal language and disordered language. In order to make this distinction, the

TABLE 5.2 *Examples of Double Scoring*

Item	Spanish (%)	English (%)	Spanish and English Combined Results (%)
Vocabulary	71	95	**98**
Nouns	75	92	92
Adjectives	61	94	100
Verbs	88	100	100
Adverbs	66	100	100
Morphology	54	73	73
Noun, verb, adjective and derivational suffix "er", "ero"	0	90	90
Adjective and suffix "est," "el mas, la mas"	100	100	100
Noun and suffix "ist," "ista"	100	0	100
Noun number	50	100	100
Pronouns	66	88	**100**
Verbs	66	61	66
Prepositions	50	33	**66**
Interrogatives	66	100	100
Syntax	58	83	83
Simple imperative sentence	50	50	50
Noun-verb agreement	0	50	50
Complex sentence with independent clause and adjectival clause	100	100	100
Direct-indirect objects	100	100	100
Noun phrase wth modifiers	100	100	100
Complex imperative with conditional clause	100	100	100
Complex imperative using neither/nor	0	100	100
Compound imperative	100	100	100

sample has to be systematically compared to the abilities of other children who come from the same community and who have had similar cultural and linguistic experiences. General statements about length of sentences in words (not morphemes), diversity of vocabulary, use of past, present, and future tense markers can be made.

Some behaviors, especially nonverbal behaviors, are relatively universal, and others can be understood across cultures. When a child does not respond to others or appears separated from peers who speak the same language and come from the same background, then there is a need for concern. Mattes and O'Mark (1991) listed some behavioral observations that may be indicative of communicative disorders. These include the following:

1. Child rarely initiates interactions, verbal and nonverbal, with peers.
2. Peers rarely initiate interactions, verbal or nonverbal, with child.
3. Child's communication has little or no effect on the actions of peers.
4. Child does not engage in dialogue or action (play) with peers.
5. Child often uses gestures when speech would be a more effective means of communication.
6. Facial expressions and other nonverbal aspects of the child's communication are culturally inappropriate.
7. Facial expressions and other nonverbal aspects of peers indicate that they may be having difficulty understanding the child's communication.

In addition, Mattes & Omark (1991) suggested the use of elicited language production tasks to help differentiate a language difference from a disorder. Additional language aspects may need to be probed. The clinician may try using elicited imitation. This is the "say what I say" approach. Tasks may include a grammatic completion section in which the Hispanic student finishes an incomplete sentence by using the appropriate grammatical form. In addition, the following questions should be asked to assist in instructional placement decisions:

1. How much structure and individual attention is required for the child to acquire new language skills?
2. To what extent does the child exhibit inappropriate responses or off-task behaviors during instructional activities?
3. To what extent does the child require instructional strategies different from those used effectively with other children from a similar cultural and linguistic background?

Alternatives to inappropriate speech and language testing with Hispanic students are included in Table 5.3. As is evident in the table, no one approach is "foolproof." The SLP will have to use a combination of several

TABLE 5.3 *Assessment Alternatives*

Procedure	Pro	Con
1. Standardize existing tests on ELL Hispanic students.	1. Tests with appropriate local norms may be valid measures of language for bilingual Hispanic students.	1. New norms may be created that are lower than those of the original population. The test may be biased in its use of standard English and format. The new norms will not change this.
2. Modify or revise tests that will make them appropriate for ELL Hispanic students.	2. The modified tests with appropriate local norms may be valid measures of language for bilingual Hispanic students. The modified tests may be quicker to develop than new tests.	2. If done incorrectly, the test may become invalid. Normed results should be not be reported.
3. Use a language sample when assessing in ELL Hispanic student's language.	3. The language sample may yield repesentative results of the child's true language abilities. Samples can be taken in a variety of contexts and in both languages.	3. The sample will have to be taken in both languages/dialects. Developmental data for the other language/dialect may not be available. Procedures to elicit the sample may be biased.
4. Use criterion-referenced tests.	4. The criterion-referenced measures may yield more adequate results, i.e., freer of norm-referenced biases. The criterion can be SLP or teacher-selected. Criteria may be adjusted to reflect cultural and linguistic factors.	4. Is the criterion developmentally appropriate? Is the criterion culturally appropriate in that the child has had sufficient exposure/motivation to attain mastery?
5. Refrain from using all normed tests that have not been corrected for bias for use with ELL Hispanic students.	5. Results from the tests can be converted into criterion-referenced results; e.g., the child scored 17/20 on the oral	5. School districts like the use of standardized tests for eligibility placement criteria.

(continued)

TABLE 5.3 *Continued*

Procedure	Pro	Con
	vocabulary subtest revealing 70% correctness.	
6. Develop new tests.	6. New tests with appropriate local norms may be valid measures of language for bilingual Hispanic students.	6. The new test may be appropriate only for a limited segment of the population. Test development involves many resources (time, effort, and money).
7. Test in both languages/dialects and use a combined scoring method.	7. The results can be compared to determine if a stronger language exists. Additionally, test items that are identical can be double-scored.	7. Time-consuming and many of the problems above still exist.
8. Conduct classroom-based ethnographic observations; obtain three separate points of reference (triangulation).	8. A true picture of performance and classroom expectations may emerge. The SLP and teacher may conference and discuss the student's performance.	8 Time-consuming. No normed comparisons; descriptive information that school districts may not accept.
9. Teach test items and periodically re-test (dynamic assessment).	9. A true picture of performance may emerge over a period of time. The standard for measurement is based on learning and not static results.	9. Time-consuming.
10. Use teacher interviews, questionnaires.	10. Teachers may observe behaviors not seen by the SLP. An opportunity to confer with the teacher may result.	10. Time-consuming. Nonnormative data that does not yield standard scores.
11. Confer with other professionals from a similar cultural and linguistic background.	11. The other professionals may shed insight into cultural or language factors unknown to the SLP.	11. Time-consuming; other professionals from the child's culture may not be

of these approaches in order to achieve the least-biased assessment (Rose-berry-McKibbin, 1995).

Best Practices

A checklist of best practices prior to assessment and testing may include the following:

1. Have multiple classroom interventions been attempted prior to testing and assessment?
2. Have classroom or home observations been carried out?
3. Have others been interviewed, e.g., parents or other family members, classroom teacher?
4. Have all possible procedures been carried out (i.e., classroom interventions, parent conference, teacher conference, prereferral screening, etc.)?
5. Have referrals containing information of the problem been stated in behavioral terms?
6. Have these behavioral issues been checked for cultural relevance? Is it normal behavior for that culture or for a student experiencing similar conditions?
7. Have test items, procedures, and items used in the assessment been checked for cultural appropriateness through interviews with the parents, members of the community, or someone familiar with the particular Hispanic culture of the student (Mexican, Puerto Rican, Cuban, etc.)?

In addition, some general guidelines when evaluating a bilingual ELL Hispanic student should be followed:

1. Test in Spanish (L1) and in English (L2) as much as possible.
2. Establish rapport with the child and/or parent(s).
3. Report standardized test scores with caution. Scores should not be reported especially if the test/procedure was not standardized on a similar Spanish dialect and cultural group (Mexican, Puerto Rican, Cuban, etc.).
4. Make sure that the child understands the task.
5. Make sure that the task is one familiar to the child.
6. Encourage the child to expand upon responses.
7. Utilize language samples, speech samples, observational samples, criterion-referenced measures, rating scales, performance-based measures, judgment-based assessment, and portfolio assessment procedures.
8. Give the child extra time to respond.
9. Confer with and involve the parent(s).
10. Confer with other professionals from a similar background (Mexican, Puerto Rican, Cuban, etc.).

References

Brice, A. (1992). The Adolescent Pragmatics Screening Scale: A comparison of language-impaired students, bilingual/Hispanic students, and regular education students. *Howard Journal of Communications, 4* , 143–156.

Brice, A., & Campbell, L. (1999). Cross-cultural communication. In R. Leavitt (Ed.), *Cross-cultural health care: An international perspective for rehabilitation professionals* (pp. 83–94). London: W. B. Saunders.

Brice, A., Mastin, M., & Perkins, C. (1997). English, Spanish, and code switching use in the ESL classroom: An ethnographic study. *Journal of Children's Communication Development,19*(2), 11–20.

Brice, A., & Montgomery, J. (1996). Adolescent pragmatic skills: A comparison of Latino students in ESL and speech and language programs. *Language, Speech, and Hearing Services in Schools, 27*, 68–81.

Brice, A., Roseberry-McKibbin, C., & Kayser, H. (1997, November). *Special language needs of linguistically and culturally diverse students.* Paper presented for the American Speech-Language-Hearing Association Annual Convention, Boston, MA.

Burnette, D. (1997). Grandmother caregivers in inner-city Latino families: A descriptive profile and informal social supports. *Journal of Multicultural Social Work, 5*(3/4), 121–137.

Cazden, C. (1988). *Classroom discourse: The language of teaching and learning.* Portsmouth, NH: Heinemann.

Cummins, J. (1984). *Bilingualism and special education : Issues in assessment and pedagogy.* San Diego: College-Hill Press.

Damico, J., & Oller, J., Jr. (1980). Pragmatic versus morphological/syntactic criteria for language referrals. *Language, Speech, and Hearing Services in Schools, 11* , 85–94.

Damico, J., Oller, J., Jr., & Storey, M. (1983). The diagnosis of language disorders in bilingual children : Surface-oriented and pragmatic criteria. *Journal of Speech and Hearing Disorders, 48,* 385–394.

Dulay, H., & Burt, M. (1974). Errors and strategies in child second language acquisition. *TESOL Quarterly, 7*(2) 129–36.

Ellis, R. (1992). Learning to communicate in the classroom. A study of two language learners' requests. *Studies in Second Language Acquisition, 14,* 1–23.

Franco, F., Fogel, A., Messinger, D., & Frazier, C. (1996). Cultural differences in physical contact between Hispanic and Anglo mother–infant dyads living in the United States. *Early Development and Parenting, 5*(3), 119–127.

Fraser, B., Rintell, E., & Walters, J. (1980). An approach to conducting research on the acquisition of pragmatic competence in a second language. In D. Larsen-Freeman (Ed.), *Discourse analysis in second language research* (pp. 75–91). Rowley, MA: Newbury House.

Guthrie, L. F., & Guthrie, G. P. (1987). Teacher language use in a Chinese bilingual classroom. In S. R. Goldman & H. T. Trueba (Eds.), *Becoming literate in English as a second language.* Norwood, NJ: Ablex.

Gutierrez-Clellen, V. (1999). Language choice in intervention with bilingual children. *American Journal of Speech-Language Pathology, 8*(4), 291–302.

Halliday, M. (1978). *Language as social semiotic.* Baltimore, MD: Edward Arnold.

Haslett, B. J. (1987). *Communication. Strategic action in context.* Hillsdale, NJ: Lawrence Erlbaum Associates.

Hymes, D. (1972). Preface. In C. Cazden, V. John, & D. Hymes (Eds.), *Functions of language in the classroom* (pp. xi–viii). New York: Teachers College Press.

Langdon, H., & Saenz, T. (Eds.). (1996). *Language assessment and intervention with multicultural students.* Oceanside, CA: Academic Communication Associates.

Madding, C. (1999). Mamá é hijo: The Latino mother–infant dyad. *Multicultural Electronic Journal of Communication Disorders,1*(2). [On-line]. Available: http://www.asha.ucf.edu/madding3.html.

Mattes, O., & Omark, D. (1991) *Speech and language assessment for the bilingual handicapped* (2nd ed). Oceanside, CA: Academic Communication Associates.

Mindel, C., Habenstein, R., & Wright, R. (1998). (Eds.). *Ethnic families in America: Patterns and variations.* Upper Saddle River, NJ: Prentice-Hall.

Ortiz, A. (1990, October). *AIM for the BEST: A model for serving exceptional language minority students.* Workshop given at the Symposium on Culturally Diverse Exceptional Children, Albuquerque, NM.

Owens, R. E. (1995). *Language disorders: A functional approach to assessment and intervention* (2nd ed.). Boston, MA: Allyn and Bacon.

Prutting, C., & Kirchner., D. (1987). A clinical appraisal of the pragmatic aspects of language. *Journal of Speech and Hearing Disorders, 52*(2),105–119.

Reed, V. (1994). *An introduction to language disorders* (2nd ed.). New York: Merrill.

Rice, M., Sell, M., & Hadley, P. (1991) Social interactions of speech-and-language-impaired children. *Journal of Speech and Hearing Research, 34,* 1299–1307.

Roseberry-McKibbin, C. (1995). *Multicultural students with special language needs.* Oceanside, CA: Academic Communication Associates.

Simon, C. (1985). *Communication skills and classroom success: Therapy methodologies for language-learning disabled students.* San Diego: College-Hill Press.

Wolfson, N. (1989). The social dynamics of native and nonnative variation in complimenting behavior. In M. Eisenstein (Ed.), *The dynamic interlanguage: Empirical studies in second language acquisition* (pp. 219–236). New York: Plenum.

6

Socialization Practices of Latinos

Carolyn Conway Madding, Ph.D.

Setting the Scene:
Delineations and Distinctions

The writer who approaches such a broad subject as the socialization practices of Latinos must begin the process by setting parameters and defining terms. Fundamental to that procedure is clarification of the differing terminology used to describe component groups within the Latino spectrum, as well as an explanation of the heterogeneity of the population.

Latino and *Hispanic* are terms used to refer to, or describe, persons who have come to the United States from many different countries. They are Mexicans, Cubans, Nicaraguans, Salvadorians, Panamanians, Puerto Ricans, Dominicans, Guatemalans, Costa Ricans, Ecuadorians, Peruvians, and others whose roots are in Central and South America and the Caribbean. It is only in the United States that they are known by the aggregate terms *Latino* and *Hispanic* (García-Preto, 1996).

The word *Hispanic* was coined by the United States government for the 1980 Census as a collective name for individuals of Mexican, Cuban, Central American, Spanish, and Puerto Rican heritage (de Paula, Laganá, & Gonzalez-Ramirez, 1996; García-Preto, 1996). According to García-Preto (1996), the creation and continued use of *Hispanic* has been a source of conflict within some groups who are defined by it.

In the 1960s, some Mexican Americans chose to refer to their group as *Chicanos* and *La Raza; Latino* has replaced those expressions of Latin solidarity and is the nomenclature most often used in the western United

States today. *Hispanic,* although widely accepted, is most prevalent in the eastern and southern sections of the country.

The Latino population consists of people with distinctive cultures and with diverse geopolitical and sociopolitical backgrounds. They are individuals whose families have inhabited lands in New Mexico, Arizona, Texas, Florida, and California for many generations; others with varying lengths of residency; as well as recently arrived immigrants and those who are undocumented (de Paula, Laganá, & Gonzalez-Ramirez, 1996; García-Preto, 1996; Glover, 1999; Holman, 1997). Latinos cover the spectrum of age, education, race, level of acculturation, and socioeconomic status. Although nearly 9 of 10 live in just 10 states and 1 in 3 in California, Latinos reside in all of the 50 U.S. states (Hernández, 1997).

The diversity of Latinos, not only from group to group but within group, precludes all-encompassing descriptions of their behaviors and socialization patterns. There are, however, a number of unifying factors recognized by many researchers and scholars that may be used to discuss Latinos in the aggregate. Common to nearly all Latino groups are the Spanish language, familism, religiosity/spiritualism, love of children and high hopes for their future, and interdependence of family and fictive kin (de Paula, Laganá, & Gonzalez-Ramirez, 1996; Glover, 1997; Juarbe, 1996; Kayser, 1998; Pérez, Pinzón, & Garza, 1997; Varela, 1996). Around these nearly universal components and values, Latinos live and socialize their offspring. In addition, each group under the Latino umbrella has its idiosyncratic mores, either implicitly or explicitly passed on to its children.

Language

Language is the principle means through which the socialization process is accomplished (Madding, 1999). It is one of the most powerful and pervasive purveyors of culture. Inextricably enmeshed in the fabric of every culture, language plays a fundamental role in the transmission of beliefs, values, and customs. As such, it is not merely a vehicle for communication, but a rich endowment of each speaker's heritage (Madding, 2000b). (Refer to Chapter 4 for a further discussion.)

For Latinos, the Spanish language exists as a common bond and is a symbol of solidarity within a diverse population. It represents a cultural link despite its many dialects and transmutations (Kalyanpur & Harry, 1999; Massey, Zambrana, & Bell, 1995). According to Massey, Zambrana, and Bell (1995), a majority of Latinos are either bilingual or monolingual speakers of Spanish; thus the unique role played by the Spanish language in every aspect of Latino life in the United States cannot be underestimated.

Most Latino parents want their children to be bilingual. They recognize the value of English and would like their progeny to be highly skilled in that language and to "feel comfortable with American culture and traditions" (Rodríguez, 1999, p. 13). At the same time, however, they want their children to speak Spanish and retain their Latino identity (Rodríguez, 1999; Valdés, 1996). Spanish is valued as the language of emotions and as a source of comfortable communication within the home (Gumperz, 1982; Rodríguez, 1999), whereas English is the language of education and commerce and as such is the way one may *abrirse paso en la vida* ("get ahead in life") (Valdés, 1996, p.136).

A considerable amount of confusion exists across all segments of the Latino culture in regard to which language or languages should be used during a child's developmental years. Parents and other caregivers may speak in Spanish, in English, or may code switch and/or code mix between the two languages (Brice, Mastin, & Perkins, 1997). Some have strong convictions about speaking to children in one language or the other, but these beliefs are seldom based on linguistic research. Conflicting advice from family, friends, teachers, and others may exacerbate the situation (Madding, 2000a).

Although most linguists and scholars who specialize in language development emphasize the importance of building heritage language proficiency in order to establish a strong base for learning English as a second language (Brice, 2000; Gutierrez-Clellen, 1999; Holman, 1997), parents are often swayed by teachers and other advice-giving adults, who suggest that a child in the United States should learn English first. If this advice is followed, children may receive less-than-optimum language input from parents who are not fluent in English. The best model, the language with the highest level of proficiency and the one that carries cultural overtones, is the heritage language. Parents who are native speakers of Spanish, but who attempt to socialize the child through the medium of English, will not only provide an inferior model but will also jeopardize the emotional, cultural connection within the family (Madding, 2000a; Roseberry-McKibbin, 1995).

In reality, a mélange of languages is encountered within the diverse Latino family structures encountered across the United States. Puerto Ricans in New York, Cubans in Florida, and Mexicans in California speak to varying degrees in Spanish, English, and "Spanglish." In multigenerational homes, it is not uncommon to hear grandparents speaking Spanish, parents conversing in a combination of Spanish and English, and school-age children chattering to each other in English (but answering questions proffered by adults in Spanish). The television may be broadcasting cartoons in English and novelas in Spanish (de Paula, Laganá, & Gonzalez-Ramirez, 1996; Juarbe, 1996; Valdés, 1996; Varela, 1996). This is the language environment amidst which many Latino children are socialized. Although there are also many Latino households in which only Spanish or only English is spoken, influences from the "other" language pervade the atmosphere. It is clear, therefore, that Latino children in the United States learn language and assimilate culture through myriad models and that one cannot speak of language socialization practices from a generalized point of view.

Familism

Webster's New World Dictionary (1999, p. 512) defines familism as "a form of social structure in which the needs of the family as a group are more important than the needs of any individual family member." The Latino family is often characterized by its adherence to the fundamentals of familism, whereby each individual's rights and his or her independence are surrendered for the good of the family unit (Brice & Campbell, 1999; McDade, 1995). Hurtado (1995) reports that Latinos, regardless of their roots and places of origin, show strong dedication to the family. "Even among the most acculturated individuals, Latinos' attitudes and behaviors are still more familistic than Anglos" (Hurtado, 1995, p. 49). According to Pérez, Pinzón, and Garza (1997), self-esteem and self-identity are byproducts of strong Latino family ties. Among Latinos, *familia* is "synonymous with security, nurturance, love, and comfort" (Mayo, 1997, p. 53) and the concept of family is idealized as something sacred (Rodríguez, 1999).

As reported by de Paula, Laganá, and Gonzalez-Ramirez (1996), familism "dictates that family comes first" (p. 214) for Mexican Americans. Families are united, loyal, and give assistance to each other, as needed, to maintain the reputation and solidarity of the group. Interpersonal relationships are often characterized by affection, intimacy, and respect, with clearly defined roles within the more traditional family networks (de Paula, Laganá, & Gonzalez-Ramirez, 1996). In the 10 Mexican American families studied by Valdés (1996), familistic values were deeply entrenched. All families in her study "viewed their life chances as primarily being a function of ligatures, that is, of family bonds" (p. 186). Furthermore, "centralizing" women were the core around which family gatherings occurred and during which the family ideology was communicated (Valdés, 1996).

Cubans and Puerto Ricans are also reported to be family-oriented, with strong ties to extended family (Juarbe, 1996; Varela, 1996). Mayo (1997) submits that all blood and fictive kin can find acceptance and sustenance in the Puerto Rican family system.

Embedded within the concept of "familism" are a number of specific attributes that family members are expected to incorporate in their relationships. Primary among these is *respeto* ("respect"). This encompasses not only respect for elders and their wisdom but also for the family structure, the culture, and for each individual (de Paula, Laganá, & Gonzalez-

Ramirez, 1996; Kayser, 1998). Children learn *respeto* in order to conform to and comprehend the roles filled by family members. In the study by Valdés (1996), she observed that even small children were expected to understand their roles and those of their parents and siblings. They were expected to be obedient and not to add to the work burden of their parents. A recurring theme across literature on several Latino cultures is that children are raised to be obedient and respectful (de Paula, Laganá, & Gonzalez-Ramirez, 1996; Juarbe, 1996; Valdés, 1996; Varela, 1996).

Especially in Mexican American and Puerto Rican extended families, grandparents, blood relatives, and fictive kin are actively involved in child socialization and disciplinary practices (McDade, 1995). Grandparents, other family, and trusted friends may be consulted and may actively participate in various family decisions or activities related to school, health, or other matters of concern (Pérez, Pinzón, & Garza, 1997; Valdés, 1996).

Compadrazgo

Extended family units frequently include *compadres* ("godfathers") and *comadres* ("godmothers"), confidants who have assumed a coparenting role (Hurtado, 1995; Kalyanpur & Harry, 1999). The fictive kin system of *compadrazgo* ("coparenthood") originated in the tradition of Roman Catholicism, wherein the parents of a newborn selected godparents for their infant. Those accepting the role of *padrino* ("godparent") became second parents, responsible for the spiritual and worldly needs of the child. Although the lives of Latinos are evolving, *compadrazgo* endures as an interfamily system of support, affection, and friendship. *Compadres* and *comadres* are often lifelong members of the family, participating in life passages, in everyday activities, and serving as advisers and close friends to various members of the family (López, 1999; Rodríguez, 1999).

Mothers

Traditionally, Latina mothers have been respected and honored as the heart of the family (Rodríguez, 1999). They usually exert considerable influence over family members and enjoy lifelong reverence from their children. Mothers have the expectation of close personal relationships with all of their children and presume that reciprocal relationships will endure with daughters as the latter reach adulthood (Glover, 1999). Juxtaposed to Glover's contention is the assertion by Rodríguez (1999) that Latina mothers are matriarchs of the family, with especially strong bonds to their sons. Although Latino fathers are made to feel that they reign supreme in the home, in reality it is the mothers who head the clan (Rodríguez, 1999).

Many Latina mothers who have acculturated to the customs of the United States and fulfill nontraditional roles by working outside the home are developing increased independence and expect their husbands to be more egalitarian than in the past (Rodríguez, 1999). They retain their esteemed role as mothers, however, despite social and economic changes (de Paula, Laganá, & Gonzalez-Ramirez, 1996; Rodríguez, 1999).

Mother–child dyadic formations may not be an archetype in the Latino family as it is in Anglo society. The mother–child dyad may coexist with the sibling–child dyad, the *comadre*–child dyad, the aunt–child dyad, or the grandparent–child dyad (Kalyanpur & Harry, 1999; Madding, 1999). Multiperson socialization and care of children is more the norm than the exception in both traditional Latino families and in the growing number of those headed by single mothers (Battle, 1997; Burnette, 1997).

Several authors have found in their studies that Mexican-descent mothers present little teaching, rely heavily on nonverbal instruction, use slow pacing and negative feedback, speak to their children with high percentages of adult wording, and do not ask children to recite or perform. "Testing" children to ascertain information learned is seldom encountered in this population. Only babies learning their first words are encouraged to regurgitate their repertoire on demand. These requests, or label quests, appear to cease once a child has gained a modicum of language. Evidence points to the fact that many Latinas of Mexican origin see themselves as mothers and caregivers, not as teachers (Kayser, 1995; Madding, 1999; Valdés, 1996; Wong-Fillmore, 1982).

In a study of 80 Mexican American mothers' socialization strategies, Cousins, Power, and Olvera-Ezzell (1993) found that the low-income mothers studied used directive techniques to control their children's behavior, seldom accompanied by rationales for the desired result. Madding's (1999) study of 30 Latina mother–infant dyads showed that mothers tended to be nonverbal or directive when interacting with their children. The mothers were uncomfortable playing on the floor with their children, although they complied with the requests to do so when guided by professionals in an early-intervention play-based program.

Franco, Fogel, Messinger and Frazier (1996), in a study of 52 mother–infant dyads, found that Latina mothers "showed more close touch and more close and affectionate touch compared to Anglo mothers, who showed more distal touch" (p. 119). Indeed, Latinos place a high cultural value on touching, accompanied by *abrazos* ("hugs") and *besos* ("kisses") (Rodríguez, 1999).

Entrée to a network of supportive relationships was shown by de Leon Sianz (1990) to give Mexican American migrant mothers the sustenance they needed to be open and accepting of their children. A study by La Roche, Turner, and Kalick (1995) corroborated the findings of de Leon Sianz (1990), indicating that a supportive social environment was "a powerful variable influencing the well-being of mothers and toddlers" (p. 382).

Valdés (1996) reports that the Mexican mothers in her study demonstrated no anxieties in regard to the rearing of children. Latina mothers seemed more tolerant of disruptive behavior of their children, such as fussing and crying or lack of attentiveness, according to Madding (1999). Madding's (1999) study also revealed that Latinas showed little response to the successful attempts of their children to speak, manipulate an object, take turns, and the like. That is, they did not readily clap, smile, or praise the child for each attainment until they had adapted and conformed to the reactions of professionals.

Some authors have reported that Latinas seldom teach their preschool children to memorize the alphabet, learn to count, begin to read, or know body parts or shapes (Kayser, 1995; Madding, 1999). When queried as to who will teach their children these concepts, the most common response was that teachers would do it (Madding, 1999). A few added that siblings and parents might help. Of the 30 mothers in Madding's study, there were only a handful who confirmed the presence of children's books in their homes. The books possessed, however, were most frequently in English, even though the mother and child were monolingual in Spanish. When questioned about the appropriate age to begin reading to children, the majority of the mothers believed that when the child was three to five years of age, she/he would understand well enough to be read to. Many mothers thought that reading should not begin until the child was five years of age (Madding, 1999).

It is apparent that the Latino children in the studies delineated above were not socialized by their mothers along the guidelines usually encountered in European American mother–infant dyads. It must be acknowledged, however, that the body of knowledge derived from research on Latino families is limited and that change occurs with increasing levels of acculturation. Nevertheless, because schools in the United States operate on the assumptions of European American standards, it appears that many Latino children will not meet those standards of preschool knowledge upon entering school. They may begin the educational process at a disadvantage, often exacerbated by the inability to speak English. Recognizing this fact does not mean that educators and European American society should regard Latino socialization and teaching practices as inferior, but rather that methods should be examined that could "level the playing field." As aptly stated by Kalyanpur and Harry (1999, p. 82), "the dual assumptions of universality and deficiency tend to affect parent–professional interactions adversely." As an alternative to the "Latino deficit" model and to the assumption that the European American model is universal and best, perhaps professionals will continue to gather data on Latino socialization practices, refrain from judgment or unfavorable comparisons, and search for new avenues for the provision of services that are as culturally appropriate as possible, while preparing the Latino child for success in the diverse cultural milieu of the United States (Madding, 1999).

Fathers

Traditionally, fathers have been the head of the Latino household and have exercised authority over all members of the family. Mexican American and Cuban men have been expected to be strong, in control, and to be the provider for the family (de Paula, Laganá, & Gonzalez-Ramirez, 1996; Varela, 1996). To other cultures, the dominance of the father and submissiveness of the mother have created a stereotype of the Latino male as the exemplification of "machismo," synonymous with brutishness. Historically, however, machismo held the connotation of virility, strength, bravery, honor, and integrity (de Paula, Laganá, & Gonzalez-Ramirez, 1996; Mayo, 1997). Despite the lingering effects of machismo, most Latino families share decision making and are more egalitarian in conjunction with role fulfillment than in the past (de Paula, Laganá, & Gonzalez-Ramirez, 1996). Research has shown that Latino fathers frequently enjoy an emotional closeness to their offspring (Mayo, 1997). In a study by López and Hamilton (1997), more Mexican American women than European American women reported that their fathers provided love.

Siblings

Older siblings, and especially females, have played an important role in the socialization and care of Latino infants. López and Hamilton (1997) report that Mexican American sisters often babysit and care for their siblings. In the Mexican American families studied by Valdés (1996), older siblings taught skills to younger children, without being asked by mothers to do so. Parents assumed that children would learn activities of daily living by observing their older siblings as they accomplished these tasks. As children matured, they seemed to take on the responsibility for teaching younger children. When the babies and toddlers were ready to learn, the siblings simply taught them and then showed pride when a skill was acquired by the youngster (Kayser, 1998; Valdés, 1996).

Valdés (1996) reported that the Mexican American families in her study depended on children to care for younger siblings at any given moment. Moreover, they expected the children to be kept out of harm's way and out of mischief. Mothers or others were never observed to teach older children how to take on or execute these responsibilities. It was assumed that children would learn from watching others in the household. In families with several children present, the eldest female child automatically took responsibility for the others. Furthermore, the older child or children possessed implicit authority to impose family rules. Hierarchical imposition of power among siblings was respected during a variety of activities. For instance, younger children would not respond to many adults, but looked to the elder child, who made the response for them (Valdés, 1996).

Latino siblings are socialized to perform a dual function as both sister or brother and pseudoparent. It has been observed that the sustenance and teaching provided by Mexican American siblings closely approximates the support given to European American children by their mothers (Volk, 1999).

Latino Children

Role of Children

"To be Hispanic is to value children" (Rodríguez, 1999, p. 3). The literature is replete with evidence to corroborate this statement and to state the importance of children in all Latino populations. Latino children, in general, are cherished, loved, and nurtured in a protective environment (de Paula, Laganá, & Gonzalez-Ramirez, 1996; Juarbe, 1996; Rodríguez, 1999; Valdés, 1996). Children are central to the cultural concept of *familia* and their presence validates the marriage of their parents.

Many family activities and celebrations are centered around children and are inclusive of them. Children not only attend all functions, such as weddings, receptions, and parties, but they are proudly displayed and encouraged to take an active part in the festivities and dancing. *Bautismos* ("baptisms"), *quinceañeras* (girl's 15th birthday celebration), and *cumpleaños* ("birthdays"), with the ever-present piñata, are typical Mexican celebrations centered on children (Rodríguez, 1999).

Much attention is showered on infants, who are perceived as mutual possessions of blood relatives and fictive kin. Babies are the center of attention, often held and fondled by adults as well as by older siblings, cousins, and others in the extended family (Rodríguez, 1999; Valdés, 1996).

In some Cuban, Puerto Rican, and Mexican American homes, male children are socialized to take on an independent, competitive, and strong persona. They are taught to be protective of the family, and especially so of their mothers and sisters. Girl children learn to be supportive and caring and, in more traditional families, to be submissive (de Paula, Laganá, & Gonzalez-Ramirez, 1996; Juarbe, 1996; Varela, 1996).

As do parents of other world cultures, Latinos want the best for their children. For those who value familism and interdependence, children may be reared to contribute to the strength of the family as a whole rather than to set their sights on lofty educational goals and independence (Kayser, 1998; Valdés, 1996). Although education is respected by all Latino cultures, each group may have different expectations as to the level, value, and use of outcomes.

Teaching Through *Dichos*

Latinos still use the centuries-old method of teaching behavioral standards, cultural values, and virtues, by incorporation of *dichos*. These are sayings or proverbs that are interspersed randomly in everyday speech or in writing and are intended to inculcate desired behavior. Among the hundreds of *dichos* used in Latino culture are the following:

> *Saber es poder.* ("Knowledge is power.")
> *No hay mal que por bien no salga.* ("Something good comes from every bad situation.")
> *Más vale pájaro en mano que ciento volando.* ("A bird in the hand is worth a hundred in the sky.")
> *El que adelante no mira, atrás se queda.* ("The person who doesn't look ahead, remains behind.")
> *El que sabe dos idiomas, vale por dos.* ("One who speaks two languages has the value of two people.")
> *El que nada debe, nada teme.* ("One who owes nothing, has nothing to fear.")
> *Acompáñate con los buenos y serás uno de ellos.* ("If you hang around with good people, you will be like them.")
> *El hombre propone y Diós dispone.* ("Man proposes and God arranges/takes care of matters.")

Discipline

Although Latino parents accept that it is important for "children to be allowed to be children" (S. Vásquez-Wrtaza, personal communication, June 20, 2000; Valdés, 1996), they encourage children to develop respect for authority and for the roles of adults within the confines of the family (Glover, 1999). It is assumed by most Latinos that young children will learn quickly to be *bien educado* ("well-behaved"). Begging for attention, interrupting adult conversations, or making demands, especially in the presence of guests, is usually frowned upon. A raised eyebrow or slight nod of the mother's head may be used as a signal to the errant child, as well as to any supervising sibling, that the behavior must cease (Valdés, 1996).

Juarbe (1996) reports that Puerto Rican mothers take an active role in disciplining children, using both positive and negative reinforcement, which may involve corporal punishment. Cuban mothers may use less corporal punishment and more verbal threats (Escobar & Escobar, 1981). The Mexican Americans studied by Valdés (1996) indicated that physical punishment by the father was the solution of last resort for misbehavior. These parents expressed concern about societal repercussions for perceived child abuse and were worried about controlling their children without final recourse to physical means. In the study by McDade (1995), however, there were no Latino parents who found threats of physical punishment, or spanking with an object, to be acceptable forms of punishment for children.

McDade (1995) revealed that the Latino parents in her study were in agreement that the community has a stake in how parents raise their children. Supporting these findings are those of Valdés (1996), who reports that the Mexican American families she studied expected adults to take an interest in the behavior of their own children as well as the conduct of other children in the community. Furthermore, her respondents agreed to the acceptability of reprimands from nonfamilial adults when misbehavior was observed. Rodríguez (1999) concurs, stating that if a child in the Latino culture misbehaves, adults are obligated to correct him or her and show the correct way to comport oneself.

Disability

Some cultures or subcultures hold very strong beliefs in regard to children born with or subsequently acquiring a handicapping condition. These beliefs about the nature, cause, and manifestations of the condition will have an effect upon the family as a whole, on interactions among siblings, and most of all on the affected child.

In the United States, European American beliefs and attitudes pervade the social, educational, and medical models around which services for the handicapped are provided. Latinos who access these systems to obtain services for a handicapped child are subjected to and immersed in the European American system. Their basic beliefs, which may be contrary to those encountered in the system, are thus tempered and perhaps muted, but not necessarily changed. There are data from various Latino groups, revealing culture-specific convictions, that may influence socialization of handicapped Latino children. Professionals who come into contact with these children and their families may provide more culturally competent services by becoming acquainted with some of these beliefs before they are encountered.

According to Juarbe (1996), Puerto Ricans often believe that the mother is at fault when a child is born with genetic defects. Mothers are blamed for not taking proper care of themselves during pregnancy. Sometimes, illnesses or disabilities are attributed to past sins of the parents, for which punishment is meted out to the offspring. If the child is severely involved, he or she will be cared for at home, with the women of the household taking charge.

Although most Cubans are reported to have higher levels of education than other Latino groups, and thus to understand modern medical theories, there are still some who hold on to folk beliefs about illness and disability. Varela (1996) cites the Cuban idea that evil spells or voodoo magic may be a cause for such eventualities. Genetic defects are believed to be caused by heredity, or perhaps by pregnancy-related trauma. It is sometimes believed, as well, that a mother who looks at a handicapped child will produce an infant with the same disability.

Those of Mexican descent may cling to a mosaic of folk beliefs about illness and disability, as related by de Paula, Laganá, and Gonzalez-Ramirez (1996) and Kayser (1998). *Mal de ojo* ("evil eye") is cast by a jealous person who gazes strongly at a child or pregnant woman, causing the child to be ill or disabled. People with green eyes are especially feared, as are those who admire an infant without touching. Failure of a pregnant woman to satisfy *antojos* ("cravings") is believed to result in a defect or injury to the unborn child. *Susto* ("shock") is thought to be initiated by an earthquake or any other jolt to the system and to cause wasting, a defective fetus, or to precipitate stuttering in a child. Some believe that a woman who does not have a safety pin under her clothing for protection against a full moon or an eclipse will bear a child with a cleft palate.

In her research, this author has encountered numerous Mexican mothers of handicapped children who have related firmly entrenched beliefs about the cause of their child's disability. Among these is a woman who asserted that her son was afflicted with Down syndrome during the 8th month of her pregnancy when she was shocked to hear that her husband had been in an automobile accident. Another, whose husband left a former wife to marry her, believed that all her children would be hexed by the *mal de ojo* she had received from the ex-wife. When her first child was born with Down syndrome, her fears were realized.

Following the tenets of the church, Latino Catholic parents may resign themselves to a child's disability, invoking the hand of God as either the deliverer of a cross to bear or as having chosen them to be parents of a special child. There is stigma attached to the birth of a disabled child, which may cause the parents to keep the child at home and to hide her or him from visitors. Mexican disabled children will seldom be institutionalized, regardless of the severity of their handicapping condition. On the other hand, they may be coddled by the extended family and given privileges and freedoms not available to other children (de Paula, Laganá, & Gonzalez-Ramirez, 1996; Kayser, 1998; Steinberg, Davila, Collazo, Loew & Fischgrund, 1997). McCord and Soto (2000) state that most Latino families with whom they have worked "do not consider caring for their child with a disability to be a burden, expect to continue caring for their needs into adulthood, and do not view the disability as something to be fixed" (p. 10).

Outside the parental realm, however, lies an unfortunate behavior among some Mexicans and Mexican Americans, which is epitomized by the tendency to mock the disabled child in not-so-subtle ways. Children with Down syndrome have been reportedly called "Little Monkey" by both adults and children. Others with facial or body disfigurements are sometimes mocked and jeered within the culture. More benign, but still discomforting, are the diminution and denial of personhood resultant from being called *el sordito* ("the little deaf one"), *la muda* ("the one who doesn't speak"), or *el tonto de María* ("Maria's little stupid one"). Steinberg et al. (1997) reported that deaf Latino children were sometimes barred from play with hearing children because mothers of the latter group feared that the problem might be contagious. Other Latinos encountered by the deaf children showed pity for them.

Most Latinos are either Catholic, follow an ever-more-popular evangelistic faith, or are Mormon. In addition to their profound heritage in religious ideals, there are strong ties to various types of folk beliefs. Many Mexican Americans make consistent border crossings to visit relatives and seek services of *curanderos* ("folk healers"). Using herbs, incantations, massage, and ritualized litanies, *curanderos* attempt to heal the sick, ease the disabled, and cleanse the soul (de Paula, Laganá, & Gonzalez-Ramirez, 1996; Kayser, 1998). Similarly, Puerto Ricans may call upon *espiritistas* ("spiritual healers"), who heal with the use of herbs, ointments, and prayers, in conjunction with Western medicines (Juarbe, 1996). When Cubans feel that healing by Western medical techniques and religion are not sufficient, they may call upon a Santero priest (Brice, 1993). Ceremonies involving spells, voodoo magic, and animal sacrifice are held in individual homes (Varela, 1996).

Mexican mothers may make *mandas* ("promises") to the Virgin of Guadalupe, vowing not to cut a child's hair until a miracle is performed to heal the disability (Zuniga, 1998). A male Mexican child with spina bifida was observed by this author to reach pre-school years with unshorn, long black hair, allowing him to be looked upon by newcomers as a girl. When the healing miracle was not forthcoming, the mother finally permitted the child to have a haircut.

Whether Latino parents of handicapped children seek healing or solace from standard religious faith, folk practices, or a syncretization of the two, they demonstrate the belief that a cure or remedy is possible through divine or other intervention.

Best Practices

Educators who comprehend the family's needs and cultural beliefs, and can lend support without making judgment, will usually find acceptance of their efforts to help the child (Zuniga, 1998). The following general Best Practice suggestions will assist SLPs and educators in working with Hispanic and Latino families:

1. By spurning overgeneralizations and stereotypes of Mexicans, Cubans, Puerto Ricans, or other Latinos, teachers and other educational personnel can guide all children toward realization of goals. Best practices dictates, however, that educators go beyond rejection of aggregation by ethnicity toward an open-minded realization of the necessity for change.
2. Educational practices, child behavioral and learning expectations, and socialization of children can no longer be viewed from European American models.
3. Everyone working in a school environment where Latino children are present, including teachers, specialists, administrators, and support personnel, should be involved in ongoing inservice education. A systematic, well-organized program of learning, based on data and input by recognized authorities on Latino families and socialization practices, spreads knowledge, stimulates thought, and ultimately creates a more Latino-friendly school environment.
4. Best practices also suggests that educators view themselves as ethnographers. Keeping notes on observed behaviors of Latino children, parents, siblings, and extended family may result in a valuable compendium of cultural and linguistic information.

It is only through a thorough grounding in the totality of the socialization milieu from which the Latino child emerges onto the school scene that we, as educators, can begin to address the needs of the child. He or she stands before us, full of anxiety, excitement, and anticipation. Perhaps Juan speaks only Spanish, Beatriz just arrived from Puerto Rico, and Pedro quakes from fear of being away from the family. A Latino-friendly school filled with caring, knowledgeable personnel can provide a welcome to all, thus setting the stage for fulfilling, culture-affirming educational experiences.

Summary

America, always a place of evolving ethnic mixture, is entering its Latino era. In California, Latinos make up the largest ethnic enclave, and many school districts show Latino enrollments of 90% or more (California Department of Education, 1999). The Latino era is a rolling wave, however, destined to sweep over the country and bring profound changes during the 21st century. Riding on this wave are diverse Latino families, who with their children will be part of the largest ethnic group in the United States sometime before the middle of the century (Rodríguez, 1999). Although English will continue to be the language of the country, Spanish is sure to be omnipresent, perhaps gaining the prestige it deserves and has often been denied. Native speakers of Spanish are now the third-largest cohort among world languages, supplanting the position of native English speakers, now in fourth position (Famighetti, 2000). The influence of language, value systems, beliefs, and mores held dear by the various Latino cultures will undoubtedly affect all ethnic groups in the country.

By acquaintance with socialization practices of Latinos, as we know them through ethnographic studies and first-hand reports, educators, medical personnel, social workers, and other professionals can work more effectively to provide appropriate speech and language services, learning outcomes, and community support for Latinos and, increasingly, by Latinos.

References

Battle, J. (1997). Academic achievement among Hispanic students from one- versus dual-parent households. *Hispanic Journal of Behavioral Sciences, 19*(2), 156–170.

Brice, A. (2000, March). Which language for bilingual speakers? Factors to consider. *American Speech-Language-Hearing Association Special Interest Division 14, Communication Disorders and Sciences in Culturally and Linguistically Diverse Populations, 6*(1), 1–7.

Brice, A. (1993). *Understanding the Cuban refugees.* San Diego: Los Amigos Research Associates.

Brice, A., & Campbell, L. (1999). Cross-cultural communication. In R. Leavitt (Ed.), *Cross-cultural health care: An international perspective for rehabilitation professionals* (pp. 83–94). London: W. B. Saunders.

Brice, A., Mastin, M., & Perkins, C. (1997). English, Spanish, and code switching use in the ESL classroom: An ethnographic study. *Journal of Children's Communication Development, 19*(2), 11–20.

Burnette, D. (1997). Grandmother caregivers in inner-city Latino families: A descriptive profile and informal social supports. *Journal of Multicultural Social Work, 5*(3/4), 121–137.

California Department of Education, E.D.U. (1999). *Statewide enrollment in California public schools by ethnic group.* [On-line]. Available: http://star.cde.ca.gov.

Cousins, J., Power, T., & Olvera-Ezzell, N. (1993). Mexican-American mothers' socialization strategies: Effects of education, acculturation, and health locus of control. *Journal of Experimental Child Psychology, 55,* 258–276.

de Leon Sianz, M. (1990). Maternal acceptance/rejection of Mexican migrant mothers. *Psychology of Women Quarterly, 14,* 245–254.

de Paula, T., Laganá, K., & Gonzalez-Ramirez, L. (1996). Mexican Americans. In J. Lipson, S. Dibble, & P. Minarik (Eds.), *Culture & nursing care: A pocket guide* (pp. 203–221). San Francisco: UCSF Nursing Press.

Escobar, K., & Escobar, O. (1981, Fall). *Comparison of childrearing practices of Anglos, Cuban-Americans, and Latin Americans.* Paper presented at the Florida Atlantic University Public Forum.

Famighetti, R. (Ed.). (2000). *The World Almanac and Book of Facts 2000.* Mahwah, NJ: Primedia Reference.

Franco, F., Fogel, A., Messinger, D., & Frazier, C. (1996). Cultural differences in physical contact between Hispanic and Anglo mother–infant dyads living in the United States. *Early Development and Parenting, 5*(3), 119–127.

Garciá-Preto, N. (1996). Latino families: An overview. In M. McGoldrick, J. Giordano, & J. Pearce (Eds.), *Ethnicity and family therapy* (pp. 141–154). New York: The Guilford Press.

Glover, G. (1999). Multicultural considerations in group play therapy. In D. Sweeney & L. Homeyer (Eds.), *The handbook of group play therapy* (pp. 282–294). San Francisco: Jossey-Bass Publishers.

Gumperz, J. (1982). *Discourse strategies.* New York: Cambridge University Press.

Gutierrez-Clellen, V. (1999). Language choice and intervention with bilingual children. *American Journal of Speech-Language Pathology, 8*(8), 291–302.

Hernández, M. (1997). *A profile of Hispanic Americans. Executive summary.* Princeton, NJ: Population Resource Center.

Holman, L. (1997). Working effectively with Hispanic immigrant families. *Phi Delta Kappan, 6,* 47–49.

Hurtado, A. (1995). Variations, combinations, and evolutions: Latino families in the United States. In R. Zambrana (Ed.), *Understanding Latino families: Scholarship, policy, and practice* (pp. 40–61). Thousand Oaks, CA: Sage Publications.

Juarbe, T. (1996). Puerto Ricans. In J. Lipson, S. Dibble, & P. Minarik (Eds.), *Culture & nursing care: A pocket guide* (pp. 222–238). San Francisco: UCSF Nursing Press.

Kalyanpur, M., & Harry, B. (1999). *Culture in special education: Building reciprocal family–professional relationships.* Baltimore, MD: Paul H. Brookes Publishing.

Kayser, H. (1998). *Assessment and intervention resource for Hispanic children.* San Diego: Singular Publishing Group.

Kayser, H. (1995). *Bilingual speech–language pathology: An Hispanic focus.* San Diego: Singular Publishing Group.

LaRoche, M., Turner, C., & Kalick, S. (1995). Latina mothers and their toddlers' behavioral difficulties. *Hispanic Journal of Behavioral Sciences, 17*(3), 375–384.

López, L., & Hamilton, M. (1997). Comparison of the role of Mexican-American and Euro-American family members in the socialization of children. *Psychological Reports, 80,* 283–288.

López, R. (1999). Las comadres as a social system. *Affilia, 14*(1), 24–41.

Madding, C. (2000a, April). *Least-biased assessment. . . Is this a quixotic view?* Paper presented at the California State University Fullerton Fifth Annual Multicultural Conference, Fullerton, CA.

Madding, C. (2000b). Maintaining focus on cultural competence in early intervention services to linguistically and culturally diverse families. *Infant-Toddler Intervention: The Transdisciplinary Journal, 10*(1), 9–18.

Madding, C. (1999). Mamá é hijo: The Latino mother–infant dyad. *Multicultural Electronic Journal of Communication Disorders,1*(2). [On-line]. Available: http://www.asha.ucf.edu/madding3.html.

Massey, D., Zambrana, R., & Bell, S. (1995). Contemporary issues in Latino families. In R. Zambrana (Ed.), *Understanding Latino families: Scholarship, policy, and practice* (pp. 190–204). Thousand Oaks, CA: Sage Publications.

Mayo, Y. (1997). Machismo, fatherhood and the Latino family: Understanding the concept. *Journal of Multicultural Social Work, 5*(1/2), 49–61.

McCord, S., & Soto, G. (2000). Working with low-income Latino families: Issues and strategies. *American Speech-Language-Hearing Association Special Interest Division 14, Communication Disorders and Sciences in Culturally and Linguistically Diverse Populations, 6*(2), 10–11.

McDade, K. (1995). How we parent: Race and ethnic differences. In C. Jacobson (Ed.), *American families: Issues in race and ethnicity* (pp. 283–300). New York: Garland Publishing.

Pérez, M., Pinzón, H., & Garza, R. (1997). Latino families: Partners for success in school settings. *Journal of School Health, 67*(5), 182–184.

Rodríguez, G. (1999). *Raising nuestros niños: Bringing up Latino children in a bicultural world.* New York: Fireside.

Roseberry-McKibbin, C. (1995). *Multicultural students with special language needs.* Oceanside, CA: Academic Communication Associates.

Steinberg, A., Davila, J., Collazo, S., Loew, R., & Fischgrund, J. (1997). "A little sign and a lot of love. . .": Attitudes, perceptions, and beliefs of Hispanic families with deaf children. *Qualitative Health Research, 7*(2), 202–222.

Valdés, G. (1996). *Con respeto: Bridging the distances between culturally diverse families and schools.* New York: Teachers College Press.

Varela, L. (1996). Cubans. In J. Lipson, S. Dibble, & P. Minarik (Eds.), *Culture and nursing care: A pocket guide* (pp. 91–100). San Francisco: UCSF Nursing Press.

Volk, D. (1999). "The teaching and the enjoyment and being together. . ." : Sibling teaching in the family of a Puerto Rican kindergartner. *Early Childhood Research Quarterly, 14*(1), 5–34.

Webster's New World College Dictionary (4th ed.). (1999). M. Agnes (Ed.). New York: Macmillan.

Wong-Fillmore, L. (1982). Minority students and school participation: What kind of English is needed? *Journal of Education, 164,* 143–156.

Zambrana, R. (Ed.). (1995). *Understanding Latino families: Scholarship, policy, and practice.* Thousand Oaks, CA: Sage Publications.

Zuniga, M. (1998). Families with Latino roots. In E. Lynch & M. Hanson (Eds.), *Developing cross-cultural competence: A guide for working with children and their families* (pp. 209–250). Baltimore, MD: Paul H. Brookes Publishing.

7

Clinician as a Qualitative Researcher

Qualitative Research and Speech–Language Pathology

Qualitative research is becoming more a part of the repertoire that speech–language pathologists are using in research and/or clinical practice (Cole & Taylor, 1990; Crago, 1990; Crago, Eriks-Brophy, Pesco, & McAlpine, 1997; Damico & Damico, 1997; Damico, 1990; Foster, Barefoot, & DeCaro, 1989; Katz, 1990; Kovarsky 1990; Kovarsky & Duchan, 1997; Kovarsky & Maxwell, 1997; Maxwell, 1990; Ripich & Spinelli, 1985; Sturm & Nelson, 1997; Westby, 1997; Westby, 1990). Without realizing it, speech–language pathologists are already familiar with the practices and methodology of qualitative research and its benefits through their existing clinical practice. Use of language samples, use of classroom-based assessment and portfolio assessment, observation of student performances in classrooms, interviews with general classroom and English as a second language teachers, and use of questionnaires are common methodologies in qualitative research.

The SLP may ask herself/himself three questions: (a) what is the need? (b) what gains do I obtain, and, (c) how can I make this an integral part of my assessment repertoire? Any SLP who has assessed an English-language-learning bilingual student will clearly know that standard assessment practices do not work well with this population (Rose-berry-McKibbin, 1995; Langdon & Cheng, 1992; Langdon & Saenz, 1996). Therefore, the need is to incorporate different assessment practices that reveal the true abilities of bilingual Spanish–English-speaking children in order to distinguish between a language difference and a language disorder. It is believed that use of qualitative practices may allow the clinician to make these appropriate distinctions. What is to be gained is that a wider scope of what the student can and cannot do will be revealed in light of classroom and school performance. And finally, the SLP can gain a truer sense of classroom expectations than what is gained through the use of traditional tests and procedures. This true sense of academic expectations will enable the SLP to serve bilingual students in the best fashion, that is, by giving the students the ability to succeed in the classroom.

Qualitative research may evoke several different meanings for speech–language pathologists involved in research; for example, the terms *ethnography* and *case studies* are often associated with qualitative research. However, ethnography and case studies are simply subsets of the different qualitative approaches that are available (Bogdan & Biklen, 1992; Glesne & Peshkin, 1992).

The purpose of this chapter is to present a tutorial on the use of qualitative research in speech–language pathology. First, qualitative research will be compared with quantitative research. Next will follow a discussion of qualitative research methods such as interviews, document research, ethnographic methods, and case studies. Specific applications of these methods to clinical practice will be made, with examples from various areas, such as working with multicultural clients. A brief review of ethnographic methods in a specific study will be presented. The goals of this chapter are for speech–language pathologists (SLPs) to (a) see how they are already using qualitative research methods in their daily clinical activities and (b) learn some new qualitative methods that they can apply to make daily clinical practice more successful with a variety of clients from diverse backgrounds, particularly Hispanic clients.

Qualitative Versus Quantitative Research

Qualitative research is descriptive research. Vin (1984) stated that qualitative methods "are the preferred strategy when 'how' or 'why' questions are being posed, when the investigator has little control over events, and when the focus is on a contemporary phenomenon within some real life context"(p. 13). Qualitative research can be concerned with group diversity, through the belief that group diversity can contribute to the acquiring of new perspectives. Qualitative research is concerned with an interpretevist paradigm (versus a positivist approach in quantitative research, which will be defined later). The interpretevist paradigm involves a socially constructed approach where observations and measurement occur through the researcher's personal involvement in the study. Because the researcher is personally involved, the task of ensuring researcher objectivity is foremost. With qualitative research, the notion of objectivity is explicitly acknowledged and through this acknowledgment, bias can be reduced (Bogdan & Biklen, 1992; Glesne & Peshkin, 1992; Lancy, 1993; Tesch, 1990).

Qualitative research also involves an inductive approach, where the researcher enters the situation with no preconceived hypotheses or questions and usually studies small numbers of participants in great depth and detail. The researcher observes, and does not manipulate the participants and the research setting as she or he tries to understand the naturally occurring phenomena. Qualitative research involves understanding the participants in a study and the setting and social construct that revolve around the participants (understanding the context is crucial). Qualitative research involves an in-depth, long-term approach to the investigation of a problem in which the researcher becomes the instrument (Glesne & Peshkin, 1992). Data in qualitative research explore the range of human behaviors and are gathered and interpreted in words.

Thus, qualitative research can be an excellent means of gathering data and information about culturally and linguistically diverse populations because of its ability to ask "how"and "why"questions. This is particularly critical when little developmental and normative data exist for culturally and linguistically diverse populations (Roseberry-McKibbin, 1995). Qualitative research is also sensitive to group diversity, making it even more appropriate as a means of understanding culturally and linguistically diverse populations. One specific way that SLPs can use qualitative research is to understand the cultural values of a new cultural group that has moved to their area. Because local SLPs have not had training or experience in working with Hispanic families, qualitative research can be used to understand Latino culture, language, and perceptions of disabilities and rehabilitation. (A reading list of qualitative articles and chapters is provided in Appendix A for the SLP unfamiliar with some aspects of qualitative investigations. This list should provide some additional help on "how to" information.)

In contrast to qualitative research, quantitative research involves a positivist approach, which is concerned with positive and measurable facts and phenomena. Quantitative research involves the use of a hypothetical–deductive approach, where the researcher enters a situation with pre-formulated questions and hypotheses. The researcher's task is to test the hypotheses experimentally, and the researcher expects specific outcomes from the study. Variables are specified beforehand, and there is manipulation and control of these variables. For example, the researcher controls subject variables such as age and socioeconomic status. A major goal of quantitative research is to control for and eliminate confounding variables that might impact the results of the study. The researcher is concerned with reliability, or replicability of the study, and with external validity, or the ability of the study's results to be generalized to similar populations. Large numbers of subjects can be studied through the gathering of quantitative data. Data in quantitative research involve numbers, not words, and meaning is derived from statistical manipulation of the numbers. (Refer to Table 7.1 for a comparison of qualitative and quantitative research.)

TABLE 7.1 *Qualitative Versus Quantitative Research Differences*

Qualitative Research	Quantitative Research
1. Focus of study is understanding behaviors.	1. Focus of study is understanding the causes of phenomena or the seeking of facts.
2. Discovery orientations.	2. Verifying orientations.
3. Subjectivity.	3. Objectivity.
4. Data gathering involves observations, typically nonobtrusive.	4. Data gathering involves controlled manipulation of variables.
5. Research questions introduced by the inside participants (emic perspective).	5. Research questions introduced by the outside researcher (etic perspective).
6. Process-oriented.	6. Product-, outcome-oriented.
7. Real, rich, deep, authentic data.	7. Reliable and valid data.
8. Ungeneralizable studies (high internal validity).	8. Generalizable studies (high external validity).

Qualitative research can be combined with quantitative research (Patton, 1990; Reichardt & Cook, 1979); many researchers believe that true research value lies in using a variety of methods (Eisner, 1981; Firestone, 1987; Howe, 1988; Mercurio, 1979). (Refer to Table 7.2 for a description of the advantages of qualitative and quantitative research.) What follows is a description of the various qualitative approaches available to the clinician researcher or SLP who wishes to utilize these methods to improve service delivery to clients from a variety of backgrounds. It should be noted that many of the qualitative methods (interviews, reviewing documents, observations, and gathering of samples such as language samples) are already used by SLPs in their clinical work and therefore should not pose difficulties in their implementation. Thus, SLPs should be able to implement more detailed and extensive qualitative research methods into their clinical practice with diverse populations with relative ease.

Types of Qualitative Research

Interviews

The interview is the most widely used qualitative research method (King, 1994). The purpose of the qualitative interview is to view the research topic from the perspective of the interviewee and not necessarily to obtain quan-

TABLE 7.2 *Qualitative Versus Quantitative Research Advantages*

Qualitative Research	Quantitative Research
1. Ideal for complex phenomena about which little is known.	1. Ideal for complex phenomena about which a base of information already is known and for which causes and relationships between the phenomena are sought.
2. The task is to discover and formulate hypotheses.	2. The task is to verify and test hypotheses.
3. The participants are small in number.	3. The subjects are large in number.
4. Little intrusion in the research process; observation of cases.	4. Manipulation and control of variables.
5. Investigator is aware of her or his biases.	5. The investigator's bias is controlled for, reduced, or eliminated.
6. Long investigations.	6. Short investigations.

tifiable responses (Cassell & Symon, 1994; King, 1994). Interviews are characterized by a low degree of structure, a focus on general questions, and also a focus on specific questions. Conducting an interview can be similar to obtaining case history information from a client. Thus, SLPs have had experience and specific training in this area.

Document Research

The term *document* has been used to describe artifact data (Merriam, 1990). Document research is retrospective analysis of written records kept by or on participants in a particular social group. Although valuable, data found in documents typically have not been established for research purposes and therefore may be incomplete. In addition, the documents may come to the researcher in forms that are not easily understood. Speech–language pathologists have had experience investigating individual education plans (IEPs), admittance records, and case history questionnaires. Thus, SLPs have had clinical experience investigating documents. They can apply the concept of document research to enhance the validity of the documents they use in making clinical decisions through asking the following questions that are asked in qualitative research:

a. What is the history of the document?
b. How did the researcher obtain it?

c. What is the authenticity of the document? How valid is the document?

d. Is the document complete?

e. Has it been altered, tampered with, or edited?

f. What is the purpose of the document?

g. Do other documents exist that may reveal similar or additional information?

In asking these questions, SLPs can ensure that clinical decisions based on their investigation of documents such as IEPs, diagnostic reports from previous clinicians, and reports from other professionals will be more valid.

Ethnographic Methods

The process of an ethnographical or qualitative study is described in further detail elsewhere (Bogdan & Biklen, 1992; Glesne & Peshkin,1992; Plante, Kiernan, & Betts, 1994). Thus, only a brief review of the various aspects involved in ethnographic research shall be given here. (Please refer to Appendix A, the reading list, for further readings and elucidation of ethnography. Also, refer to Chapter 10 for a discussion of ethnography in evaluation and diagnostics.) Qualitative research is descriptive research. Hence, words are used to describe the findings instead of numerical data (Bogdan & Biklen, 1992; Glesne & Peshkin, 1992). The data that are gathered are obtained via observations and the taking of field based notes over an extended period of time, that is, the repeated observations of variables across time. Validity of the data, or authenticity, is obtained through ethnographic triangulation (i.e., three separate data points of the observations).

The terms associated with qualitative research come from various disciplines. Anthropologists employ the term *ethnography,* while sociologists have used the terms *field study* and *ethnomethodology* (Bogdan & Biklen, 1992; Glesne & Peshkin, 1992; Lancy, 1993). All these terms and disciplines concern themselves with qualitative research, or the study of the group as the unit of analysis (Stake, 1995). The study of individual units or cases is case study research. Case studies are detailed examinations that may include one subject, one setting, or one particular event.

The case study method involves gathering data about a single subject (e.g., a student, a teacher, one school) or about one bounded area of study (e.g., one classroom) (Plante, Kiernan, & Betts, 1994; Stake, 1995). Hartley (1994) states that "case study methodology is an underutilized research strategy"(p. 208). The case study can implement both quantitative and qualitative methods; however, the emphasis is generally on qualitative methods (Hartley, 1994). The methods of data collection are the same as in larger-scale ethnographic field studies, which can include observation and interviews. Hence, the levels of observation can be the same as in the ethnographic field study (i.e., from observer, observer as participant, participant as observer, or participant points of view). These terms are defined later.

Ethnography, which comes from the anthropological tradition (Glesne & Peshkin, 1992), is the study of larger events, such as an entire community. It involves a long immersion in the field (data site). The researcher collects data primarily through participant observation and interviewing. Data are gathered through participant research, document collection, and interviewing of participants (the term *participants* is used instead of *subjects* because in ethnography, as opposed to quantitative experimental research, the persons under investigation play an active role in the data collection and the research).

Researcher observation exists along a continuum. On one end the researcher is mostly an observer, whereas at the other end the researcher is an active and vital member in the community. Thus, one can divide this continuum into four types of participant researchers: (1) observer, (2) observer as researcher, (3) researcher as observer, and (4) member. (*Note:* The qualitative and ethnography literature uses the term *participant* to refer to both the subjects and the researcher. In order to minimize confusion, this term shall be applied only to those being studied.) These roles can be defined as follows.

In the role of "observer," the researcher has little or no interaction with those being studied. In the role of "observer as researcher," the researcher is primarily an observer but has some interaction with the study participants. In the role of "researcher as observer," the researcher is an intermediary advocate (the researcher also acts as a proponent for the participants), while the researcher as member is a functioning affiliate of the community managing two conflicting roles of community member and researcher. It is not uncommon as a study continues for a qualitative researcher to begin as an observer and move to observer as member (even to small degrees) due to contact with the participants. An example of the member category is the SLP working in a school district studying the language use of his or her students in various classroom settings. The SLP is a member in managing his or her caseload, an advocate for the students on the caseload, a member of the school faculty (member as observer), and also a researcher in wishing to obtain more information about the students' level of functioning and the contextual contributing factors to the disorder.

Whether or not the qualitative researcher is an observer or observer as member, the goals of the research are the same. The qualitative researcher seeks to understand the research setting (e.g., the English as a second language classroom), its participants (e.g., the students, teachers, and teacher aides), and their behaviors (e.g., dual language use in lessons). The qualitative researcher wishes to make the unknown familiar (Glesne & Peshkin, 1992). That is, the researcher attempts to take phenomena that might appear confusing to observers and make these phenomena understandable. For example, a school-based SLP might be inundated with referrals from classroom teachers who do not know how to teach bilingual children and thus want the SLP to take these children onto her or his caseload for "remediation." As well as educating teachers about the appropriateness of these referrals, the SLP might advocate for more bilingual classrooms in his or her school district. The district administration may be confused as to what actually occurs in bilingual classrooms; therefore, the SLP attempts to make the nature of bilingual classrooms understandable to the district administrators. When the administrators understand the nature of bilingual classrooms more clearly, and the strange becomes known, they may be willing to allocate more resources toward the creation of more of these classrooms.

In ethnographic research, the setting must be established beforehand, whether it consists of a hospital emergency room, a treatment room in rehabilitation care, an outpatient waiting area, or a school classroom. The setting must be described according to who the participants are (e.g., age, ethnicity, what they say, and/or who interacts with whom). The qualitative researcher takes notice of special versus daily events, acts within the events (for example, conversations among emergency room doctors upon receiving a patient), and what gestures and communication types are occurring.

Taking notes is an essential aspect of qualitative research. The collection of notes, often referred to as "field notes," forms a field notebook or field log where collection of the field notes is stored. Field notes may incorporate written, on-site notes of what is occurring or mental notes, where the researcher remembers and later writes down occurrences that happened previously. Field notes may incorporate descriptive notes, analytic notes, information from informants (informal interviewing), and examples of documents (for example, this can be similar to portfolio documents, such as a classroom reading test). Field notes may be formal or informal: informally, the researcher can jot down observations on a legal pad and later formally reorganize the information at the end of the day; formally, the researcher can establish categories (setting, behaviors, participants, context, interpretation) beforehand and structure the notes according to these predetermined categories.

Another aspect of qualitative research is interviewing. Interviews may be the principal form of data collection in an ethnographic study or may supplement field observations. Speech–language pathologists can use the following paradigm provided by Glesne & Peshkin (1992) for assisting the ethnographer in developing appropriate interview questions:

1. Questions must match and fit the topic. The questions must be relevant to the interviewee.

2. The questions must clarify the topic of investigation.

3. The questions must be anchored in the cultural reality of the participants.

4. The questions must be drawn from the participants' lives.

Ethnographers attempt to limit the extent to which a linear format is used in questioning. They try to remain flexible, knowing that the topics and questions posed may change as the interview proceeds. A naturalistic approach to questioning develops; this departs from the clinical, linear medical model of questioning that most SLPs are familiar with. Speech–language pathologists may apply the naturalistic approach especially to their interviewing activities with culturally and linguistically diverse clients. These clients may come from cultures where, for example, interview questions about birth and development are considered personal and intrusive. In another example, members of some cultures do not believe in rehabilitation, feeling that the communicative disorder is the will of a Supreme Being and thus should not be treated (Roseberry-McKibbin, 1997). Speech–language pathologists then, should use the naturalistic approach to questioning in terms of anchoring questions in the cultural reality of the interviewees and making sure the questions are relevant to the interviewees.

An issue in all qualitative research is the trustworthiness of the data that are collected. The trustworthiness of the data is dependent upon several factors: the length of time involved in collecting the data (generally the longer the better), the descriptiveness of the data, and a method of data collection that is based on at least three different points (triangulation). Triangulation may be obtained by having more than one observer, by conducting separate observations, and by having interviews. Each of the above contains one different data point (refer to Figure 7.1 illustrating the triangulation process). Speech–language pathologists can apply the concept of triangulation to their practice by relying on multiple sources of information before drawing conclusions and making decisions. For example, a young student might state, "My mother hits me." Rather than call a protective services agency right away, the SLP might interview the student's siblings, check the student's files for previous reports of abuse, and interview the student's teacher regarding his or her perception of the situation. In this way, the SLP checks on the veracity of the student's statement and is then able to take appropriate action. Due to time constraints, it is difficult for many SLPs to apply the concept of triangulation to their daily clinical activities. However, as most experienced SLPs have found, the use of triangulation when making clinical decisions is a valuable use of time and sometimes results in avoidance of embarrassing errors.

Ethnography, then, utilizes a variety of methods, such as triangulation, to study individuals or participants in groups. Although ethnography

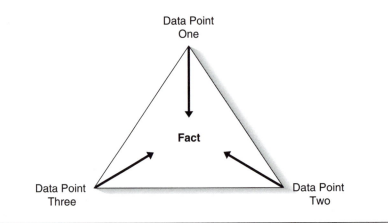

FIGURE 7.1 *Triangulation from Three Different Data Points*

typically involves group studies, researchers may also use the qualitative research method of case studies.

Qualitative Research Example

To illustrate the aspects of qualitative research just described, I will use a previously reported ethnographic field study (Brice, Mastin, & Perkins, 1997a; Brice, Mastin, & Perkins, 1997b). The purpose of this study was to investigate the types of language functions observed in an English as a second language (ESL) classroom. The pragmatic or functional language categories generated from the field observations were the basis of this study.

The qualitative research method employed was an ethnographic field study. Although interviews were conducted and some documents were examined, these were not the primary means of collecting data. Therefore, this study does not strictly fit the interview or document qualitative research method. In addition, an entire classroom was studied with the language of the teacher, teacher aide, and students under observation. The focus was not on a singular case and therefore this was not truly a case study but rather involved group-based research.

The research paradigm used in this study was that of non-obtrusive observer. The observers entered the ESL classroom and sat in one corner and collected the field notes with minimal interaction with the students or teachers as class lessons were given. However, toward the end of the study, the two observers did interact with some of the students when approached. Thus, a small shift toward the observer–researcher end of the spectrum occurred.

The setting was primarily an English as a second language classroom in a small urban elementary school. The school and community were located in a small rural area of southwestern Minnesota. The elementary school was 30% Hispanic/Latino (Amato, 1996). All of the students enrolled in the ESL classroom spoke Spanish as their first language. As is typically found in many ESL classrooms, the students were transitioned into an all English inclusive classroom after two to three years of ESL instruction (Brice & Montgomery, 1996). Thus, their English skills were a major focus of content instruction.

The data, in the form of field notes, were gathered over a period of four months. An overall total of 38 hours and 10 minutes was observed. The field notes were gathered using a formal or prearranged form that included sections for the following: (a) date, (b) time of observation, (c) context , (d) speaker, and (e) interpretation. Thus, information about the context of the lessons, who the speaker was, and the purpose of the message was recorded in the field notes. A total of 1,654 codings for 1,573 utterances were obtained and analyzed.

Informal interviews with the teacher and teacher aide were conducted over the period of the four months. A formal final exit interview was conducted at the end of the study with the teacher and teacher aide.

The participants in this study included the ESL teacher, the ESL teacher aide, and approximately 20 Spanish–English-speaking K–5 students. The teacher was partially proficient in Spanish, while the teacher aide was highly proficient in Spanish (Spanish was her first and native language). English was the language for most classroom instruction; however, Spanish was also noted in classroom instruction. In addition, numerous instances of language alternations (code switching and code mixing) of Spanish and English were noted.

The students were observed mostly in small-group instruction. The class size ranged from five to twenty students. Up to three different sessions occurred simultaneously with the teacher, teacher aide, and helpers. Small groups that were observed ranged from two to eight students. Classroom lessons varied from reading, writing, mathematics, social studies, and history. Triangulation was achieved by having two separate observers collect data over an extended period of time (resulting in multiple observations) and by conducting interviews with the teacher and teacher aide.

The results of this study yielded 50 different student and teacher classroom language functions, consisting of (listed in order of the most to the least number of functions and the total frequency of occurrence): questions, commands, feedback, reinforcement, informative, answering/responding, starting a lesson, ending a lesson, seeking clarification, speaking out loud, and other code functions.

From this ethnographic study, two practical clinical applications for the field of speech–language pathology were found. First, the languages of choice for instruction and personal use in this study were English, Spanish, and a code-switched/mixed (i.e., alternation and concurrent use of both languages within and across sentences) variety. One observation was that code switching and code mixing were normal and natural occurrences whenever two languages coexisted and so should not be viewed by SLPs as indicators of a language disorder in and of themselves (Cheng & Butler, 1989; Reyes, 1995). Code switching and code mixing were observed in all major language functions (e.g., questioning feedback, commands, etc.) by the teacher, teacher aide, and students in formal and informal language interactions. Hence, code switching and code mixing were natural sequelae of bilingual environments and, in most instances, were examples of high-level language usage.

A second application of this study related to SLP school-based practitioners was a better understanding of how language was used in one particular classroom environment. Through observations, the researchers were able to gauge students' classroom performance in a systematic manner, thus yielding useful information about everyday language functioning. The practical application is that if SLPs know which behaviors to observe, then a systematic and natural examination of that student's language performance in the classroom is possible. Multiple observations of the same student by the teacher and speech–language pathologist may yield a more reliable estimate of the student's pragmatic and language abilities than typical standardized testing.

Conclusions

The purpose of this chapter has been to introduce qualitative research to speech–language pathologists. Qualitative research is one method of inquiry currently available to speech–language pathologists. It is a type of investigation that yields answers to questions about what is occurring in given situations. With some practice and a base of knowledge, SLPs should be able to employ qualitative and ethnographic research techniques to clinical investigations, thus improving their services to a diverse range of clients. Speech–language pathologists already employ interviews, document information gathering, and sampling techniques. Application of qualitative research for use with culturally and linguistically diverse populations is appropriate and has been used by SLPs (Brice, Mastin, & Perkins, 1997b; Brice & Perkins, 1997; Crago, Eriks-Brophy, Pesco, & McAlpine, 1997).

Best Practices

Qualitative research methods can be applied to active assessment (as opposed to static assessment). These include:

1. *Interviewing of others.* Interview the general education teacher, the ESL teacher, other teachers (e.g., special education teacher), and other professionals (e.g., the school psychologist) who come into contact with the Hispanic child. Administer questionnaires to these professionals for further information. [Appendix B provides such a questionnaire that has been undergoing trial since 1990 by Brice and Brice (1999).]

2. *Use of documents.* Gather information from existing case histories, school records, school reports.

3. *Sampling techniques.* Gather and analyze samples of behavior through language samples, narrative story tells and retells, classroom portfolios, and classroom-based samples of work.

4. *Triangulation.* Gather at least three different data sets (or points of view that are different from each other) to establish a trend.

5. *Gathering of data over an extended period of time.* Collect the information over several sessions.

6. *Formulation of the hypothesis after the data have been collected and analyzed.* Formulate the hypothesis, e.g., this Spanish–English-speaking child does not present with a language disorder, only after all the data have been gathered and analyzed. Spend time thinking and reviewing all the facts before making a decision.

References

Amato, J. A. (1996). *To call it home. The new immigrants of southwestern Minnesota.* Marshall, MN: Crossing Press.

Bogdan, R. C., & Biklen, S. K. (1992). *Qualitative research for education: An introduction to theory and methods.* Boston, MA: Allyn and Bacon.

Brice, A., & Brice, R. (1999, September). *Assessment and intervention with bilingual students: A collaborative effort.* Workshop presented to the Henrico County School District, Richmond, VA.

Brice, A., Mastin, M., & Perkins, C. (1997a). English, Spanish, and code switching use in the ESL classroom: An ethnographic study. *Journal of Children's Communication Development,19*(2), 11–20.

Brice, A., Mastin, M., & Perkins, C. (1997b). Bilingual classroom discourse skills: An ethnographic study. *Florida Journal of Communication Disorders,17,* 11–19.

Brice, A., & Montgomery, J. (1996). Adolescent pragmatic skills: A comparison of Latino students in ESL and speech and language programs. *Language, Speech, and Hearing Services in Schools, 27,* 68–81.

Brice, A., & Perkins, C. (1997). What is required for transition from the ESL classroom to the general education classroom? A case study of two classrooms. *Journal of Children's Communication Development, 19*(1), 13–22.

Cassell, C., & Symon, G. (1994). (Eds.). Qualitative methods in organizational research. A practical guide. London, UK: Sage.

Cheng, L. R., & Butler, K. (1989). Code switching: A natural phenomenon versus language deficiency. *World Englishes , 8,* 293–309.

Cole, P., & Taylor, O. (1990). Performance of working class African-American children on three tests of articulation. *Language, Speech, and Hearing Services in Schools, 21*(3), 171–176.

Crago, M. (1990). Development of communicative competence in Inuit children: Implications for speech–language pathology. *Journal of Childhood Communication Disorders,* *13*(1), 73–84.

Crago, M., Eriks-Brophy, A., Pesco, D., & McAlpine, L. (1997). Culturally based miscommunication in classroom interaction. *Language, Speech, and Hearing Services in Schools,* *28*(3), 245–254.

Damico, J. (1990). Prescriptionism as a motivating mechanism: An ethnographic study in the public schools. *Journal of Childhood Communication Disorders, 13*(1), 85–92.

Damico, J., & Damico, S. (1997). The establishment of a dominant interpretive framework in language intervention. *Language, Speech, and Hearing Services in Schools, 28*(3), 289–296.

Eisner, E. (1981). On the differences between scientific and artistic approaches to qualitative research. *Educational Researcher,10* (4), 5–9.

Firestone, W. (1987). Meaning in method: The rhetoric of quantitative and qualitative research. *Educational Researcher,17*(7), 16–21.

Foster, S., Barefoot, S., & DeCaro, P. (1989). The meaning of communication to a group of deaf college students: A multidimensional perspective. *Journal of Speech and Hearing Disorders, 54*(4), 558–569.

Glesne, C., & Peshkin, A. (1992). *Becoming qualitative researchers.* White Plains, NY: Longman.

Hartley, J. F. (1994). Case studies in organizational research. In C. Cassell & G. Symon (Eds.), *Qualitative methods in organizational research.* London, UK: Sage.

Howe, K. (1988). Against the quantitative–qualitative incompatibility thesis, or dogmas die hard. *Educational Researcher, 17*(8), 10–16.

Katz, K. (1990). Clinical decision making as an ethnographic process. *Journal of Childhood Communication Disorders, 13*(1), 93–100.

King, N. (1994). The qualitative research interview. In C. Cassell & G. Symon (Eds.), *Qualitative methods in organizational research. A practical guide* (pp. 14–36). London, UK: Sage.

Kovarsky, D. (1990). Discourse markers in adult-controlled therapy: Implications for child centered intervention. *Journal of Childhood Communication Disorders, 13*(1), 29–42.

Kovarsky, D., & Duchan, J. (1997). The interactional dimensions of language therapy. *Language, Speech, and Hearing Services in Schools, 28*(3), 297–307.

Kovarsky, D., & Maxwell, M. (1997). Rethinking the context of language in the schools. *Language, Speech, and Hearing Services in Schools, 28*(3), 219–230.

Lancy, D. (1993). *Qualitative research in education: An introduction to the major traditions.* New York: Longman.

Langdon, H., & Cheng, L. (1992). *Hispanic children and adults with communication disorders.* Gaithersburg, MD: Aspen.

Langdon, H., & Saenz, T. (Eds.). (1996). *Language assessment and intervention with multicultural students.* Oceanside, CA: Academic Communication Associates.

Maxwell, M. (1997). Communication assessments of individuals with limited hearing. *Language, Speech, and Hearing Services in Schools, 28*(3), 231–244.

Maxwell, M. (1990). The authenticity of ethnographic research. *Journal of Childhood Communication Disorders, 13*(1), 1–12.

Mercurio, J. A. (1979). Community involvement in cooperative decision making: Some lessons learned. *Educational Evaluation and Policy Analysis, 6,* 37–46.

Merriam, S. B. (1990). *Case study research in education. A qualitative approach.* San Francisco, CA: Josey-Bass Publishers.

Patton, M. (1990). *Qualitative evaluation and research methods* (2nd ed.). Newbury Park, CA: Sage.

Plante, E., Kiernan, B., & Betts, J. (1994). Method or methodology: The qualitative/quantitative debate. *Language, Speech, and Hearing Services in Schools, 25*(1), 52–54.

Reichardt, C., & Cook, T. (1979). *Qualitative and quantitative methods in evaluation research.* Beverly Hills, CA: Sage.

Reyes, B. A. (1995). Considerations in the assessment and treatment of neurogenic disorders in bilingual adults. In H. Kayser (Ed.), *Bilingual speech language pathology. An Hispanic Focus* (pp. 153–182). San Diego, CA: Singular Publishing.

Ripich, D. N., & Spinelli, F. M. (1985). An ethnographical approach to assessment and intervention. In D. N. Ripich & F. M. Spinneli (Eds.), *School discourse problems* (pp. 199–218). San Diego, CA: College-Hill Press.

Roseberry-McKibbin, C. (1997). Working with culturally and linguistically diverse clients. In K. G. Shipley (Ed.) *Interviewing and counseling in communicative disorders* (pp. 151–173). Needham Heights, MA: Allyn & Bacon.

Roseberry-McKibbin, C. (1995). *Multicultural students with special language needs. Practical strategies for assessment and intervention.* Oceanside, CA: Academic Communication Associates.

Stake, R. (1995). *The art of case study research.* London, UK: Sage.

Sturm, J., & Nelson, N. (1997). Formal classroom lessons: New perspectives on a familiar discourse event. *Language, Speech, and Hearing Services in Schools, 28*(3), 255–273.

Tesch, R. (1990). *Qualitative research.* Bristol, PA: Falmer Press.

Vin, R. (1984). *Case study research: Design and methods.* Newbury Park, CA: Sage.

Westby, C. (1997). There's more to passing than knowing the answers. *Language, Speech, and Hearing Services in Schools, 28*(3), 275–287.

Westby, C. (1990). Ethnographic interviewing: Asking the right questions to the right people in the right ways. *Journal of Childhood Communication Disorders, 13*(1), 101–112.

Appendix A

Qualitative Research and Ethnographic Reading List

Agar, M. (1986). *Speaking of ethnography*. Beverly Hills, CA: Sage.

Alausuutan, P. (1995). *Researching culture: Qualitative methods and cultural studies*. Thousand Oaks, CA: Sage.

Coffey, A., & Atkinson, P. (1996). *Making sense of qualitative data*. Thousand Oaks, CA: Sage.

Coulon, A. (1995). *Ethnomethodology*. Thousand Oaks, CA: Sage.

Hamel, J., Dufour, S., & Fortin, J. (1993). *Case study methods*. Newbury Park, CA: Sage.

Hymes, D. (1996). Discourse: Scope without depth. *International Journal of the Sociology of the Language, 57*, 48–89.

Irvine, J. (1979). Formality and informality in communicative events. *American Anthropologist, 18*, 773–790.

Kirk, J., & Miller, M. (1986). *Reliability and validity in qualitative research methods*. Beverly Hills, CA: Sage.

Morgan, D. (1988). *Focus groups as qualitative research*. Beverly Hills, CA: Sage.

Psathas, G. (1994). *Conversation analysis: The sociolinguistic analysis of natural language*. Newbury Park, CA: Sage.

Riessman, C. (1993). *Narrative analysis*. Newbury Park, CA: Sage.

Saville-Troike, M. (1989). *The ethnography of communication*. Oxford, UK: Basil Blackwell.

Yin, R. (1989). *Case study research: Design and methods*. Newbury Park, CA: Sage.

Appendix B

The Multicultural–Multilingual Assessment Form (Brice & Brice, 1999)

RETURN THIS FORM TO:_____

Student Information:

Name_____ Age_____
Grade_____ School_____
Date_____

1. Student's first or home language background_____
2. Indicate student's English language proficiency level from 1 to 5 (1= limited, 5=native like)_____
3. Student's cultural background (e.g., Anglo-American, African-American, Hispanic, Asian-American, American-Indian)_____
_____
4. Indicate the number of years the student has been in schools in the United States_____

Teacher Information:

1. Teacher or specialist's name_____
2. Indicate teacher's area (e.g., ESL, General classroom, speech-language pathologist, special education)_____
3. Teacher's first language background_____
4. Proficiency in another (non-English) language (Yes/No)?_____
5. If yes indicate what language_____
6. Indicate Teacher's proficiency level from 1 to 5 (1= limited, 5=native like)_____
7. Teacher's cultural knowledge/awareness in another culture?_____
_____
8. Indicate Teacher's cultural knowledge/awareness level of other culture from 1 to 5 (1= limited, 5=native like)_____

For the Teacher or Diagnostician:	*Place a check:*		
State what language(s) the student prefers to use:	*English*	*Native*	*Not Present*
interacting socially with friends	____	____	____
asking questions of the ESL teacher	____	____	____
giving information to the ESL teacher	____	____	____
working with classmates	____	____	____
asking questions of the inclusion/regular teacher	____	____	____
giving information to the inclusion/ regular teacher	____	____	____
speaking with a friend of the same culture and language background	____	____	____
speaking with an adult of the same culture and language background	____	____	____

What type of instructional services is the student currently enrolled in?

____Full time inclusion (general education classroom, classes)

____Part time inclusion with pull out ESL instruction

____Full time ESL instruction

In what language is the student receiving instruction in:	*English*	*Native*
Reading	____	____
Writing	____	____
History, Geography, Social Studies	____	____
Science	____	____
Mathematics	____	____

Which language would you judge the student to be most proficient in:		
Reading	____	____
Writing	____	____
History, Geography, Social Studies	____	____
Science	____	____
Mathematics	____	____
Social language (in the lunchroom, in the hallway with friends, at Phy. Ed. or recess)	____	____

Compared to other English language learners from the same culture and language background in your class does she/he:	Yes	No	Not Observed
Work well in group activities?	_____	_____	_____
Work well in individual activities?	_____	_____	_____
Follow personal instructions given to the group?	_____	_____	_____
Follow personal instructions given individually?	_____	_____	_____
Follow classroom instructions to complete a task?	_____	_____	_____
Begin to work on the activity before the instructions are finished?	_____	_____	_____
Respond to questions in the expected time frame?	_____	_____	_____
Answer questions or provide information?	_____	_____	_____
Perform tasks in the expected time frame?	_____	_____	_____
Ask frequent questions?	_____	_____	_____
Behave within expected limits when something demanding is asked of him/her?	_____	_____	_____
Express her/himself adequately?	_____	_____	_____
Express him/herself to be understood in classroom speaking tasks?	_____	_____	_____
Express him/herself to be understood by others in conversation?	_____	_____	_____

Oral Language- *Language used in interpersonal communication (Basic Interpersonal Communication Skills). Put a plus (+) by the language in which this task is accomplished, put a minus (-) if it is not accomplished or not present. Does the student:*

	English	Native	Not Present
1. Function well in conversation with teachers or friends?	_____	_____	_____
2. Interpret nonverbal communication appropriately: anger, frustration, excitement, approval, disapproval?	_____	_____	_____
3. Participate in interpersonal conversations on topics such as movies, previous events, holidays?	_____	_____	_____
4. Initiate and respond to common greetings?	_____	_____	_____
5. Initiate conversations?	_____	_____	_____
6. Ask and respond to questions appropriately?	_____	_____	_____
7. Follow personal conversations?	_____	_____	_____
8. Communicate important information?	_____	_____	_____

Academic Language- Language used for learning and academics in the classroom (Cognitive Academic Language Proficiency). Does the student:

	English	Native	Not Present
1. Tell about school subjects, establish appropriate content and sequence of events (e.g., can tell about and answer questions about a math problem)?	_____	_____	_____
2. Follow a sequence of verbal commands containing four or five critical elements?	_____	_____	_____
3. Accurately repeat verbal directions when requested containing four or five critical elements?	_____	_____	_____
4. Listen to stories and accurately retell events of the story?	_____	_____	_____
5. Tell their own story or narrative containing the following: Setting, initiating event, internal response, attempt to solve dilemma, consequence of attempt, ending?	_____	_____	_____
a. Add an ending to an unfinished story ?	_____	_____	_____
6. Listen to lesson and repeat or retell key points?	_____	_____	_____
7. Ask and answer questions regarding topic discussions, lesson, etc.?	_____	_____	_____
8. Follow along during oral conversation by the teacher or classmate(s)?	_____	_____	_____
9. Ask for clarification during structured tasks?	_____	_____	_____

8

The Importance of Classroom Pragmatics to Academic Success

Enrollment of students in the United States, Australia, and the United Kingdom from varying cultural and linguistic backgrounds has significantly increased over the last few years (Australian Bureau of Statistics, 1997; Bauman, 1996; Campbell, 1996; U.S. Department of Commerce, 1990). One can therefore assume that the changing demographics in these countries also indicates the changing home language and culture of students entering schools today. These students exhibit various levels of functioning within the context of the school culture; specifically, they are acculturating to the culture of the U.S., Australian, or U.K. school system and they are also learning English. Some students from families and community backgrounds with cultural perspectives different from the dominant school culture may have had little experience with the values, activities, and other components of school life in the United States (Gutierrez-Clellen, 1996; Langdon, 1996). In addition, many speech–language pathologists (SLPs) may have had limited experience and training in evaluating and treating culturally and linguistically diverse (CLD) students who are bilingual and English language learning (ELL) (Roseberry-McKibbin & Eicholtz, 1994). SLPs serving school-age children face the challenge of how best to provide therapeutic services for those whose are bilingual.

Available information about evaluating CLD students is frequently presented in the form of general principles or recommendations (e.g., using a team approach, making naturalistic observations), but, typically, specific, concrete, practical, and immediately applicable suggestions are not given. There is scant information about treating CLD students with speech and language problems, and, unfortunately, information on appropriate inter-

vention for bilingual students lags behind assessment information (Brice &
Montgomery, 1996; Cheng, 1991; Gutierrez-Clellen, 1996; Hamayan &
Damico, 1991; Langdon & Saenz, 1996; Peña, Quinn, & Iglesias, 1992;
Roseberry-McKibbin, 1995). Thus, school-based SLPs continue to use less
than ideal practices when evaluating and treating CLD students who are
bilingual and English language learning (Roseberry-McKibbin, 1995).

Bilingualism is defined here as the ability to use two languages with
varying degrees of proficiency and in different contexts (e.g., listening,
speaking, reading, and writing) (Cummins, 1984; Skutnabb-Kangas, 1981).
When students from bilingual backgrounds enter the public schools, they
enter a system designed to meet the needs of an English-speaking and
mainstream-culture student population (i.e., white middle class), but the
system may not meet their diverse language and learning needs (Brice-
Heath, 1986; MacArthur, 1993). Students who are bilingual and ELL are
often quickly enrolled full-time into general education classrooms after limited English as a second language (ESL) instruction (Brice & Montgomery,
1996). Administrators with general education backgrounds may expect
these transitional students from bilingual and ELL backgrounds to perform
well in all aspects of language including pragmatics (Cummins, 1984). The
period of English as a second language instruction may not be sufficient for
students with culturally and linguistically diverse backgrounds to acquire
all the necessary oral, written, and academic language skills (Collier, 1987;
Cummins, 1984).

Brice-Heath (1986) indicated that the school environment influences
behaviors and affects how successful students will be in all aspects of language (including pragmatics of language). This feature of language will be
defined in the next section. Demands of the classroom may produce development of communication skills in some students, while at the same time
producing communication deficits in other students who may cope less successfully with the extra demands of the school system (Simon, 1985).

Pragmatics of Language

In a discussion of the features of language, Levinson (1983) stated that syntax (i.e., sentence structure) is the study of associative properties of sentence structure, semantics is the study of word meanings, while pragmatics
is the study of language usage. Hymes (1972) stated that there exists "a
structure of language that goes beyond the aspect of structure dealt with in
grammars"(p. xxii). This structure is commonly referred to as pragmatics.

The study of the ability to use language (i.e., pragmatics) is concerned
with speaker–listener interactions. It is the study of behaviors in contexts.
Simon (1985) also suggested that pragmatics performance in school is influenced by many connecting factors, such as knowing what to say to

whom, how it is to be said, why it is said, when, and in what situations the expression is said. This point was emphasized by Hymes (1972) when he indicated that children may experience difficulties in school

> if the language of their natural competence is not of the school; if the contexts that elicit or permit use of competence are absent in the school; if the purposes to which they put language, and the ways in which they do so, are absent or prohibited in the school. (p. xx)

Apparently, pragmatics intimately involves the speaker and listener and the nature of their interactions and the contexts in which those interactions take place. Students must choose language appropriate to social encounters with others, that is, appropriate to the school setting in teacher interactions and in interactions with other classmates.

Bates (1976) stated that pragmatics is dominant over semantics and syntax. Others have argued that investigating pragmatics is a better indicator of a language disorder in bilingual children than investigating the other aspects of language (i.e., syntax, semantics, etc.) (Brice, 1992; Brice, Mastin, & Perkins, 1997a; Brice, Mastin, & Perkins, 1997b; Brice & Montgomery, 1996; Damico & Oller, 1980; Damico, Oller & Storey, 1983). Guthrie and Guthrie (1987) reiterated this point when they stated:

> How teachers and students use language, rather than particular linguistic aspects of speech, *may have more to do with the way children learn* [emphasis added], and the miscommunication, misunderstanding, and educational difficulty students encounter (p. 206).

Simon (1985) reported that language proficiency and academic success are dependent on the degree to which the student is capable of matching the learning–teaching style incorporated in the classroom. The student is capable of high academic success if he or she learns the social language and learning patterns in the classroom.

Hence, the first part of this chapter will be concerned with bilingual student pragmatics in classroom settings. The second part will review studies of teacher pragmatics in dealing with bilingual students. Strategies specific for therapy with bilingual and ELL students will also be given.

Student Pragmatics

Brice (1992) developed a pragmatics scale to investigate student performance in various classroom contexts. A developed pragmatic screening scale, the *Adolescent Pragmatics Screening Scale* (APSS), Appendix A, was used to measure pragmatics performance of students from three adolescent groups: monolingual language-disordered, bilingual (i.e., Spanish–English speaking), and monolingual general education students. The findings of this study indicated that the language-disordered students had difficulties in expressing themselves, establishing greetings, initiating and maintaining conversations, and listening to a speaker. These difficulties placed the language-disordered students at risk for following and completing classroom lessons and participating in classroom discussions. The language-disordered students displayed difficulties with oral (spoken) language, particularly oral language that involved more grammatical and semantic aspects of language (e.g., Describes Personal Feelings in an Acceptable Manner). The language-disordered students seemed to be carrying over their general language deficit into pragmatic behaviors, thereby affecting their pragmatics (interactive language) performance. The bilingual students also displayed difficulties, particularly in making requests of others and in listening to a speaker. These difficulties placed them at risk for cooperative learning situations in the classroom.

It is recommended that the SLP coach, model, and possibly directly teach the behaviors of making requests and actively listening (in order to increase listening comprehension and follow-through on tasks). The SLP should initially focus on the behaviors of actively listening so that this knowledge may assist in learning the behaviors of making requests. Since many of the behaviors may be affected by an inadequate control of English grammatical structures, it is recommended that the SLP also focus on the grammatical aspects of language, including syntax, semantics, and morphology, to improve pragmatic skills.

In a follow-up study, Brice and Montgomery (1996) used the APSS to investigate the pragmatics performance of students from two adolescent groups: nondisordered English language learning (ELL) students receiving English as a second language (ESL) classroom instruction and bilingual students receiving speech–language (BSL) therapy. The findings of this study indicated that the BSL students differed from the ELL students in expressing themselves, establishing greetings, initiating and maintaining conversations, listening to a speaker, and cueing the listener regarding topic changes. Both groups of students had difficulties regulating others through language. Thus, even language-intact students may have difficulty acquiring this European American pragmatics feature of language. Academic failure and possible school dropout may result for the BSL students as a result of their difficulties.

The bilingual students with speech and language disorders may face alienation from their peers by not being able to appropriately greet others, to begin and terminate personal discussions, to listen attentively to what others say, and to move among topics of conversation with ease. This places these bilingual students enrolled in speech and language therapy at risk for academic failure and possible school dropout (Brice, 1992; Simon, 1985). Pragmatics in the school classroom is often viewed in an even broader context (Wong-Fillmore, 1992). For example, Wong-Fillmore (1992) notes the teacher's oral directions, written directions, and classroom groupings are often culturally based and can have a profound effect on academic success.

Rules of classroom interaction and use of strategies, provided by SLPs, may be required for bilingual Hispanic students enrolled in speech and language therapy. Several suggestions for school and classroom remediation for these students taken from the literature (Allwright, 1980; Chesterfield, Chesterfield, Hayes-Latimer, & Chavez, 1983; Odlin, 1990; Pica, 1991; Pica & Doughty, 1985; Pica, Young & Doughty, 1987; Pienemann, 1984; Schmidt & Frota, 1986; Swain, 1985; Veltman, 1988; Wong-Fillmore, 1992; Zobl, 1980) provide a basis for modifying instruction to enhance English learning and pragmatics learning. They include:

1. The speech–language pathologist should use teacher strategies such as encouraging Latino students to ask questions. Students should seek clarification and ask for repetitions and the SLP should reinforce these behaviors.
2. Speech–language pathologists should rely less on modeling as a form of correction. Bilingual students in initial learning stages should be allowed to make mistakes. SLPs should also employ more pauses and wait time for responses to allow students to monitor and reflect on their language.
3. Bilingual and ELL students need (1) reasons to communicate; (2) interaction and opportunities to speak with proficient English speakers (peers, teachers, or community members); (3) interaction, support, and feedback from others; and (4) close and continued interaction with others lasting three or four years.
4. Bilingual and ELL students need to have increased student-to-teacher interactions to encourage regulatory, heuristic, informational, and instrumental language.
5. Bilingual and ELL students need opportunities to share information with other students to express, initiate, and maintain conversations.
6. Practicing an activity prepares the Latino student to later talk about it.
7. SLPs should ask open-ended clarification questions, that is, questions that allow for expansion and elaboration, to encourage heuristic (i.e., information-seeking) language.
8. The use of grammar drills and direct instruction—teaching specific skills such as note-taking, for example—is beneficial for the adolescent student. A naturalistic approach can be used to reinforce learned skills.
9. Bilingual and ELL students can benefit from peer grouping with other students of similar ability levels to practice classroom interaction skills.
10. Bilingual and ELL students should have more practice at formalized, structured speaking situations to encourage classroom discourse skills.

The pragmatics problems of bilingual students receiving speech and language intervention must be identified early to prevent the problems from becoming an overall pervasive disorder and possibly leading to school failure (Brice-Heath, 1986; Garcia & Ortiz, 1988; Hymes, 1972). Early identification and remediation of pragmatics disorders in English language learning students appears to be a critical factor for school success. It is important for school personnel to be aware of student pragmatics in order to assist students in their education, particularly adolescents at risk of academic failure or social adjustment problems. It is also critical that there be a better understanding of teacher pragmatics. A complete picture of student pragmatics and teacher pragmatics is necessary in order to understand the true nature of classroom interactions. A review of teacher pragmatics with bilingual ELL students follows.

Teacher Pragmatics

Brice, Mastin, and Perkins (1997a) were interested in how language by teachers was used in an English as a second language classroom. Their first ethnographic study reported the various pragmatic uses of language that the ESL teacher and teacher aide used in teaching normally developing (without any language disorders) bilingual ELL students. Results from that study revealed that the teachers used language according to 50 different language functions (or pragmatics); the 50 classroom language functions are presented in Appendix B.

The following results can be drawn from the ESL classroom observations (Brice, Mastin, & Perkins, 1997b): (a) questioning occurred with the highest frequency (28.17%), followed by (b) the use of commands (16.99%), with (c) giving information (14.33%), (d) giving feedback (13.90%), and (e) answering and responding (9.5%) rounding out the top five ESL classroom pragmatic functions. Hence, most of the language that occurred in the ESL classroom was seen in the more general pragmatic functions of questioning, commands, feedback, informing, and answering. The other language functions occurred with less frequency.

Brice and Perkins (1997) investigated the teacher use of language, i.e., pragmatics, in two separate classrooms. These classrooms consisted of an ESL second grade classroom and a second grade general education classroom. The purpose of their study was to determine what aspects of language were crucial for bilingual students transitioning from the ESL classroom to the mainstream classroom. Ethnographic methodology was utilized. Brice and Perkins asked the questions: What language skills must the bilingual student possess in order to succeed in the general education classroom and what skills should the SLP be aware of in assessing bilingual students? Their study found that bilingual students in the general classroom needed to shift and adapt their language uses to meet the demands of the classroom. The general classroom proceeded at a fast pace of instruction, which necessitated fast mental processing abilities and more independent student follow-through. Learning was dependent on precise understanding of long teacher utterances. Many teacher utterances were spoken within a short time period, with few opportunities for clarification or seeking of help. Brice and Perkins (1997) determined that the student in the ESL classroom who is also enrolled in the general classroom is using three language systems: listening to and speaking Spanish, listening to and speaking English, and a mixed series of Spanish and English code-switched and code-mixed language. Language alternation was seen to serve as a bridge between Spanish and English and was not determined to be an indicator of a language disorder or language confusion. It was typically used by the teachers, aides, and the students. The findings of this study suggest that language evaluations should incorporate ethnographic observations to obtain a "truer" picture of what occurred, where it occurred, how it occurred, why it occurred, and how often it occurred.

Conclusions

Pragmatics for students in school is an important aspect of functioning within the classroom. Pragmatics skills are critical to academic progress and building of peer relationships. English language learning students and bilingual students with communication disorders may need instruction in pragmatics skills. This instruction may take the form of direct instruction (i.e., teaching to the task). In addition, teachers and SLPs need to be aware of the language demands that classrooms place upon students and that their teaching practices may have to be modified to match the learner's special needs.

Best Practices

Several best practices strategies are recommended in order to facilitate learning. The following seven tips were adapted from the Institute for Educational Research (cited in *American Teacher*, 1990):

1. Provide written copies of directions and assignments to complement oral instruction (to assist the pragmatic behaviors of listening actively and following directions).

2. Be an example of correct language. Correct ELL students' errors only during formal instruction (to assist syntax acquisition for regulatory language and personal language).
3. Don't restrict ELL students to the basics. Keep expectations high and engage students in tasks that require higher-level thinking (to encourage metalinguistic language skills).
4. Students who may seem proficient in conversational English (oral, spoken language skills) may still need help with academic language tasks, including following instructions and understanding subject-specific vocabulary.
5. Build lessons on understanding background knowledge for text-book readings (to assist following directions and listening actively).
6. Keep ELL students involved by asking prediction questions, such as "What do you think . . . ?"(to encourage metalinguistic language and expression skills).
7. Teach self-study skills such as note-taking, self-questioning, organizing, and test-taking (to encourage metalinguistic language skills).

In summary, the preceding suggestions may assist SLPs working with all ELL students in achieving school and classroom success.

References

Allwright, R. (1980). Turns, topics, and tasks: Patterns of participation in language learning and teaching. In D. Larsen-Freeman (Ed.), *Discourse analysis in second language research* (pp. 165–187). Rowley, MA: Newbury House.

Australian Bureau of Statistics. (1997). *Permanent and long-term migration.* Canberra, Australia: Author.

Bates, E. (1976). *Language and context: The acquisition of pragmatics.* New York: Academic Press.

Bauman, G. (1996). *Contesting culture: Discourses of identity in multi-ethnic London.* Cambridge, England: Cambridge University Press.

Bloom, B. (1956). *Taxonomy of educational objectives: The classification of educational goals by a committee of college and university examiners.* New York: McKay.

Brice, A. (1992). The Adolescent Pragmatics Screening Scale: A comparison of language-impaired students, bilingual/Hispanic students, and regular education students. *Howard Journal of Communications, 4,* 143–156.

Brice, A., Mastin, M., & Perkins, C. (1997a). Bilingual classroom discourse skills: An ethnographic study. *Florida Journal of Communication Disorders,17,* 11–19.

Brice, A., Mastin, M., & Perkins, C. (1997b). English, Spanish, and code switching use in the ESL classroom: An ethnographic study. *Journal of Children's Communication Development,19*(2), 11–20.

Brice, A., & Montgomery, J. (1996). Adolescent pragmatic skills: A comparison of Latino students in ESL and speech and language programs. *Language, Speech, and Hearing Services in Schools, 27,* 68–81.

Brice, A., & Perkins, C. (1997). What is required for transition from the ESL classroom to the general classroom? A case study of two classrooms. *Journal of Children's Communication Development, 19*(1), 13–22.

Brice-Heath, S. (1986). Sociocultural contexts of language development. In D. Holt (Ed.), *Beyond language: Social and cultural factors in schooling language minority students* (pp. 142–186). Los Angeles, CA: Evaluation, Dissemination, and Assessment Center.

Campbell, P. R. (1996). *Population projections for states by age, sex, race, and Hispanic origin: 1995 to 2025.* Washington, DC: U.S. Bureau of the Census, Population Division, PPL-47.

Canagarajah, A. S. (1995). Functions of codeswitching in ESL classrooms: Socialising bilingualism in Jaffna. *Journal of Multilingual and Multicultural Development, 6*(3), 173–195.

Cheng, L. (1996). Enhancing communication: Toward optimal language learning for the limited English proficient students. *Language, Speech, and Hearing Services in Schools, 27*(4), 347–354.

Chesterfield, R., Chesterfield, K. B., Hayes-Latimer, K., & Chavez, R. (1983). The influence of teachers and peers on second language acquisition in bilingual preschool programs, *TESOL Quarterly, 17*(3), 401–419.

Collier, V. (1987). Age and rate of acquisition of second language for academic purposes. *TESOL Quarterly, 21*(4), 617–641.

Cummins, J. (1984). *Bilingualism and special education: Issues in assessment and pedagogy.* San Diego: College-Hill Press.

Damico, J., & Oller, J., Jr. (1980). Pragmatic versus morphological/syntactic criteria for language referrals. *Language, Speech, and Hearing Services in Schools, 11,* 85–94.

Damico, J., Oller, J., Jr., & Storey, M. (1983). The diagnosis of language disorders in bilingual children: Surface-oriented and pragmatic criteria. *Journal of Speech and Hearing Disorders, 48,* 385–394.

Fitch, K., & Hopper, R. (1983). If you speak Spanish they'll think you're German: Attitudes toward language choice in multilingual environments. *Journal of Multilingual and Multicultural Development, 4*(2–3), 115–127.

Garcia, S., & Ortiz, A. (1988). *Preventing inappropriate referrals of language minority students to special education. (Focus, 5).* Wheaton, MD: National Clearinghouse for Bilingual Education.

Grosjean, F. (1982). *Life with two languages. An introduction to bilingualism.* Cambridge, MA: Harvard University Press.

Guthrie, L. F., & Guthrie, G. P. (1987). Teacher language use in a Chinese bilingual classroom. In S. R. Goldman & H. T. Trueba (Eds.), *Becoming literate in English as a second language.* Norwood, NJ: Ablex.

Gutierrez-Clellen, V. (1996). Language diversity: Implications for assessment. In K. Cole, P. Dale, & D. Thal (Eds.), *Advances in assessment of communication and language* (pp. 29–56). Baltimore, MD: Brookes Publishing.

Hamayan, E., & Damico, J. (Eds.). (1991). *Limiting bias in the assessment of bilingual students.* Austin, TX: Pro-Ed.

Hymes, D. (1972). In C. Cazden, V. John, & D. Hymes (Eds.), *Functions of language in the classroom* (pp. xi–ivii). New York: Teachers College Press.

Institute for Educational Research (1990). Accommodating diversity. *American Teacher, 8*(74), p. 2.

Kamwangamalu, N. M., & Lee, C. L. (1991). Chinese–English code-mixing: A case of matrix language assignment. *World Englishes, 10*(3), 247–261.

Langdon, H. W. (1996). English language learning by immigrant Spanish speakers: A United States perspective. *Topics in Language Disorders, 16* (4), 38–53.

Langdon, H., & Saenz, T. (Eds.). (1996). *Language assessment and intervention with multicultural students.* Oceanside, CA: Academic Communication Associates.

Levinson, S. (1983). *Pragmatics.* Cambridge, England: Cambridge University Press.

MacArthur, E. K. (1993). *Language characteristics and schooling in the United States, a changing picture: 1979 and 1989.* Washington, DC: National Center for Education Statistics.

Mahecha, N. (1990). *The perception of pre-switch cues by Spanish–English bilinguals.* Unpublished doctoral dissertation, City University of New York, New York, NY.

Odlin, T. (1990). *Language transfer.* Cambridge, England: Cambridge University Press.

Peña, E., Quinn, R., & Iglesias, A. (1992). The application of dynamic methods to language assessment: A nonbiased procedure. *The Journal of Special Education, 26*(3), 269–280.

Pennington, M. C. (1995). *Eight case studies of classroom discourse in the Hong Kong secondary English class.* Research Report Number 42. Hong Kong Department of English. City University of Hong Kong.

Pfaff, C. W. (1979). Constraints on language mixing: Intrasentential code switching and borrowing in Spanish/English. *Language, 55,* 291–318.

Phillips, J. M. (1975). *Code-switching in bilingual classrooms.* Masters thesis, California State University, Northridge (ERIC Document Reproduction Service No. ED 111222).

Pica, T. (1991). Classroom interaction, participation and comprehension: Redefining relationships. *System, 19*(4), 437–452.

Pica, T., & Doughty, C. (1985). The role of group work in classroom second language acquisition. *Studies in Second Language Acquisition, 7*(2), 233–248.

Pica, T., Young, R., & Doughty, C. (1987). The impact of interaction on comprehension, *TESOL Quarterly, 21*(4), 737–758.

Pienemann, M. (1984). Psychological constraints on the teachability of languages. *Studies in Second Language Acquisition, 6*(2), 186–214.

Poplack, S. (1980). Sometimes I'll start a sentence in Spanish y termino en español: Toward a typology of code-switching. *Linguistics, 18,* 581–618.

Roseberry-McKibbin, C. (1995). *Multicultural students with special language needs. Practical strategies for assessment and intervention.* Oceanside, CA: Academic Communication Associates.

Roseberry-McKibbin, C., & Eicholtz, G. E. (1994). Serving limited English proficient children in schools: A national survey. *Language, Speech, and Hearing Services in Schools, 25*(2), 156–164.

Schmidt, R. W., & Frota, S. N. (1986). Developing basic conversational ability in a second language: A case study of an adult learner of Portuguese. In R. R. Day (Ed.), *Talking to learn* (pp. 237–326). Rowley, MA: Newbury House.

Simon, C. (1985). *Communication skills and classroom success: Therapy methodologies for language-learning disabled students.* San Diego, CA: College-Hill Press.

Skutnabb-Kangas, T. (1981). *Bilingualism or not. The education of minorities.* Clevedon, England: Multilingual Matters.

Swain, M. (1985). Communicative competence: Some roles of comprehensible input and comprehensible output in its development. In S. Gass & C. Madden (Eds.), *Input in second language acquisition* (pp. 235–256). Rowley, MA: Newbury House.

Tay, M. W. J. (1989). Code-switching and code-mixing as a communicative strategy in multilingual discourse. *World Englishes, 8*(3), 407–471.

Timm, L. (1975). Spanish-English code switching: El porque y how-not-to. *Romance Philology, 28*(4), 473–482.

U.S. Department of Commerce. (1990). *Current population.* Washington, DC: Bureau of the Census.

Veltman, C. (1988). *The future of the Spanish language in the United States.* New York: Hispanic Policy Development Project.

Wong-Fillmore, L.W. (1992). *When does 1 + 1 = <2?* Paper presented at Bilingualism/Bilingüismo: A Clinical Forum, Miami, FL.

Zobl, H. (1980). The formal and developmental selectivity of L1 influence on L2 acquisition. *Language Learning, 30*(1), 43–57.

Appendix A

The Adolescent Pragmatics Screening Scale (APSS)

The Adolescent Pragmatics Screening Scale (APSS)

Student Information:

Name _____ Age _____ Grade _____
School _____Date _____

1. Indicate the student's first language background _____
   _____

2. Indicate the student's home language background if different from first language _____

3. Indicate student's English language proficiency level from 1 to 5 (1= native-like, 2= near native-like, 3= medium, 4= limited, 5= very limited) _____

4. Indicate the student's cultural/ethnic background (e.g., European-American, African-American, Hispanic, Asian-American, Native-American or the student's specific cultural background) _____
   _____

5. Indicate the number of years the student has been in schools in the United States _____

Teacher/Rater Information:

6. Indicate your professional background (Speech-language pathologist, bilingual teacher, ESL teacher, general education teacher, special education teacher) _____

7. Indicate your first language background _____

8. Indicate your proficiency level from 1 to 5 in English (1= native-like, 2= near native-like, 3= medium, 4= limited, 5= very limited) _____

9. Are you proficient in a language other than English (Yes/No)?

_____

10. If yes, indicate what language _____

11. Indicate your proficiency level from 1 to 5 in your other language (1= native-like, 2= near native-like, 3= medium, 4= limited, 5= very limited) _____

12. Are you culturally knowledgeable or aware about another culture?

_____

13. Indicate your cultural knowledge/awareness level of the other culture from 1 to 5 (1= native-like, 2= near native-like, 3= medium, 4= limited, 5= very limited) _____

14. Indicate which culture or cultures _____

Test Score Information :

Scoring : Mean Topic Scores (M.T.S.)
Topic 1 Sum of the individual behaviors ___ divided by 11= ___ No. 1. **MTS**
Topic 2 Sum of the individual behaviors ___ divided by 7 = ___ No. 2. **MTS**
Topic 3 Sum of the individual behaviors ___ divided by 4 = ___ No. 3. **MTS**
Topic 4 Sum of the individual behaviors ___ divided by 6 = ___ No. 4. **MTS**
Topic 5 Sum of the individual behaviors ___ divided by 7 = ___ No. 5. **MTS**
Topic 6 Sum of the individual behaviors ___ divided by 3 = ___ No. 6. **MTS**

Sum of ALL the individual behaviors ___ divided by 39 = ___ **Total Score (T.S.)**

15. Do you feel that this student's performance was influenced by the student's cultural backgound? ___ Yes ___ No

If the answer is yes, please indicate which behaviors lead you to this conclusion by making a notation in the **Observation** section next to the corresponding behavior and score.

The Adolescent Pragmatics Screening Scale (APSS)

Name: _____ Page One

A. Performance Rating Scale

Please indicate the student's level of behavior using the scale below

1. Behavior is highly appropriate.
2. Behavior is moderately appropriate.
3. Behavior is borderline appropriate.
4. Behavior is moderately inappropriate.
5. Behavior is highly inappropriate.

B. Observations

This section is reserved for performance observations that you feel are pertinent to your rating.

1. Affects listener's behavior through language   SCORE   OBSERVATIONS

1. Asks for help (e.g., "I don't know how to do this problem", "Can you show me how to look up a word in the dictionary ?", "How do you spell _?")   1. ____   _____

2. Asks questions (e.g., "How many times does 9 go into 72?" , "How does a President get elected?")   2. ____   _____

3. Attempts to persuade others (e.g., "I really think John is the best candidate because_", "I don't think I should have to do this because_")   3. ____   _____

4. Informs another of important information (e.g., "Teacher, someone wrote some bad words on the wall outside", "I saw a snake in the boy's bathroom down the hall.")   4. ____   _____

5. Asks for a favor of a friend/classmate (e.g., "Can you give me a ride to school?", "Will you ask Sally out for Friday night for me?")   5. ____   _____

6. Asks for a favor of the teacher (e.g., "Can I redo the homework assignment?", "Can I get out of class five minutes early so I can catch the new bus?")   6. ____   _____

7. Asks for teachers' and/or adults' permission (e.g., going to the bathroom, asking to get a drink of water, asking to sharpen a pencil)   7. ____   _____

8. Asks for other student's permission (e.g., "Can I invite John to go with us?", "Can I ask your girlfriend for her phone number?")   8. ____   _____

	SCORE	OBSERVATIONS

9. Able to negotiate, give and take, in order to reach an agreement ("I'll give you a ride to school if you pay me five dollars a week for gas", "I'll help you with your Algebra homework if you help me paint the signs for homecoming.")   9. ____   _____

10. Is able to give simple directions (e.g., telling how to find the Spanish teacher's classroom or how to find the bathroom.)   10. ____   _____

11. Rephrases a statement (e.g., "You meant this, didn't you?" "Did you mean this _?")   11. ____   _____

____ TOPIC 1. SUM OF SCORES

2. Expresses self	SCORE	OBSERVATIONS

1. Describes personal feelings in an acceptable manner (e.g., says, "I wish that this English class wasn't so boring" "I'm feeling really frustrated by all the setbacks on my homework.")   1. ____   _____

2. Shows feelings in acceptable manner (e.g., taking audible breaths to contain one's anger or smiling with enthusiasm to show pleasure)   2. ____   _____

3. Offers a contrary opinion in class discussions (e.g., "I don't believe that Columbus was the first to discover America, Leif Ericson was said to have reached Greenland and Nova Scotia before Columbus", "I don't believe that the two party system really offers a choice to voters.")   3. ____   _____

4. Gives logical reasons for opinions (e.g., "I believe that the two party system offers a wider choice than the one party system_", "I think we should work on something else; we did something like this yesterday.")   4. ____   _____

5. Says that they disagree in a conversation (e.g., "I don't agree with you", "We can't agree on this one.")   5. ____   _____

6. Stays on topic for an appropriate amount of time.   6. ____   _____

7. Switches response to another mode to suit the listener (e.g., speaks differently when addressing the principal than when addressing a friend, speaks differently to a younger child of 2–3 years than addressing peers of the same age.)   7. ____   _____

____ TOPIC 2. SUM OF SCORES

3. *Establishes appropriate greetings*	SCORE	OBSERVATIONS
1. Establishes eye contact when saying hello or greeting.	1. ____	_____
2. Smiles when meeting friends	2. ____	_____
3. Responds to an introduction by other similar greeting.	3. ____	_____
4. Introduces self to others ("Hi, I'm _", "My name is_, what's yours?")	4. ____	_____

____ TOPIC 3. SUM OF SCORES

4. *Initiates and maintains conversation*	SCORE	OBSERVATIONS
1. Displays appropriate response time	1. ____	_____
2. Asks for more time (e.g., "I'm still thinking", "Wait a second", "Give me some more time.")	2. ____	_____
3. Notes that the listener is not following the conversation and needs clarification or more information (e.g., "There's a thing down there, down there, I mean there's a snake down in the boy's bathroom down the hall.")	3. ____	_____
4. Talks to others with appropriate pitch and loudness levels of voice (e.g., uses appropriate levels for the classroom, physical education, the lunchroom, or after school.)	4. ____	_____
5. Answers questions relevantly (e.g., Nine goes into 72 eight times", "The President gets elected by the people.")	5. ____	_____
6. Waits for appropriate pauses in conversation before speaking.	6. ____	_____

____ TOPIC 4. SUM OF SCORES

5. *Listens actively*	SCORE	OBSERVATIONS
1. Asks to repeat what has been said for better understanding (e.g., "Could you say that again?", "What do you mean?")	1. ____	_____
2. Looks at teacher when addressed (e.g., through occasional glances or maintained eye contact)	2. ____	_____
3. Listens to others in class (e.g., head is up, leaning toward the speaker, eyes on the speaker.)	3. ____	_____

	SCORE	*OBSERVATIONS*

4. Changes activities when asked by the teacher (e.g., is able to put away his or her paper and pencil or close a book or pull out something different without having to be told personally).   **4.** ____   _____

5. Acknowledges the speaker verbally (e.g., says "Uh-huh, yeah, what else?")   **5.**____   _____

6. Acknowledges the speaker nonverbally (e.g., looks at the speaker through occasional glances, maintained eye contact or nodding.)   **6.**____   _____

7. Differentiates between literal and figurative language (e.g., the student knows that the expression "John is sharp as a tack" actually means that John is very smart, or that if "Sally's leg is killing her" it does not mean that Sally will die.)   **7.** ____   _____

____ TOPIC 5. SUM OF SCORES

6. Cues the listener regarding topic shifts	*SCORE*	*OBSERVATIONS*

1. Waits for a pause in the conversation before speaking about something else (e.g., waits for a pause of approximately 3–5 seconds at the end of a thought or sentence.)   **1.** ____   _____

2. Looks away to indicate loss of interest in conversation (e.g., looks away and maintains this look for approximately 3–5 seconds.)   **2.** ____   _____

3. Makes easy transitions between topics (e.g., the listener does not question what they are talking about.)   **3.**____   _____

____ TOPIC 6. SUM OF SCORES

Appendix B

Definitions and Examples of the Fifty Classroom Language Functions*

Questioning

Questions are one significant aspect of teacher instruction in the traditional classroom. Hence, the use of questions is a high-occurrence language function of classrooms.

1. *Task question.* This question directs the other person—the student, for example—to the task. It is a more global type of question than a procedure question. Example:
   a. SLP: "Anybody want to read it?"
2. *Rhetorical question.* A rhetorical question does not truly seek an answer. The purpose of the question is to alert the listener to information that is to be presented. Example:
   a. SLP: "You know what? You need to leave a space for the answer. *Vas a dejar un espacio, aqui vas a poner la repuesta.*" (You are going to leave a space; here you are going to put the answer.)
3. *Procedure question.* This is a single-action type of question. It implies that movement is to occur from one task to another. It is a question that implies that steps are to be taken. Example:
   a. SLP: "What are you supposed to do with them when you come into my room, M.?"
4. *Asking permission.* This question involves the person asking seeking to obtain authorization from another individual. Example:

---

*From "English, Spanish, and code switching use in the ESL classroom: An ethnographic study" by A. Brice, M. Mastin, & C. Perkins, 1997, *Journal of Children's Communication Development, 19,* 11–20. Copyright 1997 by PRO-ED, Inc. Reprinted with permission.

a. SLP: "Can I use it?" (Asking M. to borrow his pencil.)
5. *Factual question.* This is similar to Bloom's (1956) knowledge question. It requires a simple answer. Example:
   a. SLP: "How much is here? How much money?"
6. *Comprehension question.* The person needs to understand the information in order to proceed with the lesson or task. Example:
   a. SLP (from a mathematics counting lesson): "M., you counting? Well, what do you think? Do you have enough?"
7. *Content question.* The content question may follow a comprehension question or vocabulary question. It addresses information related to classroom content lessons. Example:
   a. SLP: "What language is 'mille lacque'?"
8. *Vocabulary check.* This question type addresses vocabulary understanding and use for students. Example:
   a. SLP: "*Sabes que quiere decir* 'team'?" (Do you know what "team" means?)
9. *Information check.* With information check, the question is a simple comprehension check. The asker wishes to know if the message was conveyed and understood. Example:
   a. SLP: "Oh, you made something at the beach. What is this? Castle. *Sure?*"
10. *Higher-level question (application, analysis, synthesis, evaluation).* The higher-level questions are taken from Bloom's (1956) taxonomy of application, synthesis, and evaluation. Example:
    a. SLP: "What if I want to put your names in alphabetical order?"
11. *Personal question.* The personal question is one in which the information is not strongly related to classroom content or procedures. For the SLP it is a nonpedagogical classroom question. Example:
    a. Student: "Now what is she going to do with it?"

Commands

Commands fall under the realm of requests. Requests are language acts that ask or command a response from others.

1. *Direct task request.* The direct task request function is a specific request. Typically, the SLP asks students to perform a direct request. It is clear and obvious what the request is and who should carry it out. Example:
   a. SLP: "M., you need a pencil."
2. *Indirect task request.* An indirect request alludes to the task to be performed. Example:
   a. SLP: "Now everyone has to help me do our writing."

3. *Redirection to task.* The student is off-task and needs to be redirected to the in-progress appointed task. Example:
   a. SLP: "E., you need to follow along."
4. *Seeking response with a fill-in answer (cloze).* The SLP seeks for the students to complete the answer. She or he allows for a pause and gives clear indication that the students need to give a verbal response. A rise in final pitch and intonation also may accompany this feature. Example:
   a. SLP: "*Once les quitas cinco son ___?*" (Eleven take away five is ___?)
5. *Directing to lesson.* This request is more specific than the direct task request. It is content-based, whereas the former is task-based. It is a prompt to the lesson. Example:
   a. SLP: "I think you're going to put three forward."
6. *Personal request.* The personal request is a plea outside of task or classroom functions. Example:
   a. Student: "*T., me puedes ayudar con esto.*" (T., can you help me with this one?)

Feedback (Reinforcement)

SLPs provide feedback and reinforcement to students.

1. *Reprimand.* The reprimand is a verbal admonishment. Example:
   a. SLP: "*Ella te dijo que trajera el papel.*" (She, the teacher, told you to bring the paper.)
2. *Enticement (prompting, positive reinforcement).* Enticement may take several different forms such as prompting, or providing some positive reinforcement. The positive reinforcement is usually verbal and immediate. The purpose of the enticement is to keep students involved and going. Example:
   a. SLP: "Oh, you made something at the beach. What is this?"
   b. Aide: "How about one more, *otro mas* (another one)?"
3. *Correction.* A correction is usually immediate and takes the form of correcting mistakes. Example:
   a. Aide: "What is a wolf?" (Student barks.) "That's a dog."
4. *Acknowledgment (confirming, e.g., yes/no response).* The acknowledgment is a type of feedback where the speaker, e.g., the SLP, confirms a response with words similar to "right," "sure" or may provide feedback to the correctness or truth-value of the response. Example:
   a. Aide: "You know what, M., you need to fix these."
5. *Reiteration.* In reiterations, the speaker repeats what was said for emphasis. It may be used for different levels: vocabulary reiteration (i.e., "Do you understand the word?"), comprehension reiteration (e.g., "Do you grasp the material, do you understand the instructions?"),

task reiteration (e.g., "Do you understand the task?"), or content reiteration (i.e., "Do you understand the content or scope of the material?"). Example:

a. SLP: "Why is he afraid of the ball? *Tiene miedo* (He is afraid). R., *he is afraid of the ball.*"

6. *Reiteration from other's statement.* The speaker repeats what the other person has previously said in the form of a response. Example:

a. Aide: "The ones that are wrong." Student: "*Los que están mal* (The ones that are wrong).*"

7. *Giving an example.* Exemplars are used. It may involve giving more than one answer or multiple ways of dealing with the material. Example:

a. SLP (from mathematics lesson): "Oh, go like this: eight and two more."

Informative

This function heading deals with information being disseminated. The general heading of "Informative" corresponds to the category of transmitting information.

1. *Declaration (commenting).* The speaker provides a comment, point of view related to the task or lesson. Example:

a. Aide: "Good, you're all finished."

2. *Explaining.* SLPs may emphasize key elements through explanation. Explaining involves detailed dissemination of information that may involve two or more facts or bits of information; hence teachers give more than one thought. Example:

a. SLP: "The blue whales are the largest. Can anybody find anything about the humpback whales? Here it is, the humpback whales."

3. *Informative (content/task related).* The informative function involves giving small pieces of information, that is, one fact. Example:

a. SLP (lesson on the U.S. Civil War): "The South attacked Ft. Sumter. Do you know what it means to attack?"

4. *Informative personal.* Personal information less related to the task or classroom lesson is given. Example:

a. SLP: "*Ahorita vengo* (I shall return soon). I'll be right back."

5. *Giving the answer.* The teacher or aide provides the answer to a problem or question. This function typically follows the SLP's question. Example:

a. SLP: "*Te acuerdas lo que quiere decir* less (Do you know what "less" means)? *Menos.*"

Answering/Responding

Answering and responding deals with content aspects and structuring lessons.

1. *Translating a response.* The speaker translates a response previously said by the other person. This may involve a one-word translation, especially when, for example, the SLP may ask a vocabulary-related question. Example:
   a. SLP: "Do you know what *near* means?" Student: "*Tocar* (touch)."
2. *Choral response.* The group answers or responds in unison to the SLP request. Example:
   a. SLP: "They go fishing on the what ___ ? They go fishing on the big water, ___. What?" Students: "Ocean."
3. *Answering out loud, talking out loud (without being called on).* The student answers without being called on or volunteers the information without any call from the SLP. The SLP may prompt for an answer but does not directly call on anyone. Example:
   a. Student: "Six. *Me faltan dos* (I have two left)."
4. *Answering in response to other's question.* This is similar to answering questions in teacher-fronted instruction. Example:
   a. SLP: "I think that's an antelope. What do you call it?" Student: "*Chivo* (goat)."

Starting a Lesson

SLPs use language to prepare students for preclass instruction or lessons, similar to opening the class. Starting a lesson details those aspects that allow for preclass instruction.

1. *Lead statement.* Lead statements serve the language function of opening the class to prepare students for preclass instructions or lessons. The lead statement is found at the beginning of a lesson. It distinctively cues the listener as to what is to occur. The SLP proceeds in a verbal handholding, with the students being led along. The example given provides the first step and leads to the next statement or step. Example:
   a. SLP: "Okay, let's go do a little bit of math and then you can look at this, M."
2. *Shifting topics.* The class lesson is in place and the SLP moves to a new lesson. This involves a transition to a new lesson or aspect of the lesson. Example:
   a. SLP: "You can take out your reading books. We're going to do the story about the star."

3. *Starter-filler.* Use of words such as *okay, uh-huh, a ver, pues* as seen in conversation do act as interjections, starters, or fillers. As a starter, the word serves to alert the listener that new or important information is to be given. As a filler, words like *okay* indicate that the speaker is processing information or that she or he may still be holding the conversational floor. Example:
  a. SLP: *"Okay, tu tienes que poner partes, fraciones* (you have to put parts, fractions).*"*

Ending a Lesson

The SLP, in an effort to finish the lesson, expedites through overt cues to the students.

  1. *Cuing to leave.* The person gives information that it is time to leave and transition out of the classroom. Example:
  a. SLP: "Know what, everyone put away your books. *It's time to leave.*"
  2. *Cuing to finish.* Cuing to finish consists of language attempted to alert the student about finishing the lesson. In specific, information is given to terminate and bring the lesson to a closure. Example:
  a. SLP: *"Know what? Everyone put away your books.* It's time to leave."

Seeking Clarification

Seeking clarification is one means to gather information and elucidate understanding.

  1. *Clarification.* In clarification, the speaker seeks to define and illuminate some information. Example:
  a. Aide: *"Que quieres?* (What do you want?)*"*
  2. *Translating.* Simple translation allows SLPs to translate words and concepts from one language to another. In translation, information in one language is to be transferred to the other via oral or written modes. Example:
  a. (The SLP is translating a story directly from the written English to spoken Spanish): *"Entonces, Henny Penny se fueron a la carrera a avisarle al rey que se va caer el cielo."*
  3. *Seeking help.* The student asks for help in order to perform an activity. Specifically, the student seeks assistance. Thus, seeking help may take direct or indirect forms. Example:
  a. Student: "Hey, Mrs. E., Mrs. E."

Speaking Out Loud

This refers to the function of private speech or the overt use of language and speaking during cognitive tasks. This overt language pragmatics is used to plan, guide, and monitor the use of language. Specifically, speaking out loud also seems to include practicing along with the planning functions.

1. *Self-talk.* No SLP prompt is given for the person to engage in self-talk. It is not in response to a question, such as in answering out loud. Example:
   a. Student: "Now, I gonna try it out. Let me see how many words I get."
2. *Practicing.* In response to the SLP example, the student practices a response. Example:
   a. SLP: "What's this? Look. B-b-bump. Now you guys bump heads." Student: "*B-b-b.*"

Other Code Moves

This consists of a general category of functions not identified by headings. However, the first three functions (we code, anticipation code switching, and diglossia) are particular to code switching.

1. *We code.* This serves as a rapport function—that is, as an in-group code—signifying that the mother tongue serves a solidarity function. Examples:
   a. SLP (a man comes into the room and starts talking with the SLP. She then turns to the observer and states, switching to Spanish): "*El es mi hijo* (He is my son)."
2. *Anticipation code switching.* The speaker anticipates a code switch; for example, speaking Spanish may trigger a switch to that language. Example:
   a. SLP: "Mask, drum, worm. Know what worms are? Do you know in Spanish? *Sabes que es*? (Do you know what it is?)."
3. *Diglossia.* Specific words for specific contexts may be used. The words do not appear to be borrowed words since both the Spanish and English equivalents are used interchangeably, the words do not fill particular linguistic niches, and the particular diglossia words seem to reflect school subjects. Example:
   a. Student: "*Se me revantaron* six (Six burst)."
4. *Apologizing.* The person excuses or makes amends. Example:
   a. Student: "*Vamos a ver el mapa de color,* sorry (Let's see the color map, sorry)."

5. *Reading.* This is a general category involving all reading, writing, literate aspects of language. Reading and literate aspects of language are an integral part of school learning. Example:
   a. (SLP is reading a book): "Ronald Morgan goes to bat (also the name of the book). Is Ronald Morgan a good player?"
6. *Turn-taking.* Turn-taking is verbalized. Example:
   a. SLP: "Okay M., your turn."

9

The Pragmatics of Bilingual Classrooms

A Meta-Ethnography of Qualitative Research

Code Switching and Code Mixing

Language alternation is a normal, common, and important aspect of bilingualism (Grosjean, 1982; Kamwangamalu, 1992; Pennington, 1995). Bilingualism is defined here as the ability to use two languages in varying degrees of proficiency and in different contexts such as reading, writing, listening, and speaking. For the bilingual student, the process of code switching (alternating of two languages) requires a nonrandom, sophisticated cognitive and linguistic manipulation of the two languages (Aguirre, 1988; Miller, 1984). Four classifications of bilingual speaking abilities according to language performances are outlined in Table 9.1. To illustrate, suppose a child is attempting to communicate a request, for example, "I want to be picked up from school early today." If the child is able to provide the appropriate message in both the first language (L1) and the second language (L2), she or he might be considered Bilingually Advantaged. Communication in either language does not differ significantly and the speaker is viewed as a competent communicator; the use of the code switching, or code mixing, may also be present. However, if the student knows the request in L1 but not in L2, it may be said that the child is L1 Advantaged and he or she is viewed as a more competent communicator in the primary language (e.g., Spanish) than in the second language (e.g., English). Alternatively, if the student knows how to say the request in L2 (e.g., English) but not in L1 (e.g., Spanish), it may be viewed that he or she is a more compe-

TABLE 9.1 *Classifications of Bilingual Speaking Abilities According to Language Performance*

Language Act	Language 1 (Native)	Language 2 (English)	Performance
Request	Expressed	Expressed	Bilingually Advantaged
Request	Expressed	Not expressed	L1 Advantaged
Request	Not expressed	Expressed	L2 Advantaged
Request	Not expressed	Not expressed	Bilingually Disadvantaged

tent communicator in the foreign language (L2, English in this example). Either of these conditions would illustrate that a language lag in either L1 or L2 is present. A student in this classification does not present with a language disorder because she or he has exhibited competency in at least one language. On a standardized assessment normed on monolingual English-speaking peers the L1 (Spanish) Advantaged may not perform well within the expected parameters, while the L2 (English) Advantaged student may perform well. Given the nature of the standardized test, in effect the L2 Advantaged student knows the correct response while the L1 Advantaged student may be unable to express the concept verbally in English.

It should also be noted that in and of itself use of alternation is not indicative of a language disorder (Cheng & Butler, 1989; Reyes, 1995)—quite the contrary, in fact. Language alternation in the CLD speaker's discourse indicates knowledge of the two languages, including the semantic, morphological, syntactic, and pragmatic dimensions of both languages. It could be argued that language alternation (e.g., code switching or code mixing) is an indication of a sophisticated user who exhibits a sound cognitive–linguistic functioning. This point was also stated by Reyes (1995), when she said that "an unfortunate yet common misconception is to view code switching as an indicator of deficient language skills in the bilingual speaker. In fact, numerous investigations of code switching have demonstrated just the opposite" (p. 163). The deficiencies mentioned here are ones of learning, not of innate abilities. Clearly, the speaker's ability to express in one language what is not available in the other language indicates that the speaker knows the parameters of the concept. He or she is able to express the linguistic data through a maze of common language attributes (semantics, morphology, syntax, pragmatics) in order to alternate languages.

The last category of the bilingual performer, the Bilingually Disadvantaged, suggests that the speaker is deficient in comparable linguistic elements in both languages. The initial analysis might suggest that this is an individual who, when compared to normal aged peers in either language group, would not perform in the normal range. However, consider that the absence of expressive function does not necessarily mean that a language disorder is present. It may be simply a "deficiency" due to a lack of adequate instructional opportunities, life experiences, or communication interaction. In any event, intervention by either the SLP or classroom teacher is warranted with further assessment needed to define the nature and extent of the deficiency.

Types of Language Alternation

Language alternation can structurally be divided into two categories: code switching (CS) and code mixing (CM). Language alternation is a commonly observed phenomenon with bilingual speakers; it is rule governed and represents shifts to the other language within or across sentence boundaries (Poplack, 1980). Language alternation across sentence boundaries is known as *intersentential* code switching; language alternation within a sentence, code mixing, has been referred to as *intrasentential* alternation (Grosjean, 1982; Torres, 1989). Thus, embedded words, phrases, and sentences from two languages are found across and/or within sentences. For example, the Spanish–English bilingual student might say, "I'm going to be late so I know that *mi mama me va regañar* (my mother is going to scold me). Am I going to be in trouble."

There is a difference of opinion in the literature whether CM and CS should be looked at as different phenomena (D'Souza, 1992; Sridhar & Sridhar, 1980; Tay, 1989). The prevailing view is that the two are not different and should be understood as variations of a unique process in language alternation.

Gumperz (1992) and Miller (1984) noted that CS is motivated by the listener and/or the purpose of the speech act. CS is typically situation motivated. A change in the social situation can motivate a change in code—the arrival of a new speaker or change in the focus of the topic may facilitate a switch to the other language. For example, a speaker may change on the arrival of a new listener: "*Sabes qué Tomas viene a la sesión?* (Did you know that Thomas is coming to the session?) Oh, hi Tom."

CM is also a highly structured bilingual communicative device. It is commonly observed to involve the mixing of various linguistic units, such as morphemes, words, and phrases, from two different languages within the same sentence.

A third form of language alternation is know as "borrowing." Borrowing is a linguistic strategy employed by both bilingual and monolingual speakers. It entails integration of the word or phrase from one language into the other; the borrowed word or phrase therefore becomes a part of the other language and is assimilated into the second language. Borrowed words and phrases take on their own phonological and morphological characteristics (Gumperz, 1982; Kamwangamalu, 1992). Gumperz (1982) points out that "borrowing can be defined as the introduction of single words or short idiomatic phrases from one variety into the other" (p. 66). Borrowing sometimes fills in lexical gaps of the second language.

It is important to note that borrowing may occur in the speech of monolingual and bilingual speakers alike. CS and CM occur only in the speech of bilinguals. Borrowed words often follow the grammatical rules of the new host language. For example, borrowed words in Spanish taken from English include *beisbol* ("baseball"), *futbol* ("football"), and *yanqui* ("yankee"). Alternatively, some words have come to the English language from Spanish, including stirrup *(estribo)*, lasso *(lazo)*, and corral *(corral)*.

While CS, CM, and borrowing all have their identifiable characteristics in terms of use and function, it is clear that these functions are all part of the normal communicative process for the CLD student. That is, the presence of these linguistic usages does not indicate a language disorder. Table 9.2 presents a summary of the CS, CM, and borrowing aspects typically found in alternating language usage. A review and summary of linguistic and functional aspects of language alternation follows.

TABLE 9.2 *Summary Features of Code Switching, Code Mixing, and Borrowed Words*

Feature	Code Switching	Code Mixing	Borrowed Words
Language shift	Yes	No	No
Situational alternation	Yes	No	No
Langauge alternation	Yes	Yes	Yes
Occurs with bilingual speakers	Yes	Yes	Yes
Occurs with monolingual speakers	No	No	Yes
Occurs at sentence level	Yes	Yes	No
Occurs at phrase and word level	No	No	Yes
Fills in lexical gaps in L1	No	No	Yes
Change in phonology	No	No	Yes
L1 equivalent exists	Yes	Yes	No

Classroom Language and Code Switching

Aguirre (1988) noted that researchers have been very cautious in depicting the role of language alternation in bilingual classrooms. What has been reported has pertained to general classroom discourse (Chaudron, 1988; Moskowitz, 1971; Sinclair & Couthard, 1975). However, some researchers have investigated both classroom talk and the role of code switching and code mixing (Merritt, Cleghorn, Abagi, & Bunyi, 1992; Pennington, 1995).

Merritt, Cleghorn, Abagi, & Bunyi (1992) observed three primary bilingual English, Swahili, and mother tongue classrooms in Kenya. Their findings indicate that code switching and code mixing can serve specific classroom functions, for example, as linguistic markers to indicate topic shifts, providing translations, or giving word substitutions instead of a full definition.

Pennington (1995) investigated both teacher and student discourse in an English as a foreign language (EFL) classroom. She found that the students' functional uses of Cantonese involved five distinct functions: (a) discussing with peers, (b) talking to the teacher at desks, (c) answering questions in teacher-fronted instruction, (d) asking questions in teacher-fronted instruction, and (e) translating sentences. She suggested that certain compensatory uses of code switching may be present for the students. For example, such uses may be: (a) when students cannot understand instructions given in English (Guthrie and Guthrie's clarification), (b) when lesson times are short, and (c) when explicating ideas. Other code switching uses may be related to student solidarity.

Teacher Uses of CS/CM

Code switching and code mixing in the classroom can take two forms: as part of a planned curriculum approach in instruction or as a result of more spontaneous language use. The use of CS and CM as curriculum pedagogy has been documented in the bilingual education literature (Aguirre, 1988; Faltis, 1989; Giaque & Ely, 1990; Lin, 1990; Pennington, 1995) as well as its natural and spontaneous use (Brice, Mastin, & Perkins, 1997; Guthrie & Guthrie, 1987; Merritt, Cleghorn, Abagi, & Bunyi, 1992; Pennington, 1995; Phillips, 1975).

Aguirre (1988) suggested that if the school professional (e.g., the SLP or teacher) believes that the student possesses similar and equal ability in both languages, then she or he may want to purposely alternate languages with the student to enhance syntactic complexity and word knowledge. If the SLP believes that the student is alternating languages because of confusion, then she or he may employ code switching as a deliberate strategy to transfer concepts and linguistic symbols from one language to the other.

Faltis (1989) stated that code switching in the classroom should follow two guidelines: (a) only intersentential language mixing, i.e., code switching and not code mixing, be allowed in the classroom and (b) all language switching should be school professional initiated (this latter point may be difficult to impose). The rationale for this is that code switching, i.e., inter-sentential switching, provides students with sufficient input in both languages. It enables students with differing language proficiencies to focus on learning the classroom concepts instead of having to focus entirely on de-coding English. It provides a manner of giving each language equal prestige. It also encourages a kind of language behavior that is commonly used with bilinguals (Grosjean, 1982; Kamwangamalu, 1992; Kwan-Terry, 1992; Miller, 1984). Additional uses of code switching in planned instruction come from Giauque and Ely (1990), who stated that (a) code switching is to be used as a transition language technique to eventually all-English in-struction, (b) it addresses the language tension in learning a second lan-guage, (c) it addresses the student need to understand as much as possible of what is being taught in the second language, and (d) it motivates stu-dents to use as much of the second language as they can for real classroom communication. Therapy should have a foundation in real learning or learning that is based on context (Figueroa & Ruiz, 1997) or authentic ex-amples. Figueroa and Ruiz (1997) stated that reading, writing, listening, and speaking defines 90% of special education programs and that students need to be able to practice all of their language skills. Their advice is to let Spanish speakers take risks in using English and Spanish.

There have been several studies on the spontaneous uses of code switching and code mixing in classrooms. These studies have focused on the pragmatics or functional uses of language in ESL or bilingual classrooms (Brice, Mastin, & Perkins, 1997; Guthrie & Guthrie, 1987; Merritt, Cleghorn, Abagi, & Bunyi, 1992; Pennington, 1995).

Brice, Mastin, and Perkins (1997) reported findings from an English as a second language (ESL) classroom in the United States. The study was conducted in a small community elementary school consisting of 30% His-panics/Latinos (Amato, 1996), and the pragmatic or functional uses of lan-guage were the basis of their study. All of the students enrolled in the ESL classroom spoke Spanish as their first language. The researchers found 50 specific functional uses of classroom language. The general, macro-level code moves consisted of questions, commands, feedback, reinforcement, information, answering/responding, starting a lesson, ending a lesson, seeking clarification, speaking out loud, and other code functions. The spe-cific, micro-level pragmatics code functions particular to CS and CM in-cluded giving feedback, students seeking clarification, teachers asking vocabulary questions, teachers informing, and teachers giving commands through direct task requests.

Guthrie and Guthrie (1987) studied two teachers and their ap-proaches to language use with Chinese–English-speaking students in Cali-fornia. In this study, one teacher was bilingual (Chinese–English-speaking), while the other teacher was monolingual English-speaking. The bilingual teacher employed five distinct purposes for code switching in reading lessons: (a) for translation; (b) as a "we code," a term borrowed from Gumperz (1982) for establishing and maintaining solidarity and group membership; (c) for giving procedures and directions; (d) for clarification, especially with the introduction of new vocabulary words; and (e) as a check for understanding.

Pennington (1995) observed eight Cantonese–English-speaking secondary English classroom teachers during a writing lesson in Hong Kong. She found that the teachers' functional distribution of Cantonese use was as follows: individual talk; defining words; giving instructions; expediting lessons; explicating ideas; reading in L1; tagging an utterance; discussion; expressing solidarity (we-code); disciplining; and motivating.

In sum, teachers use communication with bilingual students to serve two major functions: to give classroom tasks and instructions and to provide strategies particular to learning a second language. It appears that teachers give commands, directions, and instructions as part of their general teaching role. Teachers instructing bilingual students seem to define words, translate, introduce new vocabulary words, and check vocabulary understanding through questions. In addition, use of two languages in the classroom also provides solidarity, as a we-code, with the students.

Purpose

What are the specific types of language pragmatics functions used in the bilingual classroom? This question needs to be investigated along with information that may assist the speech–language pathologist in making assessment and placement decisions. Thus, an outcome of this chapter is to provide a summation of the common classroom pragmatics of language functions as seen with bilingual students. This will be accomplished through meta-ethnography (Noblit & Hare, 1988), which is achieved through ethnographic coding of reported research studies. In essence, the qualitative researcher codes the studies according to a taxonomy and summarizes them.

Methods

Three qualitative ethnographic studies were performed (Brice, 1997; Brice, Mastin & Perkins, 1997; Brice & Perkins, 1997). Qualitative research is descriptive research, that is, words are used to describe the findings instead of numerical data (Bogdan & Biklen, 1992; Glesne & Peshkin, 1992). Data are typically gathered via observations and field notes taken over an extended period of time, that is, repeated observations of variables across time. Validity of the data, or authenticity, is obtained through ethnographic triangulation (three separate data points of the observations). Ethnographic triangulation of the first two studies was obtained by having two separate observers, collecting data over an extended period of time (resulting in multiple observations), and conducting mainly informal as well as formal interviews with the ESL and regular classroom teachers.

The first two studies (Brice, Mastin & Perkins, 1997; Brice & Perkins, 1997) were conducted in the English as a second language (ESL) classroom and the general education second grade classroom in a small community elementary school located in a rural area of southwestern Minnesota. At the time, the elementary school was 30% Hispanic/Latino (Amato, 1996).

The third study was a meta-ethnography (Noblit & Hare, 1988) of the research conducted with bilingual speakers, with specific reference to code switching and code mixing. The studies reviewed included: Adendorff (1993); Camilleri (1991); Canagarajah (1995); Guthrie & Guthrie (1987); Merritt, Cleghorn, Abagi, & Bunyi, (1992); Pease-Alvarez & Winsler (1994); Pennington (1995); and Polio & Duff (1994).

Results

Table 9.3 presents the cross-referencing of the meta-ethnography codings, while Table 9.4 presents a summation of the two ethnographic studies and the meta-ethnography cross-referencing study.

TABLE 9.3   *Meta-ethnography Cross-Referencing of Studies*

5 Cross-Referenced Code Functions (Pragmatic Functions)
Reiteration

4 Cross-Referenced Code Functions (Pragmatic Functions)
Direct task request
Reprimands
Enticement/reinforcement
Explaining
Starter-fillers
Translating

3 Cross-Referenced Code Functions (Pragmatic Functions)
Comprehension question
Directing to lesson
Informative
We-code

2 Cross-Referenced Code Functions (Pragmatic Functions)
Vocabulary question
Higher-level question (application, analysis, synthesis, evaluation)
Acknowledgment

TABLE 9.4 *Code Function*

	Meta-ethnography	*ESL*	*Regular Classroom*	*Total*
1. Reiteration	X	X	X	3
2. Direct task request	X	X	X	3
3. Reprimands	X	—	—	1
4. Enticement/prompting	X	—	X	2
5. Explaining	X	—	X	2
6. Starter-fillers	X	X	X	3
7. Translating	X	—	—	1
8. Comprehension question	X	X	X	3
9. Directing to lesson	X	—	X	2
10. Informative	X	X	X	3
11. We-code	X	—	—	1
12. Vocabulary question	X	X	—	2
13. Higher-level question	X	—	—	1
14. Acknowledgment	X	—	—	1
15. Answering in response to other's question	X	—	—	1
16. Declaration/commenting	—	X	X	2
17. Correction	—	X	—	1
18. Indirect task request	—	X	X	2
19. Informative personal	—	X	—	1
20. Clarification	—	X	—	1
21. Translating a response	—	X	—	1
22. Cueing to leave	—	X	—	1
23. Calling upon a student	—	X	—	1
24. Content question	—	—	X	1
25. Cueing to finish	—	—	X	1
26. Shifting topics	—	—	X	1
27. Factual question	—	X	X	2

Conclusions

The general principles gleaned from the three qualitative studies indicated the following:

1. Code switching and code mixing in classroom discourse are present even in environments which do not actively support bilingual efforts.

2. One hundred percent of the utterances are grammatically correct for Spanish, English, and Spanish–English according to the linguistic rules reported by Poplack (1980). Poplack (1980) iterates the rules of equivalence constraint (syntactic rules of each language cannot be violated) and the free morpheme constraint (language switches may not occur around a bound morpheme) within code-switched and code-mixed language. Therefore, use of code switching and code mixing in and of themselves are not indicative of a language disorder or language confusion.

3. Bilingual and monolingual classrooms seem to employ a common culture regardless of the country of origin, that is, a teacher-centered, teacher-directed approach with a focus on classroom management.

4. Common functions of language (pragmatics) found in classrooms included: direct task request, starter-fillers, enticement/prompting, directing to lesson, indirect task request, reiteration, comprehension question, informative, explaining, vocabulary question, declaration/commenting, factual question, and translating/translating a response.

5. Language assessment is not an isolated activity. Anderson (1997) indicated that

> as bilingualism is both a social and linguistic phenomenon (Hamers & Blanc, 1989), establishing language impairment in bilingual children encompasses more than analyzing language performance. It also includes carefully studying the sociolinguistic environment of each bilingual child that is referred for assessment.

Best Practices

From these results the following practices are recommended:

1. Allow for use of code switching with bilingual, Spanish–English-speaking students in classrooms and the therapy room. Code switching occurs whenever bilingual students are present (Aguirre, 1988). This will allow students to practice speaking and transition into using English at their readiness level.

2. Teach listening skills that correspond to classroom management issues; for example, opening one's book to the page number indicated by the teacher and following the list of instructions needed to com-

plete that particular activity. Teach students to distinguish critical information from noncritical information.

3. Use requests, reiterate statements, ask comprehension questions, give pertinent yet short information statements, give lengthier explanations, check for vocabulary understanding through questions, and make comments to enhance therapy or instruction. These pragmatic strategies are universal in teaching second language learners.

4. Remember that language is omnipresent in school. Use every language opportunity to instruct. To reiterate, language use is not an isolated activity.

Thus, speech–language pathologists and teachers must be knowledgeable of second-language acquisition features, how language is used in classrooms, and what different language demands are placed upon students as they function in different classroom environments.

References

Adendorff, R. (1993). Codeswitching amongst Zulu-speaking teachers and their pupils: Its functions and implications for teacher education. *Language and Education, 7*(3), 141–161.

Aguirre, A. (1988). Code switching, intuitive knowledge, and the bilingual classroom. In H. Garcia & R. Chavez (Eds.), *Ethnolinguistic issues in education* (pp. 28–38). Lubbock, TX: Texas Tech University.

Amato, J. A. (1996). *To call it home. The new immigrants of southwestern Minnesota.* Marshall, MN: Crossing Press.

Anderson, R. (1997, February). Examining language loss in bilingual children. *Communication Disorders and Sciences in Culturally and Linguistically Diverse Populations Newsletter, 3*(1), 2–5.

Brice, A. (1997, March). *The bilingual classroom protocol: Its development and use.* Paper presented at the LTRC 1997 Colloquium. Fairness in Language Testing, Orlando, FL.

Brice, A., Mastin, M., & Perkins, C. (1997). English, Spanish, and code switching use in the ESL classroom: An ethnographic study. *Journal of Children's Communication Development, 19*(2), 11–20.

Brice, A., & Perkins, C. (1997). What is required for transition from the ESL classroom to the general education classroom? A case study of two classrooms. *Journal of Children's Communication Development, 19*(1), 13–22.

Bogdan, R., & Biklen, S. K. (1992). *Qualitative research for education.* Boston, MA: Allyn and Bacon.

Camilleri, A. (1991). Cross-linguistic influence of a bilingual classroom: The examples of Maltese and English. *Edinburgh Working Papers in Applied Linguistics, 2,* 101–111.

Canagarajah, A. S. (1995). Functions of codeswitching in ESL classrooms: Socialising bilingualism in Jaffna. *Journal of Multilingual and Multicultural Development, 6*(3), 173–195.

Chaudron, C. (1988). *Second language classrooms. Research on teaching and learning.* New York: Cambridge University Press.

Cheng, L. R., & Butler, K. (1989). Code switching: A natural phenomenon versus language deficiency. *World Englishes, 8,* 293–309.

D'Souza, J. (1992). The relationship between code-mixing and the new varieties of English: Issues and implications. *World Englishes, 11*(2/3), 217–223.

Faltis, C. J. (1989). Code-switching and bilingual schooling: An examination of Jacobson's new concurrent approach. *Journal of Multilingual and Multicultural Development, 10*(2), 117–127.

Figueroa, R. A., & Ruiz, N. T. (1997, January). *The optimal learning environment.* Paper presented at the Council for Exceptional Children Symposium on Culturally Diverse Exceptional Learners, New Orleans, LA.

Giauque, G., & Ely, C. (1990). Code-switching in beginning foreign language teaching. In R. Jacobson & C. Faltis (Eds.), *Language distribution issues in bilingual schooling* (pp. 174–184). Clevedon, England: Multilingual Matters.

Glesne, C., & Peshkin, A. (1992). *Becoming qualitative researchers.* White Plains, NY: Longman.

Grosjean, F. (1982). *Life with two languages. An introduction to bilingualism.* Cambridge, MA: Harvard University Press.

Guthrie, L. F., & Guthrie, G. P. (1987). Teacher language use in a Chinese bilingual classroom. In S. R. Goldman & H. T. Trueba (Eds.), *Becoming literate in English as a second language.* Norwood, NJ: Ablex.

Kamwangamalu, N. M. (1992). Mixers and mixing. English across cultures. *World Englishes, 11*(2/3), 173–181.

Kwan-Terry, A. (1992). Code-switching and code-mixing: The case of a child learning English and Chinese simultaneously. *Journal of Multilingual and Multicultural Development, 13*(3), 243–259.

Lin, A. M. Y. (1990). Teaching in two tongues: Language alternation in foreign language classrooms. *Research Report Number 3.* Department of English, City Polytechnic of Hong Kong.

Mehan, H. (1979). *Learning lessons: Social organization in the classroom.* Cambridge, MA: Harvard University Press.

Merritt, M., Cleghorn, A., Abagi, J. O. , & Bunyi, G. (1992). Socialising multilingualism: Determinants of codeswitching in Kenyan primary classrooms. *Journal of Multilingual and Multicultural Development, 13*(1 & 2), 103–12.

Miller, N. (1984). Language use in bilingual communities. In N. Miller (Ed.), *Bilingualism and language disability: Assessment and remediation* (pp. 3–25). London, England: Croom Helm.

Moskowitz, G. (1971). Interaction analysis: A new modern language for supervisors. *Foreign Language Annals, 5,* 213.

Noblit, G. W., & Hare, R. D. (1988). *Meta-ethnography: Synthesizing qualitative studies.* Newbury Park, CA: Sage Publications.

Pease-Alvarez, L., & Winsler, A. (1994). Cuando el maestro no habla español: Children's bilingual practices in the classroom. *TESOL Quarterly, 28* (3), 507–535.

Pennington, M. C. (1995). Eight case studies of classroom discourse in the Hong Kong secondary English class. *Research Report Number 42.* Hong Kong Department of English. City University of Hong Kong.

Phillips, J. M. (1975). *Code-switching in bilingual classrooms.* Masters thesis, California State University, Northridge (ERIC Document Reproduction Service No. ED 111222).

Polio, C. G., & Duff, P. A. (1994). Teachers' language use in university foreign language classrooms: A qualitative analysis of English and target language alternation. *Modern Language Journal, 78*(3), 313–326.

Poplack, S. (1980). Sometimes I'll start a sentence in Spanish y termino en español: Toward a typology of code-switching. *Linguistics, 18,* 581–618.

Reyes, B. A. (1995). Considerations in the assessment and treatment of neurogenic disorders in bilingual adults. In H. Kayser (Ed.), *Bilingual speech language pathology. An Hispanic focus* (pp. 153–182). San Diego, CA: Singular Publishing.

Sinclair, J., & Couthard, M. (1975). *Towards an analysis of discourse: The English used by teachers and pupils.* Oxford: Oxford University Press.

Sridhar, S. N., & Sridhar, K. (1980). The syntax and psycholinguistics of bilingual code-mixing. *Canadian Journal of Psychology, 34,* 407–416.

Tay, M. W. J. (1989). Code-switching and code-mixing as a communicative strategy in multilingual discourse. *World Englishes, 8*(3), 407–471.

Practical Assessment Strategies with Hispanic Students

Raquel T. Anderson

Introduction

A continued area of discussion in the field concerns assessment and identification of communication disorders in children from culturally and/or linguistically diverse backgrounds (CLD). Discussion of issues such as the
presence of linguistic and cultural bias inherent in many of our testing instruments and procedures, and best practices for assessing CLD children,
abounds in the textbooks and journal articles. In this chapter, the focus will
be on the Hispanic child who is in a sociolinguistic context where Spanish
is the minority language and English is the dominant language. By dominant, it is meant that it is the language of power, as it permeates most social and political institutions in the country, including schools.

Although the focus of this chapter may seem narrow, it is not. The
Hispanic community is quite diverse, both culturally and linguistically. Hispanics come from various countries, and thus the Spanish dialect spoken
differs across groups (cf. Anderson, 1995; Canfield, 1981; Gutiérrez-Clellen,
Restrepo, Bedore, Peña, & Anderson, 2000; Langdon, 1992a). Furthermore,
in countries where indigenous languages coexist with Spanish, immigrants
may be bilingual speakers or primarily fluent in the indigenous language.
This can be a characteristic of some immigrants from Central and North
American countries, such as Guatemala and Mexico (cf. Bedore, 1999;
Langdon, 1992a). Particular Hispanic communities have been in this coun-

try for generations, while others are recent immigrants. Reasons for leaving the homeland also differ across Hispanic groups. The community also varies in terms of the racial configuration of its people. While Hispanics from Spanish-speaking Caribbean countries may have strong African roots, others have American Indian roots (Langdon, 1992a). These differences thus point to quite a diverse group of individuals that are called Hispanics. As a result of these differences, this chapter will not attempt to provide cultural and linguistic information, but provide guidelines for conducting sound assessments that take into consideration the variety of realities and experiences of the Hispanic community, and thus the Hispanic child.

To guide the discussion of the various topics that will be presented throughout this chapter, two case studies will be used. These will describe two different Hispanic children with varied linguistic and experiential backgrounds. They also differ in terms of the assessment questions and needs. As each topic is presented, the children will be used as examples of how to apply the information.

Cases: Benito and Consuelo

Benito

Benito Camacho is a six-year-old child of recent immigrants from the Dominican Republic. He lives in a large urban area in the eastern United States in a housing project where 60% of the residents are Hispanic, mainly Puerto Rican and Dominican. His family has resided in the United States and in this community for approximately six months. Both parents have blue-collar jobs and their income puts them below the poverty level. The parents have completed high school in the Dominican Republic. The main language spoken at home is Spanish, both parents indicating that they are fluent Spanish-speakers with limited English skills. The family is composed of both parents, the maternal grandmother, an older sister, Mariela, who is eight, and a younger brother, José, aged four.

Benito is presently in first grade in a bilingual program in a large inner-city elementary school. He has been in this program for approximately eight months. This is his first school experience. The bilingual program focuses on teaching Spanish literacy skills through second grade, with English as a separate, second language instruction. All content areas are in Spanish. The bilingual teacher, Mrs. Eva Maldonado, has referred the child to the assessment team because she is concerned about Benito's lack of progress in reading and writing in Spanish, as compared to other children in the classroom. In addition, the teacher describes him at times as difficult to understand and not talking much in class. According to Mrs. Maldonado, he follows classroom routines well and appears to understand what is said to him in Spanish. She indicated that at times he fails to show "on-task behavior," especially when working on his own. Benito gets along with other children in the classroom, all of whom are Dominican or Puerto Rican. She adds that Benito's primary language is Spanish, and he has minimal oral English skills.

Consuelo

Consuelo Ijalba is a 10-year-old child of Mexican American descent. She is Spanish–English bilingual and has been diagnosed with mild mental retardation and with a seizure disorder. She is currently on medication to control her seizures. From reports, she is described as verbal (oral) with significant functional articulation problems. Her comprehension is described as mildly impaired. According to parental and school reports, Consuelo speaks both languages and has problems in both. She has always been in English immersion programs and had English as a second language pullout instruction during kindergarten. Language and other interventions have been limited, due to frequent moves. The father is reported to be bilingual (English–Spanish) and her mother is predominantly Spanish-speaking. Consuelo was born in the United States, while both parents were born in Mexico and have resided in the southwestern United States for approximately 15 years. The father is presently attending law school. The mother is the primary caregiver and speaks to Consuelo mainly in Spanish. The parents have recently moved to a small college town and plan to be there for approximately three years. She will be beginning school there and from school reports, will be placed in a self-contained English-only classroom for children with cognitive disabilities. The parents are concerned about her poor language skills and her difficulty speaking. They are also concerned about the dual language input and don't know if they should continue to speak Spanish at home. Consuelo has two older brothers (ages 10 and 13) and a younger sister (age 5). The brothers' primary language is English, while the sister's is Spanish.

What Is the Purpose of Assessment?

A basic consideration in the development of an effective assessment plan for any child is the purpose of the evaluation; that is, why was the child referred and what are the concerns? These questions, in essence, guide assessment. In speech–language pathology, there are two basic purposes of assessment: (1) identification of a disorder and (2) describing regularities in performance (Haynes & Pindzola, 1998; Lund & Duchan, 1993; Tomblin, 2000). The instruments and/or procedures that are utilized during assessment are intimately tied to these purposes and the information that needs to be obtained for that particular child. For example, a clinician to whom

Benito is referred may have as the main purpose of the assessment establishing if he has a communication disorder. The clinician may also be interested in describing regularities in performance, but the initial question or concern is identification of a disorder. On the other hand, a clinician working with Consuelo may be more interested in describing her communication skills, including areas of strengths and deficits. This is because deficits have been identified and the purpose of the assessment is not so much identifying a disorder, but obtaining the necessary data to develop an effective treatment plan. Because of these different assessment goals, different data gathering and analysis procedures will be used.

With the Hispanic child, regardless of what the purpose is of the assessment, the process of gathering the necessary data becomes more complicated, as cultural and linguistic differences from the mainstream population, the population for which most assessment procedures have been developed, impact performance. Clinicians, then, must be cognizant of the potential bias inherent in the assessment instruments used. Two potential biases are present in any testing procedure: (1) linguistic bias and (2) cultural bias (Anderson, 1994a, 1994b, 1996; Lidz & Peña, 1996; Wolfram, 1983).

Linguistic bias pertains to the language that is used during testing and the language expected in the child's responses. For example, if a child is given a test using Standard American English (SAE), and the child speaks a different dialect, the instrument would then be biased. In this case, a child may perform differently than expected, not because of a true language disability, but because there is a mismatch between the child's dialect and the dialect of the testing instrument. As a result, such a procedure will fail in identifying a true disability, as the child's performance may be the result of a linguistic difference and not a language impairment. Because Hispanic children may be speakers of other English dialects (e.g., African American English) (cf. Zentella, 1997), be bilingual English–Spanish speakers, or have limited skills in the language used for testing, the potential for linguistic bias during the assessment of this group of children is great.

Cultural bias refers to the use of activities and items that do not correspond to the child's experiential base. Many of the procedures utilized for assessing language skills are based on typical mainstream interaction patterns between a child and an adult. If these interaction patterns do not resemble those with which the child is familiar, a potential for cultural bias will ensue. Peña, Quinn, and Iglesias (1992) reported an example of such a bias. They studied a group of low-income Puerto Rican preschoolers and their performance on a test that required them to label pictures, the *Expressive One Word Picture Vocabulary Test* (EOWPVT) (Gardner, 1990). Object labeling was not a typical language experience in the children's environment, as it is not frequent in adult–child interactions from that particular background. This contrasts with mainstream interactions, where labeling of objects in the environment is a common parent–child interaction pattern (van Kleeck, 1994). When tested, the majority of the Puerto Rican children performed poorly, not because of a true deficit in expressive vocabulary, but because the expected response did not match what would be expected in their culture. Not only are procedures potentially biased but the items chosen to assess language skills may also be biased. If a child has not had experience with that item, the clinician cannot ascertain if the child failed to respond because of language learning deficits or because of not encountering such an item previously.

The two cases of Benito and Consuelo will demonstrate the negative impact cultural and linguistic biases can have on performance. Because one of the main goals of Benito's assessment is to identify a communication disorder, utilizing activities and tasks where a potential linguistic and/or cultural mismatch may exist, the clinician will not be able to discern if his responses are the result of deficits in language learning or if they are due to differences between the language of assessment and the child's language background, as well as to lack of experience with the target items and data collection procedures. In fact, the clinician will not be able to answer the most important question posed: Does Benito have a communication disorder?

In Benito's case, various cultural and linguistic factors need to be considered. The case history information suggests that Spanish is the language most frequently used in the home and community. He has been in an English environment for a limited amount of time (eight months), thus the language of assessment will need to be Spanish. Furthermore, because he and his family are from the Dominican Republic, this Spanish dialect should be used for assessment and interpretation of the child's responses. The family has been in the United States for a short period of time and are living in a primarily Hispanic neighborhood. It can be predicted that their level of acculturation to the mainstream culture will be low, thus potential cultural biases (e.g., adult–child interaction patterns) need to be examined before utilizing any assessment instrument. In addition, Benito has had limited experience with the school culture, again suggesting that possible experiential differences may impact performance on any assessment procedure used.

Although Consuelo may indeed have a language learning disability, bias in testing will also confound the data collected. Certain information present in the case summary is of relevance. First, Consuelo is a Spanish–English bilingual. In order to obtain a clear pattern of areas of strength and areas of deficit, she must thus be tested in both languages. Furthermore, phenomena that are particular to bilingualism need to be accounted for in our testing. Examples of such phenomena include domains of use of each language (e.g., home versus school), code switching, and first language loss. These, in turn, will affect how Consuelo's performance is interpreted. In addition, cultural differences in interaction patterns may also

influence performance and make it difficult for the clinician to discern responses that may be due to differences in interaction patterns or to true lack
of skill. Any clinician working with Consuelo and attempting to describe
regularities in performance for making intervention decisions needs to be
able to determine where her deficits lie. If not, the intervention plan resulting from the assessment may not address Consuelo's deficits.

Assessing the Hispanic Child— General Considerations

Obtaining Background Knowledge

A clinician working with a Hispanic child, whether bilingual or monolingual, needs to have general background information in the following areas:
(a) second language acquisition, (b) bilingualism, and (c) sociolinguistics
(ASHA, 1985). Some of this information is provided in the present text, but
there are many additional sources of information, including books, articles,
and coursework in the area. Without this general background knowledge,
the clinician runs the risk of incorrectly assessing the language abilities of
the Hispanic child, as she or he will not have the necessary expertise for
choosing appropriate testing procedures and interpreting behavior. Because
Hispanics are a heterogeneous group, both culturally and linguistically, a
clinician should also be familiar with the particular Hispanic community
with which she or he is working. This Hispanic community can be large or
can be as small as a single-family unit.

There are various ways in which a clinician can gather information
about the language and culture of the Hispanic community she or he will
be working with, be it one child or many children. A list of possible sources
of information is presented in Table 10.1. If the community encompasses
more than one or two families, good means of gathering relevant demographic and sociocultural information about the community include using
a cultural informant, visiting the community, and researching written materials.

A cultural informant should be someone who is very familiar with the
community. Whenever possible, it should be a member of this community.
Some examples may be community leaders and professionals with extensive experience working with the Hispanic group. Because observations and
insights that an informant provides may be affected by personal biases (e.g.,
toward the Hispanic community and toward the mainstream community),
having more than one informant will provide a broader perspective and
view of the sociolinguistic and cultural characteristics of the group. This individual can also be of invaluable help as the clinician designs and chooses
assessment methods for the Hispanic children in the caseload. Relevant so-

TABLE 10.1 *Information Sources for the Target Hispanic Community*

Cultural Informant
Teachers
Community leaders/members
Other professionals

Universities/Colleges
Language departments
Linguistics/applied linguistics departments
Sociology/anthropology departments
Speech–language pathology departments
Ethnic studies

Readings
Communication disorders
Multicultural education
Bilingual education
Bilingualism/second language acquisition
Sociology
Anthropology
History

Visits to the Community
Community centers
Recreational areas
Shopping areas
Churches or religious centers

Continuing Education
University courses
ASHA convention
State conventions
Other conventions/congresses (e.g., education, applied linguistics)
Workshops

ciolinguistic information that can be obtained from the informant includes patterns of language use in the community, incidence of bilingualism, characteristics of the Spanish and English dialects spoken, and general patterns of code switching or code mixing. Cultural and demographic particulars include incidence of poverty within the community, general nonverbal patterns of communication, child-rearing practices, and attitudes toward disabilities. Recommended areas of inquiry for informants are summarized in Table 10.2.

TABLE 10.2 *Areas of Inquiry for a Cultural Informant*

1. Language interaction rules (within and across generations)
2. Attitudes of the group toward the mainstream
3. Degree of acculturation (within and across generations)
4. Extent of poverty within the community
5. Family member roles
6. Customs, values, and beliefs that are relevant for understanding the child and family's behavior
7. Typical family size
8. Experience with the American educational system
9. Differences between educational systems in the United States and the home country
10. Experience with formal education
11. Attitudes about disabilities
12. Reasons for leaving homeland and settling in the area

If the clinician is working in a setting where there is a large Hispanic community, an additional means for gathering information is to visit that community. This may include working as a volunteer in existing community centers or programs, attending special events in the community, or simply visiting stores in the neighborhood. Patterns of behavior noted by the clinician should be discussed with the cultural informant(s), as the clinician's personal worldview may affect how observations are interpreted. Besides providing the clinician with insights about the community, visiting the neighborhood also helps in establishing rapport with both the children and their families. In this manner, community members may begin to see the clinician as one who is genuinely interested in their well-being and who is open to new cultures.

Obtaining Child-specific Information

As with any child referred for an assessment, the clinician is responsible for obtaining background information. In addition to the typical data gathered via case history reports, language and school history data are essential to the assessment of the Hispanic child. Because of the possible dual language background, clinicians must gather information concerning the child's (and family's) use of Spanish and English. They must also understand the school experiences, both in terms of language and content of instruction.

Various aspects of language use and skill not touched on in traditional case history forms or interview guidelines need to be included in the background information. A summary of specific areas of inquiry is presented in Table 10.3. Parents or other family members should be asked about language use at home (Mattes & Omark, 1991). This includes the language that is spoken to the child by various family members and the language spoken by the child while interacting with them. For example, parents can indicate what language the child uses when speaking to them, their siblings, grandparents, or any other individual within the family. They can also be asked to indicate in what language(s) the child responds to each family member. Data on how often the child interacts with each person and the percent of time the child uses each language with said person should be noted. In this manner, the clinician can obtain a clear idea of the amount of time the child uses Spanish and English, thus permitting the clinician to make sound decisions concerning which language(s) to be used during assessment.

Other pertinent information concerning language use includes the amount of code switching used by the child and in what circumstances this is observed. Questions should include, when does the child code switch and with whom does she or he code switch? Such questions can aid the clinician in incorporating activities during assessment that can tap into the child's code switching skill, a skill that can provide great insight into pragmatic and grammatical skills (Brice, 2000; also refer to Chapters 4, 8, and 9).

It is also very important for the clinician to address the possibility of first language (L1) loss. This phenomenon is present when parents

TABLE 10.3 *Additional Information That Needs to Be Collected via Case History/Interview*

Language use:

- at home by the child
- at home by each family member
- language of interaction between child and each family member
- with peers
- use of each language (Spanish, English, indigenous) across settings, topics, and interactants
- changes in language use and input over time (family members, child)
- changes in language ability for Spanish and English (and when applicable, indigenous language)

Attitudes toward maintenance of Spanish skills

Education/schooling in country of origin

Previous involvement with other professionals and with the school

Access to medical care

---

and/or other family members indicate that the child's L1 skills have changed over time, and this change has resulted in a reduction of productive ability in the language, in this case Spanish (Anderson, 1999; Orellana, 1994). This is an extremely important piece of information to obtain, as L1 loss can explain a child's use of Spanish that does not correspond to what would be expected for that age and presumed Spanish experience. Parents should thus be asked if they have noted any differences in skill in both Spanish and English. They should also be asked to describe the child's relative skill in both languages. This information will aid the clinician not only in developing the assessment protocol but, more importantly, in interpreting the child's performance (Anderson, 1994b, 1999; Schiff-Myers, 1992).

The child's school history provides information concerning experience with literacy and academic-based language in Spanish and in English. With younger children, it also may provide insight as to the child's preliteracy skills. Furthermore, and regrettably in the United States, it can also indicate the quality of education to which the child has been exposed (Kozol, 1991). If the child has been in school, the clinician will need to gather information on the type of program in which the child has been enrolled. With Hispanic children, who are often in a dual language environment, it is necessary to establish if the child has attended or is attending a bilingual program. Because these programs vary in many ways (see Chapter 2), the clinician needs to gather pertinent information on the particular program the child has attended. This includes the following: (1) type of program (e.g., early exit transitional, late exit transitional); (2) length of time in the program; (3) language of instruction (e.g., only Spanish used, both Spanish and English used); (4) language used for literacy development; and (5) type of English instruction provided. If the child has attended school in the native country, data on the school system of that country may be of help, including English instruction, if any. This can be gathered via parent interview, the informant, or written reports from the country of origin. Such information will give the clinician data on the child's academic experience in each language and thus help plan assessment accordingly.

One of the harsh realities of the Hispanic community is that compared to the mainstream group and to other ethnic/racial minorities in this country, they evidence higher poverty rates. For example, the 1998 United States Census reports that approximately a quarter of the Hispanic families is poor. This fact, in turn, impacts the type and quality of schooling poor Hispanic children (and for that matter any child) may receive (Kozol, 1991). A discussion of the American public educational system and its disparities across socioeconomic levels is beyond the scope of this chapter, but the clinician needs to be aware of this phenomenon in order to understand performance, especially in using procedures that focus on academic-based language learning.

Use of an Interpreter

For monolingual clinicians working with a Hispanic population, it is essential that they seek an interpreter. In fact, interpreters should probably be used more frequently in speech–language pathology. For example, in a survey conducted by Roseberry-McKibbin and Eicholtz (1994) on service delivery models used with limited English proficient children, 90% of the respondents indicated that they were not fluent enough to provide services in the other language. In the same survey, the most frequent ethnic group served was the Hispanic, thus Spanish was the other language. An alternative to using an interpreter would be to enlist the services of a bilingual Spanish–English-speaking clinician. This alternative, although viable in some cases, may not be feasible in others. The number of clinicians who speak Spanish fluently is small in contrast with the ever-growing Hispanic population (Kayser, 1993, 1995a; Langdon, 1992a).

Several guidelines should be followed when choosing and working with an interpreter. These are summarized in Table 10.4. It is important not to use a family member as an interpreter; for example, an older sibling. Although this may seem a simple and efficient way of obtaining an interpreter, it will be counterproductive for various reasons. First, there is an intimate relationship between the family member and the child. By ascribing that individual the interpreter role, this relationship will shift, and the person may not be able to detach from the process. Second, the clinician is imposing another role on an individual who does not have that usual role with the child, thus perhaps bringing some conflict between the two roles. Third, this would be an added stress to the family member in a situation that already may be quite stressful. In sum, the end result may be that the clinician will fail to obtain the needed information via the use of such an interpreter.

A better alternative would be to train a member of the community, or someone who has native or native-like fluency in the language. In fact, the cultural informant could play a dual role by also being the interpreter. Other possible sources for interpreters include individuals within the school community, usually teacher aides who are fluent in Spanish. Regardless of whom the clinician will work with, it is essential that this person have certain skills. An interpreter should have good oral and written skills in both English and Spanish (Kayser 1995b), as she or he will need to communicate, both orally and in written form, in both languages. The individual's Spanish skill can be ascertained by requesting the help of individuals who are fluent, such as Spanish teachers in the district or community members. The individual should be familiar with the dialect or variant spoken in the community, so that the child's performance will be adequately assessed. Additional linguistic skills include being able to shift styles depending on the situation; for example, interacting with the child during play and inter-

TABLE 10.4 *General Guidelines for Working with an Interpreter*

1. Interpreter needs to have the following skills:
   - literacy in both Spanish and English
   - ability to interact properly in both languages with children and adults from the target Hispanic community
   - ability to maintain confidentiality
   - knowledge of the educational system and of relevant terminology
2. Areas of training:
   - ethical practices
   - professional terminology
   - rationale for and procedures used during the assessment process
   - implementation of the assessment procedures
3. Training strategies:
   - role-playing
   - practice administering procedure to an English speaker of the same age as the child
   - use the cultural informant as a resource for evaluating the interpreter's skills.

Source: Kayser (1995b).

viewing the parents. Community members as informants could aid the clinician in gathering such information.

The clinician working with the interpreter is responsible for providing the interpreter with necessary information about our field and scope of practice as well as the responsibilities of the interpreter during assessment (Kayser, 1993, 1995b; Langdon, 1992b). For example, the interpreter must be familiar with the terminology used in the field in order to understand the technical jargon and translate this for the family members in written and oral communications. The interpreter should also be versed in best practices in our profession, particularly with respect to assessing the school-aged child who comes from a dual language background. Here, a comprehensive explanation of why certain procedures are performed is essential, as this will enable the intrepreter to understand what information needs to be gathered and thus be able to gather it. It is also important that the clinician familiarize the interpreter with ethical practices in our profession (Kayser, 1993, 1995b; Langdon, 1992b). The interpreter must understand the importance of confidentiality, as this may ultimately affect the relationship established between the clinician and the family. Ultimately, the clinician needs to inform the interpreter that the clinician is the one that makes any clinical decisions about the child; the interpreter is not expected to do this. Because the clinician is responsible for clinical management decisions, she or he must ensure that the interpreter has the necessary skills prior to aiding in the assessment process.

There are various activities or tasks where an interpreter could be of service, but prior to actually collaborating on a real case, the clinician must train the interpreter to perform the task appropriately. The interpreter can be of assistance during interactions between the clinician and family. As with any aspect of the assessment, the family needs to be informed when an interpreter will be used, and more importantly, they should be the ones to decide if they need an interpreter. Another activity where the interpreter may be helpful would be administering specific testing procedures and obtaining language samples in Spanish. Within these activities, the interpreter can also identify to the clinician specific items and/or procedures that may be culturally and/or linguistically inappropriate for the Hispanic child. The task(s) in which the interpreter will participate will depend on the child, the family, and the assessment goals.

Regardless of the task, the clinician must train the interpreter to perform the procedure. There are two main strategies that can be used for training. First, the clinician and interpreter can role-play the situation. This can be video-recorded for both verbal and visual feedback. Second, the interpreter can actually practice performing the task with an English-speaking client; for example, the parents of a child in the school or an English-speaking child of the same age range as the Hispanic child who is being assessed (Kayser, 1995b). Regardless of the training method used, the clinician must ensure that the interpreter can perform the task in a competent manner.

Parent Interview

One of the best sources of information concerning children's language skills are the parents. This is especially the case when working with the Hispanic child. In a recent study by Restrepo (1998) in which she analyzed identifiers of specific language impairment in school-aged Spanish-speaking children, it was found that one of the best identifiers of language impairment was parental concern. Thus, the need to obtain the parent's perceptions of their child's language skills is of extreme relevance when assessing Hispanic children. Others have supported the value of interviewing parents when working with this group of children (Anderson, 1994a; Kayser, 1995c).

When interviewing Hispanic parents, as with any parent, the clinician must consider their availability to come for an interview. A place and time that is convenient for the parents should be ascertained, and, if possible, alternative times and meeting places can be discussed with them. Although a case history form can be sent to the parents, a face-to-face interview should follow this up. In this way, questions that may surface from the case history information can be addressed and additional data can be collected as needed. If a case history form is mailed to the parents, care should be taken that it respects the parents' preferred language. The clinician can ascertain this by asking the parents directly or by utilizing the cultural informant. If a Spanish case history form is used, the clinician needs to ensure that the language is appropriate, both in content and structure. Some written questionnaires are available, for example, the *Bilingual Health and Developmental History Questionnaire* (Gómez-Valdez, 1988).

The content of the interview should include general case history information. These data include developmental speech, language, and motor history, pregnancy and delivery, medical history, family history, and school/academic history (Hall & Morris, 2000; Haynes & Pindzola, 1998). Of relevance is whether the parents have any concerns regarding their child's speech and/or language development. As suggested by Restrepo (1998) and Kayser (1995c), questions, whenever possible, should be direct. By this it is meant that the clinician needs to ask specific questions—for example, whether they are concerned about their child's communication skill—and then move to broader questions. If necessary, the parents should be asked to compare their child's skill with those of other children, including siblings and peers (Restrepo, 1998). It is also essential that the clinician gather information pertaining to the child's skill, experience, and use of Spanish and English. Specifically, the clinician needs to inquire about the child's skill in both languages and if the parents have noted changes in skill across time. The use of each language among family members must also be ascertained; for example, what language each individual uses when interacting with the child. These data will provide the clinician with relevant information as to the domains in which each language is used, the presence of code switching, and the possibility of language loss. This, in turn, will aid the clinician in deciding how to assess the child's skill in each language, as well as in establishing some tentative hypotheses as to expected ability in Spanish and in English. Information about the child's school experience— in particular, the type of language program attended by the child—is also important. Such particulars will aid the clinician in identifying expected literacy skills and general academic experience in each language. This, in turn, will suggest possible areas of assessment in Spanish and English.

Benito and Consuelo

Getting started with Benito and Consuelo will entail obtaining the necessary background information. If not bilingual, the clinician will also need to identify either a bilingual speech–language pathologist or train a paraprofessional to serve as an interpreter. In both cases, information concerning language background and possible cultural differences needs to be gathered. Nevertheless, the specific information, as well as the means of obtaining such information, will differ for the two children.

In Benito's case, the clinician has a rich source of information within the community. Because the child lives in a relatively large Hispanic community, the clinician can obtain an informant who lives in the child's neighborhood and who is familiar with the Dominican Spanish variant and culture. Some possible sources could be found within the school, as he is in a bilingual program. For example, the bilingual teacher may be able to provide relevant information and thus serve as a linguistic and cultural informant. The child is limited English proficient, thus, in order to complete a nonbiased assessment, Benito will need to be evaluated in Spanish. Whoever will work with the clinician must be trained in the assessment procedures that will be used, including interviewing the parents, as they also have limited English skills. Role-playing and practice with real clients can be used as training strategies.

In contrast to Benito, Consuelo lives in an environment where there is not a large Hispanic community from which to obtain a cultural and linguistic informant. Nevertheless, because she lives in a college town, a possible source of information could be found within the university; for example, the Spanish department. If an interpreter is necessary because the clinician is not bilingual, an interpreter can also be obtained by contacting graduate students in the department or faculty. Consuelo speaks both languages, thus she will have to be assessed in Spanish and in English. The interpreter will thus collaborate with the clinician during the assessment. In addition, as Consuelo's mother speaks primarily Spanish, the interpreter may also be of assistance during the parent interview. Due to Consuelo's language and school background, specific information concerning language use and school experiences must be obtained. The parents need to be asked about the child's development in both languages and changes in relative use and input of both Spanish and English. They will also need to provide information concerning their daughter's schooling, including when she was identified as presenting mental retardation. Data on how the child was assessed, including language(s) of assessment and procedures should be collected. If the parents cannot provide all the pertinent information, school records should be secured, as school experience needs to be ascertained before developing an assessment plan. This information will provide data concerning academic experience in both languages and type of services that were provided, and thus will give the clinician insights as to expected language performance.

Assessing Language Skills in the Hispanic Child

Use of Norm-referenced Tests with Hispanic Children

The use of traditional assessment procedures in the evaluation of CLD students has been the subject of many debates in the field (cf. Anderson,

1994a, 1994b, 1996; Kayser, 1996; Quinn, Goldstein, & Peña, 1996; Taylor & Payne, 1983; Wolfram, 1983). Research has attested to the potential linguistic and cultural bias of these tests and the overidentification of Hispanic children as language learning disabled (Peña, Quinn, & Iglesias, 1992; Kayser, 1995c). In spite of these potential problems, clinicians continue to rely on norm-referenced tests for the identification of children with language learning problems (Kayser, 1995c). As a result, Hispanic children continue to be misdiagnosed and thus receive inappropriate services. One of the issues concerned with the use of norm-referenced tests with the Hispanic child is the question of their validity. Although most tests present ample evidence of their inherent validity for assessing the construct they purport to test, the fact remains that validity is a relative concept; that is, what is valid for one group of people is not necessarily valid for another group.

Although bias can occur with *any* assessment procedure, most of the research has indicated that many norm-referenced tests are biased. By *biased* it is meant that the individual's demographic characteristics, not purported to affect performance, do in fact impact how the individual scores on the test. If a test differentiates between individuals on the basis of demographic characteristics, such a test is biased against the population that scores low on the test. The procedure is thus not truly assessing language ability, but how acculturated the Hispanic child is to the mainstream culture and language. As a result, the validity of the test is compromised. All norm-referenced tests thus need to be assessed for potential bias when used with the Hispanic child. Such relevant issues as the language of the test, including variant procedures for eliciting responses, specific items used (lexical and grammatical targets), and the normative sample used for ranking performance need to be studied and identified.

Several procedures can be used to assess the potential for linguistic and cultural bias inherent in an assessment instrument. Linguistic bias is assessed by careful study of the test content. An obvious first question for the Hispanic child is the language being tested—in other words, English or Spanish. In addition, the variant of each language needs to be ascertained. For example, if the test is in Spanish, what Spanish variant is being assessed? The child's linguistic background needs to match that of the test. For Spanish variants, most of the differences are observed in vocabulary and phonology while fewer differences are observed in syntax and morphology (Zayas-Bazán & Fernández, 1993). Because of this, the clinician must pay closer attention to the vocabulary items used and the expected responses. Labels must conform to the variant spoken by the child and the community. For example, in Puerto Rican Spanish, the word *carro* is used to label an automobile, while in Mexico, it is *coche* (Zayas-Bazán & Fernández, 1993); in Puerto Rico, *coche* refers to a baby carriage. If the test includes the word *coche* in reference to an automobile, this may be problematic for the child who speaks Puerto Rican Spanish because the response may be scored as incorrect. If phonological differences could impact performance, the clinician should be familiar with the common phonological patterns of the Spanish variant (cf. Canfield, 1981; Goldstein, 1995). Following the same Spanish variant, a common phonological pattern in Puerto Rican Spanish is the aspiration or "deletion" of final [s] (Anderson & Smith, 1987; Goldstein, 1995). Because final [s] can also serve as a marker for plural (e.g., *las casas* /"the houses"), plural targets with [s] may be produced with either aspiration or omission. A clinician unfamiliar with this pattern may incorrectly score such responses as incorrect when in fact the child's underlying representation does include plural marking. The end result is that the child will not be credited with evidencing plurality when in fact the child has acquired the necessary plural markers for his or her Spanish variant.

Linguistic bias can also occur if the child is being tested in English. Even if the child can speak English, the particular English variant spoken by the child's community may not be SAE, the variant used in norm-referenced tests. For example, Hispanic children may speak a vernacular English, such as African American English (AAE) (Zentella, 1997). They may also speak an English variant that may be influenced by Spanish (Zentella, 1997). In fact, they may be speakers of more than one English variant. In a comprehensive ethnographic study of a small Puerto Rican community in New York City, Zentella (1997) reported that the children and adults spoke various varieties of English, including AAE and what she termed Hispanized English, or English with Spanish influences. Thus, regardless of the child's proficiency in English, care should be taken that the test's language matches the variant spoken by the Hispanic child being tested.

A further issue compounds the use of a norm-referenced test with the Hispanic child. Many of these children are bilingual, with varied levels of relative proficiency in each language. Norm-referenced tests available to the clinician focus on one of the child's languages and treat each as independent from each other, when, in fact, the relationship between the two languages is one that is fluid and dynamic (Anderson, 1994a; Grosjean, 1982; Nicoladis & Genesee, 1997; Romaine, 1996). Because of this, norm-referenced tests may be inadequate for bilingual children for a variety of reasons. First, the norms used are typically those of children who are monolingual in the language being tested. The child's peers, then, who should be bilingual Hispanic children from similar sociolinguistic backgrounds, are not represented in the norms. Using monolingual norms may thus result in the child's language ability not being evaluated as a whole, but on how much English or Spanish the child knows. How both languages interact and are used is not evaluated. A second problem lies in the fact that these tests do not provide guidelines for interpreting responses produced in the child's other language. As a result, accepting responses in either language and later using the norms compromises the validity of comparing the child's performance with that of those represented in the normative sample. Thus, the clinician is in a quandary. If responses are accepted in either language and the test does not provide for accepting these responses, then the clinician should not use the norms for comparison purposes. The use of such a procedure for identifying a disorder is thus questionable.

Linguistic bias is, then, a potential factor that can negatively impact a Hispanic child's performance on a norm-referenced test. In order to reduce linguistic bias, the clinician needs to examine the content of any norm-referenced test and evaluate its appropriateness for the particular child to be assessed. Included in this examination are (a) adequacy of the items used for eliciting the desired response; (b) how the expected response corresponds to what would be a typical response for the child's particular language variant; and (c) the representativeness of the child's cultural and linguistic background in terms of the normative sample (including dual language learners). When investigating the adequacy of the norms, the clinician must not only evaluate if children from a similar background were represented but also if there are any data on how these children performed relative to the rest of the normative sample. Because the percentage of Hispanic children is usually small, simply having the same percent of Hispanic children as that indicated in the latest census is not sufficient. The child will thus be compared to the mainstream child, not to a Hispanic peer. If the Hispanic children differed in performance and this is not reported, then the comparison may be inappropriate. In addition, because of the linguistic and cultural heterogeneity of the Hispanic population, evidence of Hispanic children in the sample does not always translate to adequate representation.

Cultural bias is present in testing when the interaction and expected performance do not match what is the typical pattern in the child's community. The linguistic bias may be reduced by considering the child's language variant and use of two languages and by choosing appropriate target items, but if there is a mismatch between the interaction expected during testing and that which is familiar to the child, cultural bias will accrue. Like any interaction between human beings, testing is a social event (Wolfram, 1983). Because it is a social event, there are rules of interaction, which include expected responses to particular cues. The clinician, then, needs to evaluate each testing instrument for its potential cultural bias. Information concerning typical interaction patterns between adult and child in the community obtained via the informant can aid in evaluating the cultural appropriateness of the test. Having an individual from the community evaluate the procedures in terms of how well they match the community's interaction patterns, especially between children and adults, will aid the clinician in discerning potential bias. The clinician can also administer the test to other Hispanic children with backgrounds similar to that of the child referred for assessment and who are considered to have age-appropriate language skills. Studying their responses during testing can give insight into potential cultural (and linguistic) biases present in the testing instrument. In that manner, the clinician will be able to interpret the child's responses by contrasting them to those of true peers.

It is essential that the clinician using a Spanish norm-referenced test be cognizant of both linguistic and cultural bias inherent in the instrument. Even if the child is limited English proficient and Spanish is the language of assessment, using a Spanish norm-referenced test may not reduce these two types of biases. Most of the testing instruments available in Spanish are either translations or adaptations of existing English tests. For example, the *Preschool Language Scale-3* (Spanish edition) (Zimmerman, Steiner, & Pond, 1993) is an adaptation of a test constructed for English-speaking children. From a purely linguistic perspective, this is an inadequate solution to the lack of Spanish norm-referenced tests.

Using Norm-referenced Tests: Benito and Consuelo

A clinician working with Benito has the major goal of ascertaining if he has a true language disability. In theory, then, norm-referenced tests may be appropriate tools for this purpose. Nevertheless, in this case, the clinician must be certain that such an instrument is a valid measure of Benito's language ability. The norm-referenced test chosen for this purpose must be in Spanish, as this child is limited English proficient and Spanish dominant. The content of the test needs to be examined for potential cultural and linguistic biases. The test must acknowledge and conform to the Spanish variant used by Benito; that is, Dominican Spanish. Thus, the expected responses should match those predicted for that particular dialect. In addition, the specific items used and structures targeted must also be appropriate. This is especially relevant when evaluating a test that was either translated or adapted from an existing English test. The procedures used for eliciting responses will also need to be scrutinized for potential cultural bias. This will also include evaluating whether the particular items presented are familiar to the child, so that incorrect responses can be attributed to lack of skill and not to lack of experience. If the test is normed on Hispanic children, the demographic characteristics of the group need to match those of Benito. If not, the child's performance may not be compared to that of his true peers. As previously mentioned, consulting with someone familiar with the dialect and the child's community will be necessary. If the testing instrument is biased, then other alternatives for identifying a language disorder in this child need to be used.

In Consuelo's case, problems with using norm-referenced tests are exacerbated by the fact that she is bilingual, and these tests do not include in their normative sample bilingual individuals. This is problematic because a bilingual is not the sum of two monolinguals (Grosjean, 1982; Miller, 1988; Romaine, 1996), and thus any comparison between monolingual and bilingual speakers for ranking purposes is suspect. In addition, the child has already been identified as language learning disabled, thus the value of such a procedure is questionable. Recall that the main goal of norm-referenced tests is to identify a problem through comparing a child's performance with that of peers. It does not provide information for establishing treatment goals or for measuring progress (Haynes & Pindzola, 1998) and should not be used for these purposes. Because the value of the information provided by these tests will be minimal, and because their validity for testing a bilingual child is suspect, they should not be used with Consuelo. The only reason to use them would be to get an idea of how she compares to her monolingual peers (both Spanish and English) in performance on language tasks.

Criterion-referenced Procedures

Criterion-referenced procedures provide the clinician with information that cannot be obtained via more traditional testing methods, such as norm-referenced tests. They assess an individual's performance mastery of a particular skill or, in language testing, a specific grammatical structure or linguistic concept (Haynes & Pindzola, 1999). The fundamental purpose, then, is to distinguish between levels of performance (McCauley, 1996). Examples of measures that fall within a broad definition of criterion-referenced procedures that are used in our field include obtaining a percent of syllables stuttered during a speech, maximum phonation time, percent consonants correct (PCC), and mean length of utterances (MLU) (McCauley, 1996). These measures are used quite frequently by clinicians to establish treatment goals, baseline performance, and treatment efficacy. Regrettably, they are used less frequently during assessment. Because they do not compare a child's performance to that of other children, their potential for use with the Hispanic child is great. Nevertheless, as with any assessment procedure, they need to be a valid measure of the ability being tested.

Because criterion-referenced procedures are used to differentiate among levels of performance, they are developed with a relatively narrow focus. These measures evaluate skill in a particular area or domain. For example, a criterion-referenced measure may be used to assess a child's ability to use episodic structure in a story-retelling task. As such, it is developed so that the particular relevant aspects of the episodic structure during a retelling task can be scrutinized. The clinician may establish how many stories the child will retell, how many episodes each story contains, and the expected performance level, such as number of complete episodes produced. The procedure has thus been developed to assess only one language domain—episodic structure in story retelling—and does not compare the child to other children who performed the task, but to an established mastery level—in this case, number of complete episodes produced.

Why would criterion-referenced measures be a potentially valid procedure for evaluating language skills in the Hispanic child? One of the main advantages of these measures is that they can be tailored to each particular child and each particular situation. This characteristic, in turn, makes them desirable for testing children who are both linguistically and culturally diverse, as the procedures can be developed to accommodate this heterogeneity. Procedures and materials can be used that are familiar to the children and thus responses are not impacted by the child's lack of experience with the materials and by cultural differences in interaction. Establishing measures for each language and acceptable responses in either language can control language issues. This, in turn, permits the child to use both English and Spanish. The clinician, then, has control over the content of the measure and the permissible responses.

One strategy that may aid the clinician in evaluating the validity and reliability of the criterion-referenced measure she or he has developed is to administer it to a group of children from similar experiential and language backgrounds who do not present with problems and who should perform adequately. In that way, she or he can revise the format of the measure so that the child's responses will be a true reflection of ability. Another strategy is to work closely with a cultural and linguistic informant in the development of such a procedure. In fact, the procedure can be administered to adults in the community, who can be, in a sense, its reviewers. Insights from the adults can thus be used to improve the measure.

In conclusion, criterion-referenced measures are an excellent alternative to traditional norm-referenced tests because they do not compare the Hispanic child to mainstream monolingual peers. Because they can be designed by the clinician, they can be constructed so as to reduce potential linguistic and cultural bias. In addition, unlike norm-referenced tests, they can also aid in developing intervention goals. The clinician must ensure that they are valid and reliable measures of the domain being tested.

Using Criterion-referenced Measures: Benito and Consuelo

Both Benito and Consuelo would benefit from criterion-referenced measures. In Benito's case, the clinician can use absolute levels of mastery, that is, what would be expected of a 5-year-old child in terms of Spanish skill, and who speaks Dominican Spanish. Facts from an informant, as well as developmental guidelines for Spanish, such as those provided by Anderson (1995), Bedore (1999), and Merino (1992), would be helpful. Because the child has never been assessed, the clinician will need to identify areas of concern, either via parent interview, teacher interview, observation, and/or informal interactions with the child. Once these have been identified, the clinician can develop criterion-referenced measures that acknowledge cultural and linguistic diversity and that are tailored for measuring Spanish skill.

Because Consuelo has already been identified as language learning disabled, there should be information in her records concerning previous intervention and areas of deficit. This information can be used to identify language domains that need to be tested as well as the language of assessment for those domains (Spanish, English, or both). Of course, as with Benito, information from parents and teachers, as well as from observations and actual interactions with Consuelo, will be helpful. With that information, then, the clinician can develop valid and reliable procedures for assessing both Spanish and English, taking into consideration previous experience with both languages. Due to the fact that Consuelo is bilingual, the use of criterion-referenced procedures is quite relevant. As bilingual children are a mixed bag in terms of relative skill in each language and use of code switching, the expected responses can be tailored to fit her pattern of use of each language.

For both Consuelo and Benito, the criterion-referenced measures that are developed can be "field tested" with their peers. In Benito's case, his peers would be monolingual five-year-old children from a similar sociolinguistic background. Consuelo's peers are other bilingual children with similar educational experiences. The information provided via these measures can help in identifying a language disorder (Benito) as well as in establishing areas of deficit and relative skill (Benito and Consuelo). These measures should be used whenever a clinician is assessing such a child.

Ethnographic Observations

The value of ethnographic observations in the assessment of the Hispanic child has been discussed at length in Chapter 7. Thus, this section suggests general guidelines for incorporating such a strategy into the assessment process. As with any procedure, the potential for bias is always present and the clinician is responsible for ensuring that such bias is eradicated or at least minimized. As has been stressed throughout this chapter, background knowledge of the child and the child's sociolinguistic experience is essential, regardless of the evaluation approach used.

When a clinician performs observations, perception of what is occurring, and thus the interpretation of the event, is tainted by the clinician's own cultural views (Robinson-Zañartu, 1996). Individuals interpret the world from their cultural mirror. Because of this, if a clinician's worldview and interaction patterns differ from those of the child being observed, the end result is an incorrect interpretation of behaviors, usually to the detriment of the child. This, in turn, may perpetuate some of the stereotypes and incorrect perceptions the clinician may have of the community, which are then ascribed to the child.

One concern clinicians may have about conducting ethnographic observations is that these are time-consuming, more so than other measures. This is not necessarily true, if they are well planned. In addition, the amount of information they can provide suggests that it is time spent wisely. Prior to conducting any ethnographic observation, the clinician must have preplanned it; that is, its purpose and the information to be gathered must be identified. For example, is the clinician interested in observing the child's pragmatic skills during informal interactions with peers? Are the peers monolingual or bilingual speakers? What would be the best setting for gathering this information? Will the clinician need an interpreter to assist in the observation? Will the observation be videotaped? What aspects of pragmatics will be the focus? An observation that is of diagnostic value must thus be well planned.

Observations should be conducted in various school contexts, including the various classrooms or classes that the child attends. For example, if the child is in a regular classroom and a pullout ESL class, behavior in both contexts should be sampled. This will provide information concerning particular classroom dynamics that may impact the child's communicative skill. Observations should also be conducted while the child is engaged in a variety of classroom activities, such as independent and group work, as well as while different subjects (e.g., math and language arts) are being taught. Interactions with both the teacher and other students should also be assessed.

In addition to the classroom, the clinician should incorporate other school settings in the observation schedule. These include the playground and the cafeteria. These observations will provide pertinent information as to how situational context impacts the child's communication. It may be the case that the child is quite a competent interactant with peers on the playground but demonstrates a different communicative profile within the classroom. If the only data available were that of the classroom, the clinician would have an incomplete picture of the child's communicative skill, which may, in turn, result in an incorrect diagnosis of language disability (Kayser, 1990).

Because one of the linguistic realities of most Hispanic children is that they are in a dual language context, and will most probably interact with children and adults with various levels of Spanish and English proficiency, it is essential to include in the observation schedule instances where the child communicates with speakers who are monolingual (English and Spanish) and speakers who are bilingual. Such observations will provide the clinician with relevant information concerning the child's use of both languages and ability to communicate with a variety of speakers. Information concerning relative skill in both languages, use of code switching (type and function), and ability to take into consideration the listener's relative language skill can be readily gathered. This information, in turn, will give the clinician insight as to how well the child is able to use and understand both languages and how well she or he follows the sociolinguistic rules of language choice present in the community. For example, a child who recognizes the interlocutor's relative language skill and is able to accommodate to that level of skill is a more competent speaker than one who does not, which may aid in differentiating between typical and atypical language skills. In the same vein, a child who demonstrates code switching patterns that follow community norms and that conform to the sociolinguistic reality of the situation at hand (e.g., interlocutor's language competence) is also demonstrating appropriate communicative skill. Conducting observations in a variety of linguistic contexts is thus an important component of evaluating a Hispanic child who speaks, albeit perhaps with different competency levels, both languages, as these will truly show the child's ability to use both languages to communicate with different individuals.

For children who are limited English proficient, observations can provide valuable information concerning strategies the child uses for managing a new linguistic situation. It is of common knowledge in the field of child second language acquisition that children make use of a variety of strategies to cope with the task of learning a new language (Tabors, 1997). Strategies such as the silent period, where the child does not attempt to speak the new language, use of gestures, relying on routine events for deriving meaning, and learning a few general phrases in the language have been consistently reported in the literature (Wong-Fillmore, 1979; Tabors, 1997). Clinicians should thus be familiar with these strategies, including how they are manifested in the child, and with what should be expected from the child at different levels of exposure or experience with the new language—in the Hispanic child's case, English. A complete discussion of patterns of second language learning in sequential learners is beyond the scope of this chapter. Excellent discussions of these language learning strategies have been presented by Wong-Fillmore (1979) and, more recently, Tabors (1997). The reader is referred to these sources for more comprehensive information. Observations can also identify if, for the length of time in the situation, the strategies used are appropriate. In fact, if there are other children in the classroom who are also Hispanic and are also learning English as a second language, they can also be observed, thus providing the clinician with observational data that will aid in discerning between typical and atypical skills.

Ethnographic Observations: Benito and Consuelo

The value of ethnographic observations in the evaluation of both Benito and Consuelo cannot be stressed enough. In Benito's case, the child's use of

Spanish with his Spanish-speaking peers as well as with his bilingual teacher can be evaluated, and thus Spanish communicative competency can be established. In addition, as he is in the process of learning a second language, strategies used in situations where English is the language of interaction can be identified and thus evaluated as to their appropriateness. When observing Benito interacting with Spanish speakers, data can be gathered on how the child responds to others and how others respond to his productions. In that way, competence in Spanish for interaction purposes (peers) and for academic purposes (in the classroom with the teacher) can be established. In English contexts, observations can focus on determining the strategies he is using as a second language learner and their appropriateness for his age and experience. Because Benito is in a school where there are, most probably, other same-aged peers who are in a similar sociolinguistic environment, observation of other children in similar contexts will permit the clinician to evaluate Benito's communicative skill with those of his "true" peers. Ethnographic observations, then, can be useful for identifying a true language disability in a child like Benito.

Ethnographic observations will be, by necessity, an integral component of Consuelo's assessment. Based on the background information, it appears that she has skills in both languages. Both languages will need to be assessed, including her ability to code switch or use these languages according to contextual variables. This ability, in turn, provides insight into her control of both languages and her awareness of the communicative needs present in a particular interaction. One of the most efficient ways to obtain this information is by conducting various ethnographic observations where the language required for interaction differs. Observations can also provide valuable information concerning how the level of linguistic demands, in both languages, differs. For example, observations in contexts where there is contextual support for understanding what is being said—as, for example, during a game in the schoolyard—can be contrasted with one where there is less support for understanding and where she will need to be more explicit in her productions. Examples of these would include a formal classroom activity, such as group reading or group discussion of the material. In this way, the impact of context on skill can be ascertained. In addition, the clinician can gather relevant data that will indicate the child's areas of relative strengths and weaknesses for planning intervention. The clinician can also obtain important insight for developing other assessment procedures (e.g., criterion-referenced measures) or identifying areas that need to be tested more thoroughly.

Language Sampling

Many researchers and clinicians working with CLD children have supported the use of language sampling procedures as an alternative to other testing methods, such as norm-referenced testing (Anderson, 1994a; Brice & Montgomery, 1996; Kayser & Restrepo, 1995; Mattes & Omark, 1991). Such procedures provide the clinician with the opportunity to sample a child's productive skill in more naturalistic settings, thus providing information not only about the child's grammatical skill but also about how the child uses language for communication (i.e., pragmatic skill) (Damico, Smith, & Augustine, 1996). Because the clinician is flexible as to how to obtain and analyze a language sample, the procedure can be tailored to fit the child's cultural and linguistic background and simultaneously address the clinical questions that guide the assessment. At the same time, the clinician needs to be aware that, as with any assessment procedure, the potential for bias is always present.

In order to obtain adequate language samples, several factors need to be considered. As can be observed, three areas are to be evaluated. The clinician will have to identify environmental variables that may impact performance, the most suitable type of sample, and how the sample will be analyzed. Once these have been identified, the clinician can develop a plan for collecting the samples. As with any procedure, the use of language samples needs to be tailored to fit the child's background as well as assessment needs. In addition, because they are samples, the more that are collected, the more reliable and valid the data can become (Kayser & Restrepo, 1995). Because there may not be time to obtain an extensive number of language samples, the clinician must carefully plan this procedure so that the samples are indeed representative of the Hispanic child's linguistic ability.

Before collecting a language sample, there are various environmental variables that need to be identified. Of utmost importance is for the clinician to decide what language(s) will be sampled. Once this has been established, the environmental variables that impact language choice will have to be discerned. In this way, the clinician can ensure that the appropriate environmental constraints are present for collecting the sample in the target language. When working with the Hispanic child, there are three main language choices: (a) Spanish, (b) English, and (c) both English and Spanish. In addition, the clinician may be interested in collecting data that evaluate the child's use of both languages during an interaction (i.e., code switching, or use of both Spanish and English concurrently). Choice of language is dependent on the child's language ability. If the child is monolingual in either one of the languages, the samples should be collected only for that language. If, on the other hand, the child has skills in both languages, both languages should be sampled, regardless of identified level of skill. Furthermore, because code switching is an essential component of a bilingual individual's linguistic repertoire, this phenomenon should also be sampled. As mentioned in Chapters 4, 8, and 9, it provides additional information on the child's grammatical and pragmatic skill. Clinicians must remember that the goal of assessment is to evaluate how much the child knows about *language,* not English and/or Spanish.

After the language of the sample is identified, the clinician then proceeds with establishing how the sample will be collected. For example, if the target language is used in specific contexts, then the clinician must ensure that these are obtained in a manner that considers domains of use. In addition, with whom the child will interact is intimately tied to the language of the sample. It is also tied to the experiences the child has had interacting in the various contexts and with the various participants. Thus, the clinician should also establish the child's level of acculturation to the mainstream and to the school culture before any language sampling procedure is scheduled. With children who are younger and new to the school, the level of acculturation may be low, whereas older children who have attended American schools for some time may have high levels of acculturation to the school culture (Kayser & Restrepo, 1995). Accordingly, before this can be established, the child's educational history needs to be identified so that the procedure will match cultural and linguistic experience as well as school expectations.

Based on language choice and level of acculturation, the clinician will then determine the following: (1) where the sample will be collected, (2) who will interact with the child, and (3) the type of sample that will be collected. Of course, all these factors are interrelated, as the choice made in one will impact the others. The physical environment where the sample is collected should conform to where the target language is spoken by the child. This may not be possible in instances where the language in question is mainly spoken at home. Nevertheless, if the clinician is in a context where this variable can be controlled, an effort should be made to gather information in the appropriate physical context.

More important, the clinician must decide with whom the child is to interact. Of course, the target language will indicate to the clinician who should participate during the data collection. The individual should have native or near-native proficiency in the target language. In addition, if the child is bilingual and the clinician wants to sample English or Spanish, a participant who is monolingual in the language should be used. If the participant is an individual with whom the child usually interacts, then care should be taken that said interactions take place mainly in the language being sampled. When the clinician is interested in evaluating the child's use of both languages during an interaction, then a bilingual individual with native-like proficiency in both languages should interact with the child. In instances where the clinician wants to evaluate how well the child chooses the language according to the interactant, an activity could be set up where two "monolingual" speakers, one Spanish and one English, interact simultaneously with the child. In that way, the child's ability to be a bridge between two speakers can be used to evaluate both pragmatic and grammatical skill.

The child's level of acculturation and previous experience with certain situations will also determine who will interact with the child. The best partners are those with whom the child is most familiar. This is particularly the case for young Hispanic children. By "familiar" it is meant the individual with whom the child interacts the most within a conversational context. For example, in my work with preschool and early school-aged children, the best communication partners seem to be older (but not much older) siblings, especially when they are not aware that they are being observed. Because it is common in many Hispanic families for siblings to be responsible for each other and to play with each other, this situation is one that is quite familiar to the young Hispanic child. If this is not possible, the clinician should consider engaging the help of peers in the child's classroom. If the clinician, because of lack of available siblings or peers who speak the language being targeted, obtains a conversational sample with an adult (i.e., clinician or paraprofessional), care should be taken to ensure the child is comfortable in this situation. This can be accomplished by establishing an initial rapport with the child and not obtaining a sample at the outset of the assessment. Some suggested activities would be for the clinician or other adult to interact informally with the child in the classroom or during play activities and to be a familiar face to the child by visiting the classroom, playground, and/or cafeteria while the child is there. Participating in interactions with other children during this time may also ease the child's apprehension of interacting with the adult. With older children who have more experience with the school culture, interacting with an unfamiliar adult may not be at odds with their experiential base. With younger children or with children who have a limited amount of experience with the American educational system, on the other hand, care needs to be taken that the child is comfortable interacting with the adult.

The type of language samples that will be collected in each language needs to be determined. This, in addition to the variables place and interactant, will identify the type of elicitation technique the clinician will use. With preschool and school-aged children, two main types of samples are usually gathered: (1) conversational sample and (2) narrative sample, generally story retelling. Each of these types can be elicited by various means. In addition, both types of samples should be collected, because they provide different information and thus give the clinician a broader picture as to the child's language abilities. If the child has had experience in both English and Spanish with both types of samples, they should be elicited in both languages.

It is recommended that more than one conversational sample be obtained in each of the languages. These should correspond to the child's expected use of the languages. Obtaining more than one sample will ensure a more representative view of the child's productive skills. Factors such as age, experience with the procedure, and interactant will determine how the sample will be elicited. For example, with a young child, a conversational sample is best obtained during free play, especially with another child. To "stress the system," the clinician may interact with the child and elicit more information during a conversational exchange by requesting the child to elaborate ("tell me more"), explain a process ("tell me how we do this"), and/or interpret a behavior ("why would X do this?"). (For more examples, see Kayser & Restrepo, 1995.) The clinician can also engage the child in a role-playing activity that conforms to the child's experiential base. For example, the clinician can pretend to be at a fast-food restaurant and is being served by the child, or vice versa.

Any activity chosen for obtaining a conversational sample must conform to the clinician's needs and to the child's linguistic and cultural experience. As such, the materials used as stimuli must also be appropriate. The items should be familiar to the child. In that way, lack of response cannot be ascribed to lack of experience. In addition, these should be familiar in the *target language* and thus conform to the domain in which the language is used. For example, if the child uses Spanish at home and Spanish is being sampled, the items present should be those that pertain more to home interactions (e.g., kitchen utensils, certain games). If, on the other hand, English use is related to academic based activities, then the task should incorporate materials that are used mainly at school. Materials should also be culturally appropriate in that they are familiar to the child.

Narrative samples should be collected from both younger and older school-aged children. Because of the nature of a narrative, it provides data that may not be obtained via a conversational sample. Narratives require the child to express a series of events in a cohesive and sequential manner (Naremore, 1997). These events are usually placed in the past tense, as, for example, when retelling a personal event (personal narrative) or retelling a story. In Spanish, for example, narratives provide the opportunity to evaluate the child's use of aspectual distinctions in verbs [e.g., *estaba* ("was"—imperfect) versus *estuvo* ("was"—perfect)], an area that may not be sampled during a conversational exchange (Bayley, Alvarez-Calderón, & Schecter, 1998). They also furnish information concerning the child's use of more complex syntax and of cohesive devices, such as anaphoric referencing (Gutiérrez-Clellen, 1998). For children who have had experience with school-based narratives (e.g., story retelling), they also give insight into the child's use of story grammar or episodic structure, skills that have been identified as important for success in reading (Naremore, Densmore, & Harman, 1995).

Decisions as to what type of narratives to elicit will depend on child-specific variables as well as on the clinical questions posed during assessment. For the Hispanic child, care should be taken to identify contexts and topics that ensure a good representation of ability to narrate an event. Previous experience in telling stories, including types of stories, should be identified for each language. The child's parents, the cultural informant, and the teacher can provide information relevant to determining the best type of narrative to elicit as well as the topic and elicitation procedure to follow.

Several elicitation procedures can be utilized. Gutiérrez-Clellen (1998) indicates, for example, that in order to obtain an extended narrative from the Hispanic children with which she worked, she needed to provide continued prompting. Clinicians working with Hispanic children may thus need to adjust the level of prompting provided. Back-channeling responses such as "This is very interesting. Tell me more" and "What happened next?" may be appropriate. Depending on the child's age and experience, the sample should include both personal narratives and story retellings. Personal narratives may be more familiar to the Hispanic child and thus may provide a more representative context for evaluating the child's ability to narrate an event. Story retelling should be elicited by means that are most familiar to the child. For example, if the child is young and/or has had limited literacy experience in the language being sampled, perhaps a story retelling task should ask the child to retell a movie or an episode from a familiar television program. If a book is chosen, the clinician may want to consider choosing books that tell a story from the child's culture; for example, the stories of Juan Bobo in the Puerto Rican culture (Marques, 1989). Of course, the story to be retold should be in consonance with the language being targeted. The narrative task chosen for each language must conform to the child's experience telling stories in that particular language. As with the conversational sample, a certain degree of familiarity with the listener will result in a more representative narrative from the child.

Once conversational and narrative samples have been gathered, the clinician will have to choose how they will be analyzed. If this is not done properly, the clinician runs the risk of misinterpreting the valuable data obtained. First and foremost, what is typical for children from similar backgrounds needs to be identified. In some instances, developmental data are available, especially for Spanish-speaking children who have limited English skills (Anderson, 1995; Bedore, 1999; Merino, 1992). In other cases, especially with bilingual children, the clinician has to confer with the cultural informant and investigate whether the patterns evidenced by the child are typical for the background and sociolinguistic experience. If there are other children in the school with similar linguistic and cultural experiences, these can be used to obtain initial data on what should be considered typical performance. Only with this information can the clinician identify language deficits in the child via language sample analysis.

There are various analysis procedures a clinician can utilize to evaluate a language sample. Many of these have been applied to Spanish, and some are effective means of assessing English skill. Most, nevertheless, are problematic in Spanish and thus should be used with careful consideration of the child being assessed and the purpose of the analysis (Gutiérrez-Clellen et al., 2000). Some of the methodology has been adapted from procedures used for assessing English skill. As a result, they have the same problem as translated/adapted norm-referenced tests in that they may not be addressing what is genuinely important for Spanish. An example is the *Developmental Assessment of Spanish Grammar* (DASG) (Toronto, 1976), which analyzes the same forms present in the English procedure developed by Lee and Canter (1971). Other examples include the use of mean length of utterance (MLU) morphemes; such a measure was originally developed for a language—English—with a relatively small number of bound morphemes, in contrast to Spanish. Its value for analyzing Spanish grammatical skill has not been established (Gutiérrez-Clellen et al., 2000). Additionally, different researchers have established different scoring procedures for obtaining MLU-morphemes in Spanish. Clinicians, then, need to conform to a particular scoring procedure if their goal is to contrast the child's score with that of other children. Although MLU based on word count has been suggested, this alternative scoring procedure has also not been validated for Spanish. In addition, establishing what does and does not constitute a word in Spanish is an issue of contention (e.g., *Damelo* vs. *Me lo das*—"Give it to me"; reflexive constructions such as *se cayó*—"it fell itself"). If any of these measures are chosen, care must be taken to follow the established guidelines used by researchers for developing the norms the clinician will use. Even if used, though, these serve only to identify a possible language disorder, not to describe it or provide intervention goals.

Other alternatives for analyzing language samples may have more promise. In particular, T-units as measures for analysis have been used by researchers working with Spanish-speaking children (Gutiérrez-Clellen, 2000; Restrepo, 1998). Restrepo (1998) noted that the number of grammatical errors per T-unit was one of the best identifiers of grammatical deficits in a group of Spanish-speaking children with specific language impairment. It is suggested, then, that the clinician working with a Hispanic child use this measure for identifying a possible language disability (Gutiérrez-Clellen et al., 2000).

Because such a measure will not provide the clinician with information concerning the child's particular areas of deficit, additional analyses have to be performed. As with English, the clinician will need to identify morphosyntactic aspects that are typical and those that are atypical. Areas that should be evaluated in Spanish include: (a) noun phrase number and gender agreement; (b) use of pronouns; (c) verb morphology (tense, aspect, mood, person, and number); (d) use of prepositions; and (e) sentence embedding (Kayser & Restrepo, 1995). The clinician can thus identify whether the child uses the necessary morphological markers and, if the child does not use these, the pattern of error. The clinician may also note aspects that were not elicited during the sample and that may need to be probed via a criterion-referenced procedure.

When analyzing narratives, both grammatical aspects as well as story structure are assessed. Procedures similar to those for analyzing grammatical skill in conversational samples can be used with narratives. Story structure analysis must conform, nevertheless, to the cultural expectations of storytelling. Additionally, the child's experience with more mainstream narratives, if these were collected, needs to be identified prior to analyzing story grammar or episodic structure. Procedures for assessing the episodic structure of narratives, such as those described by Naremore, Densmore, and Harman (1995), with the above caveat, can be followed.

To summarize, language sampling provides excellent data on children's grammatical and pragmatic skill. To ensure that the samples are representative of the child's linguistic ability, more than one sample (both conversational and narrative) should be collected. If possible, these should be varied in terms of the context in which they are gathered. They need not be lengthy and can be collected while conducting ethnographic observations. Samples should be obtained in the languages the child uses, and opportunities for code switching should also be provided. The language that is to be sampled will dictate the circumstances under which the data will be collected. As with any procedure, the cultural and linguistic background of the child needs to be considered. In addition, care should be taken in interpreting the obtained results. As always, the children should be compared to their peers (other Hispanic children) and to community expectations. The analysis should provide not only for identifying a possible deficit but for describing patterns of strengths and weaknesses.

Language Samples: Benito and Consuelo

For both children, language sampling procedures can provide important information concerning the children's ability to use language, as well as their grammatical skill. In Benito's case, language samples need to be collected in Spanish. Because he has been in the school environment for a relatively short period and his parents are recent arrivals to the United States, the clinician can hypothesize that his level of acculturation is low. Care should be taken, then, to ensure that the interactants are familiar to Benito. In particular, if the goal is to obtain a conversational sample, the participation of his older sister, Mariela, or a Spanish-speaking friend may provide the best environment for gathering a representative sample. The clinician may also want to collect a sample while he is interacting with an adult, such as the interpreter, or the parents (if possible and culturally appropriate), so as to ascertain how the interactant impacts performance. This, in turn, may explain some of the behaviors the teacher has noted in the classroom (i.e., not talking much in class). Ethnographic observations can thus supplement the data gathered via the conversational samples.

All samples should be analyzed based on what is acceptable in Dominican Spanish. A cultural informant will be needed if the clinician does not have the necessary Spanish skill. In Benito's case, a general measure of grammatical skill, such as mean number of errors per T-unit (Gutiérrez-Clellen et al., 2000; Restrepo, 1998) can be used to discern possible deficits. Of course, the child's performance should be compared with those of his peers, and the clinician working within this community should make every effort to obtain local norms for the measures used. Nevertheless, as an initial step, Benito's performance can be contrasted to that of the children studied by Restrepo (1998). Additionally, the sample should be examined to identify patterns of errors that may enable the clinician to develop specific probes (e.g., criterion-referencing) and to identify potential intervention targets, if Benito does indeed present with a language disorder.

In Benito's case, narrative samples should be obtained as well, preferably personal narratives. As he has had limited experience with the "school culture," these samples may be more indicative of his true skill. If a story-retelling task is used, it should be retelling a movie or a television series, again considering the child's previous experience with narratives. As with any narrative, the linguistic features used and the story structure should be analyzed. The interpretation of Benito's performance should be based on comparisons with narratives made by typically developing peers who come from a similar sociolinguistic background.

Consuelo's case is more complex linguistically, as language samples need to be obtained in both languages. Conversational samples must be obtained in Spanish and in English, as she is bilingual. Samples where code switching may be evidenced (i.e., a bilingual speaker or two monolingual speakers of each language) are to be targeted as well. All methodology should conform to typical interaction patterns. For example, due to her history, adult–child interactions in Spanish may be more frequent than child–child interactions. As a result, the former interactions may be more valid for this particular child. Conversational samples with the mother, who is the one that speaks primarily in Spanish with Consuelo, or with a Spanish-speaking adult are a valuable part of the assessment. Conversational samples in English can be obtained while interacting with peers as well as with adults, as she has also had experience with the language in both contexts. As in Benito's case, some of the samples can be gathered during ethnographic observations.

Because Consuelo has been in school for a considerable period, narrative skills will need to be assessed. These should be in English, as she has not had academic experience (unless the parents are pursuing Spanish literacy on their own) mediated by Spanish. Although it should be expected that Consuelo's level of acculturation to the school culture is high, it is important to consider that she has not been in one school for a long period of time due to the family's frequent moves. This factor needs to be considered when evaluating narrative skill. If possible, samples of both personal and storyretelling narratives should be obtained. In Consuelo's case, books can be used as props for story retelling, and these should be age and culturally appropriate.

Unfortunately, the clinician does not have a Hispanic community in the school with which to compare Consuelo's performance. In this case, the clinician needs to rely on information concerning typical bilingual development, including issues such as code switching, L1 and L2 transfer, and L1 loss (see Chapters 4, 5, 6). In addition, more focus needs to be placed on how Consuelo uses language and less on the form of both Spanish and English (Kayser, 1990). Analysis should include addressing patterns of strengths and weaknesses, as this is the area of concern, not diagnosing a disability. General or gross measures will not provide needed information, unless the clinician needs to confirm the presence of a disorder. Consulting with a cultural (and linguistic) informant and having the background information on child bilingualism and second language acquisition will enable the clinician to do a comprehensive and sound analysis of Consuelo's language skills, as evidenced by the language samples that were collected.

Dynamic Assessment

The previous strategies pertain to evaluating children's ability at a particular point in time. That is, the child's performance during each of the tasks is evaluated and contrasted to what would be expected of other children in similar contexts. In a sense, then, the information gathered pertains to static performance or what the child can do at a particular point in time. It does not provide data on the child's potential for learning or acquiring the skill in question. The SLP's role during all these activities is one of examiner, who establishes the procedures needed for collecting the data, collects the data, and then analyzes the data. As such, SLPs are not actively engaged in the learning process, because they are not assessing learning, but assessing the present level of skill. Although this information is of utmost relevance in the assessment of the Hispanic child, measuring or at least gathering data on the child's ability to learn can provide great insight for both identifying a language disorder and for planning intervention when needed. This information is collected via an evaluation procedure referred to in the literature as dynamic assessment (Feuerstein, 1979; Peña et al., 1992; Ukrainetz, Harpell, Walsh, & Coyle, 2000).

Dynamic assessment is best described as a process that studies not only an individual's current performance level but how the individual can learn if provided the opportunity for learning. As such, it evaluates how specific task characteristics (e.g., number of items, types of items, complexity of task) impact performance as well as the specific strategies an individual uses for learning the task (Feuerstein, 1979). Because of its focus, clinicians can use such a procedure to discriminate between typical and atypical language learning ability (Peña et al., 1992; Ukrainetz et al., 2000), thus minimizing incorrect identification of language disability in Hispanic children whose cultural and linguistic realities may mask ability as disability (e.g., L1 loss, developmental L2 errors, differences in experiences with mainstream interaction patterns). If a child does indeed have a disability, dynamic assessment provides valuable information concerning the types of tasks and materials that result in better performance, the learning strategies used, as well as how "quickly" the child learns (Feuerstein, 1979). For example, the clinician may establish that objects and not pictures will need to be used during intervention. The clinician may also learn that a particular number of items at one time is the most to which the child will attend. Furthermore, the clinician may establish that the child shows deficits in attention or responds impulsively, thus requiring modifying learning strategies as an intervention goal. In a sense, then, dynamic assessment reduces the initial guesswork that may take place during the initial therapy sessions because the needed information for beginning intervention is in place early.

Table 10.5 summarizes the major differences between what can be termed "static" (or more traditional testing procedures) and dynamic assessment. As can be observed, there are three major differences. First, the relationship between the child and the clinician changes from one of tester–testee to one of teacher–student. In dynamic assessment, the child is actively engaged in learning, while the clinician is actively teaching a skill or concept. This results in the second major difference that pertains to the relationship between assessment and intervention. While there is no intervention during assessment when performing a static assessment, in dy-

TABLE 10.5 *Static versus Dynamic Assessment*

Static	Dynamic
1. Relationship is one of tester–testee.	1. Relationship one of student–teacher.
2. No intervention occurs during the assessment process.	2. Intervention is integrated within the assessment process.
3. Results interpreted according to an established "norm" or expected skill level.	3. Results not interpreted according to an expected "norm" or skill level.
4. Assessment is oriented toward a product (e.g., diagnosis, identifying specific skill level).	4. Assessment is oriented toward a process (e.g., learning pattern, factors that impact learning).

Source: Feuerstein (1979); Peña, Quinn, & Inglesias (1992).

namic assessment, intervention is an integral component. The third difference pertains to how the results are interpreted. In most static assessments, results are compared to a norm. This norm is not necessarily how other children performed in the task, as in the case of a norm-referenced test, but is defined in terms of what performance should be expected from that child, considering cultural and linguistic background. Because dynamic assessment involves teaching, and this teaching will be individualized to each child, the results cannot be compared to a norm, but contrasted to previous performance; that is, how does performance differ from time one to time two, with intervention mediating the experiences?

In the past decade, researchers working with CLD children have explored the value of dynamic assessment mainly as a tool for distinguishing difference versus disorder. Studies have been conducted with Hispanic children (Peña et al. 1992) and Native American children (Ukrainetz et al., 2000). These have shown that it has great potential as a nonbiased assessment procedure. Both Peña et al. (1992) and Ukrainetz et al. (2000) used a strategy that tests children's ability in a particular task, such as categorizing, then teaches the task to the children. Retesting the children's ability to perform the task without clinician cueing or aid follows this teaching sequence. Children who were truly language learning disabled failed to evidence learning in the same manner as children who demonstrated typical language skills. These results, then, point to the value of such a procedure for identifying true disability in the Hispanic child.

A clinician to whom a Hispanic child has been referred for an initial diagnosis of language learning disability should consider employing a dynamic assessment strategy to establish if the child presents language learning deficits. This can be accomplished by developing a procedure whereby the child can be tested on a particular task or even a testing instrument, like, for example, the *EOWPVT* (Gardner, 1990) as done by Peña et al. (1992). If the child performs below age expectations, the clinician can either train the child on the test-taking procedure or teach the target concept. After this has been accomplished, the child is retested. It is expected that a child with true language disabilities will experience difficulty learning language, thus the child should still perform poorly on the target task. If the child performs in a manner consistent with age expectations after training, then the child, most likely, is a typical language learner. The clinician, then, can be confident in the identification of language learning disabilities, because poor performance cannot be ascribed to lack of experience with the concept or the task.

Dynamic assessment can also be applied in cases where there is an identified disability and the clinician wants to establish the child's performance pattern, specifically, environmental factors that promote or hinder learning. Examples of these would include: (a) type of cue or feedback provided; (b) materials used, including type and quantity; and (c) the physical setting where the teaching takes place. In addition, the clinician may want to identify learning strategies used by the child that may hinder or enhance learning. In these cases, the clinician will systematically manipulate variables that may impact performance. For instance, in assessing the child's ability to learn story grammar, the clinician may change the type of stimuli used by systematically modifying the length (number of episodes) and/or complexity of the story. The information gathered from the dynamic assessment, in turn, may help in designing effective intervention strategies, not only within a clinical setting but in the classroom as well. It provides, then, for an efficient means of collaboration between the clinician and the teacher(s) working with the child.

In conclusion, dynamic assessment is an effective testing procedure for the Hispanic child. In contrast to the other testing methods presented in this chapter, such techniques provide the clinician with ample information about a Hispanic child's learning potential and the possible factors that influence learning. If a test-teach-retest methodology is employed, it can serve as a tool for differential diagnosis (Peña et al., 1992; Ukrainetz et al., 2000). If a child has already been identified, via nonbiased methods, as having a language disability, dynamic assessment is a powerful tool for developing sound treatment procedures and for providing other professionals, such as teachers, with effective intervention techniques within the classroom. A clinician working with the Hispanic population should thus consider incorporating dynamic tasks into assessment; the data gathered can potentially be of great assistance in answering the two main questions usually posed during evaluation: (a) does the child present with a language learning disability, and (b) what are the child's areas of strength and weakness?

Dynamic Assessment: Benito and Consuelo

Benito provides an excellent example of how dynamic assessment can be used as a tool for differential diagnosis. The clinician working with this child can do one of the following: (1) use a norm-referenced test, preferably one that assesses one language area, such as expressive vocabulary; or (2) develop a teaching task based on a gap in performance evidenced via other means, such as observation or language sampling. Considering that the child's primary language is Spanish, these activities should be conducted in that language. If the clinician chooses in this case to test and teach in English—for example, to see how quickly the child learns certain vocabulary or morphological inflection—a Spanish interpreter should be available to provide instructions or other relevant information in Spanish. Once it is decided what the testing will consist of, the clinician will test Benito and later teach him the skill needed to perform appropriately. After this has been completed, the clinician will retest Benito and compare performance across the two testing sessions. The training part of this procedure need not be lengthy. I would suggest at least two training sessions before retesting. In this way, the clinician can ensure that there was sufficient opportunity for learning to take place.

In Consuelo's case, a test-teach-retest methodology can also be employed if the clinician wants to confirm the initial diagnosis of a language learning disability. More important, dynamic assessment can be used to identify the best treatment methodology to follow. As the static assessment procedures are administered, the clinician will note areas of deficits. Based on these areas, the clinician will then develop a training procedure to assess how Consuelo approaches the task and what factors influence performance. With this child, English can be used as the mediating language. As in the example provided in the previous section, if she evidences deficits in story grammar, the clinician can develop a dynamic assessment procedure whereby the child is presented with different stories, of varied lengths (number of episodes) and linguistic complexity. Different stimuli, such as visual cues of the story line, can also be presented. Manipulating these variables, the clinician can identify what aspects result in improved performance and what characteristics do not. The clinician can also provide models of stories for Consuelo to follow, thus evaluating what clinician cues impact learning. This information, in turn, can be used to develop a treatment program that addresses this area of deficit. Because story retelling is an integral part of classroom instruction, the clinician can also collaborate with the teacher to develop effective classroom-based intervention strategies that are tailored to meet Consuelo's needs.

Best Practices

The goal of the previous discussion was to describe assessment alternatives that can be used with confidence when working with Hispanic children. Most of these are familiar to all clinicians and include observations, language sampling, use of criterion-referenced procedures, and dynamic assessment. These have been identified by other researchers as effective tools for evaluating the language skills of a Hispanic child (cf. Anderson, 1996; Brice & Montgomery, 1996; Kayser & Restrepo, 1995; Peña et al., 1992). Clinicians working with Hispanic children should make every effort to incorporate some or all of the procedures described in this chapter. Of course, any assessment strategy is only effective if it is well planned and executed and if the clinician interprets the behavior appropriately. In order to use these strategies effectively, the clinician needs to gather important cultural and linguistic information about the particular Hispanic community to which the child belongs. Without this knowledge, the potential for bias is still present. Any clinician working with Hispanic children must acquire that information before assessing a Hispanic child.

1. Monolingual clinicians will need to train and work closely with an interpreter.
2. All clinicians will need to be literate in the area of bilingualism and second language acquisition.
3. Most important, clinicians will have to become more flexible in how they collect the necessary assessment data as well as continue to work closely with other professionals who also work with the Hispanic community. In this manner, our field will provide the best services possible to the ever-growing Hispanic community in the United States.

References

American Speech-Language-Hearing Association. (1985). Clinical management of communicatively handicapped minority language populations. *ASHA, 27*(6), 29–32.

Anderson, R. (1994a). Cultural and linguistic diversity and language impairment in preschool children. *Seminars in Speech and Language, 15,* 115–124.

Anderson, R. (1994b). Stressing the need for inclusion of cultural and linguistic diversity within our professional preparation: A case study. *Tejas, 20,* 13–18.

Anderson, R. (1995). Spanish morphological and syntactic development. In H. Kayser (Ed.), *Bilingual speech–language pathology: An Hispanic focus* (pp. 41–74). San Diego: Singular.

Anderson, R. (1999). Impact of first language loss on grammar in a bilingual child. *Communication Disorders Quarterly, 21,* 4–16.

Anderson, R. T. (1996). Assessing the grammar of Spanish-speaking children: A comparison of two procedures. *Language, Speech and Hearing Services in Schools, 27,* 333–344.

Anderson, R. & Smith, B. L. (1987). Phonological development of two-year-old monolingual Spanish-speaking children. *Journal of Child Language, 14,* 57–78.

Bayley, R., Alvarez-Calderón, A., & Schecter, S. (1998). Tense and aspect in Mexican-origin children's Spanish narratives. In E. V. Clark (Ed.), *The proceedings of the twenty-ninth annual child language forum* (pp. 221–230). Stanford, CA: Center for the Study of Language and Information.

Bedore, L. M. (1999). The acquisition of Spanish. In O. L. Taylor and L. B. Leonard (Eds.), *Language acquisition across North America* (pp. 157–208). San Diego, CA: Singular.

Brice, A. (2000). Code switching and code mixing in the ESL classroom: A study of pragmatic and syntactic features. *Advances in Speech Language Pathology: Journal of the Speech Pathology Association of Australia, 20,* 19–28.

Brice, A., & Montgomery, J. (1996). Adolescent pragmatic skills: A comparison of Latino students in ESL and speech-language programs. *Language, Speech and Hearing Services in Schools, 27,* 68–81.

Canfield, D. L. (1981). *Spanish pronunciation in the Americas.* Chicago, IL: University of Chicago Press.

Damico, J. S., Smith, M. D., & Augustine, L. E. (1996). Multicultural populations and language disorders. In M. D. Smith and J. S. Damico (Eds.), *Childhood language disorders* (pp. 272–299). New York: Thieme.

Feuerstein, R. (1979). *The dynamic assessment of retarded performers: The Learning Potential Assessment Device, theory, instrument and techniques.* Baltimore, MD: University Park Press.

Gardner, M. F. (1990). *Expressive One-Word Picture Vocabulary Test.* Novato, CA: Academic Therapy Publications.

Goldstein, B. A. (1995). Spanish phonological development. In H. Kayser (Ed.), *Bilingual speech–language pathology: An Hispanic focus* (pp. 17–40). San Diego, CA: Singular.

Gómez-Valdez, C. (1988). *Bilingual Health and Developmental History Questionnaire.* Oceanside, CA: Academic Communication Associates.

Grosjean, F. (1982). *Life with two languages: An introduction to bilingualism.* Cambridge, MA: Harvard University Press.

Gutiérrez-Clellen, V. F. (1998). Syntactic skills of Spanish-speaking children with low school achievement. *Language, Speech and Hearing Services in Schools, 29,* 207–215.

Gutiérrez-Clellen, V. F., Restrepo, A., Bedore, L., Peña, E., & Anderson, R. (2000). Language sample analysis in Spanish-speaking children: Methodological considerations. *Language, Speech, and Hearing Services in Schools, 31,* 88–98.

Hall, P. K., & Morris, H. L. (2000). The clinical history. In J. B. Tomblin, H. L. Morris, and D. C. Spriestersbach (Eds.), *Diagnosis in speech–language pathology* (pp. 65–82). San Diego, CA: Singular.

Haynes, W. O., & Pindzola, R. H. (1998). *Diagnosis and evaluation in speech pathology* (5th ed.). Boston: Allyn & Bacon.

Kayser, H. (1990). Social communicative behaviours of language-disordered Mexican-American students. *Child Language Teaching and Therapy, 6,* 255–269.

Kayser, H. (1993). Hispanic cultures. In D. E. Battle (Ed.), *Communication disorders in multi-cultural populations* (pp. 114–157).Boston, MA: Andover.

Kayser, H. (1995a). An emerging specialist: The bilingual speech–language pathologist. In H. Kayser (Ed.), *Bilingual speech–language pathology: An Hispanic focus* (pp. 1–13). San Diego, CA: Singular.

Kayser, H. (1995b). Interpreters. In H. Kayser (Ed.), *Bilingual speech–language pathology: An Hispanic focus* (pp. 207–222). San Diego, CA: Singular.

Kayser, H. (1995c). Assessment of speech and language impairments in bilingual children. In H. Kayser (Ed.), *Bilingual speech–language pathology: An Hispanic focus* (pp. 223–242). San Diego, CA: Singular.

Kayser, H. (1996). Cultural/linguistic variation in the United States and its implications for assessment and intervention in speech–language pathology: An epilogue. *Language, Speech and Hearing Services in Schools, 27,* 385–386.

Kayser, H., & Restrepo, M. A. (1995). Language samples: Elicitation and analysis. In H. Kayser (Ed.), *Bilingual speech–language pathology: An Hispanic focus* (pp. 265–286). San Diego, CA: Singular.

Kozol, J. (1991). *Savage inequalities: Children in America's schools.* New York: Crown Publishers.

Langdon, H. W. (1992a). The Hispanic population: Facts and figures. In H. W. Langdon and L. L. Cheng (Eds.), *Hispanic children and adults with communication disorders* (pp. 20–56). Gaithersburg, MD: Aspen.

Langdon, H. W. (1992b). Speech and language assessment of LEP/bilingual Hispanic students. In H. W. Langdon and L. L. Cheng (Eds.), *Hispanic children and adults with communication disorders* (pp. 201–271). Gaithersburg, MD: Aspen.

Lee, L. L., & Canter, S. (1971). Developmental sentence scoring: A clinical procedure for estimating syntactic development in children's spontaneous speech. *Journal of Speech and Hearing Disorders, 36,* 315–340.

Lidz, C. S., & Peña, E. D. (1996). Dynamic assessment: The model, its relevance as a non-biased approach, and its application to Latino American preschool children. *Language, Speech and Hearing Services in Schools, 27,* 367–372.

Lund, N. J., & Duchan, J. F. (1993). *Assessing children's language in naturalistic contexts.* Englewood Cliffs, NJ: Prentice-Hall.

Marques, R. (1989). *Juan Bobo y la dama de occidente; pantomima puertorriqueña para un ballet accidental* (Juan Bobo and the woman from the occident; a Puerto Rican pantomime for an accidental ballet). Río Piedras, PR: Editorial Cultural.

Mattes, L. J., & Omark, D. R. (1991). *Speech and language assessment for the bilingual handicapped.* Oceanside, CA: Academic Communication Associates.

McCauley, R. J. (1996). Familiar strangers: Criterion-referenced measures in communication disorders. *Language, Speech and Hearing Services in Schools, 29,* 3–10.

Merino, B. J. (1992). Acquisition of syntactic and phonological features in Spanish. In H. W. Langdon and L. L. Cheng (Eds.), *Hispanic children and adults with communication disorders* (pp. 57–98). Gaithersburg, MD: Aspen.

Miller, N. (1988). Language dominance in bilingual children. In M. J. Ball (Ed.), *Theoretical linguistics and disordered language* (pp. 235–256). San Diego, CA: College-Hill Press.

Naremore, R. C. (1997). Making it hang together: Children's use of mental frameworks to structure narratives. *Topics in Language Disorders, 18,* 16–30.

Naremore, R. C., Densmore, A. E., & Harman, D. R. (1995). *Language intervention with school-aged children: Conversation, narrative, and text.* San Diego, CA: Singular.

Nicoladis, E., & Genesee, F. (1997). Language development in preschool bilingual children. *Journal of Speech-Language Pathology and Audiology, 21,* 258–270.

Orellana, M. F. (1994, April 4–8). *Superhuman forces: Young children's English language acquisition and Spanish language loss.* Paper presented at the Annual Meeting of the American Educational Research Association, New Orleans, LA.

Peña, E., Quinn, R., & Iglesias, A. (1992). The application of dynamic methods to language assessment: A non-biased procedure. *Journal of Special Education, 26,* 269–280.

Quinn, R., Goldstein, B., & Peña, E. D. (1996). Cultural/linguistic variation in the United States and its implications for assessment and intervention in speech–language pathology: An introduction. *Language, Speech and Hearing Services in Schools, 27,* 345–346.

Restrepo, M. A. (1998). Identifiers of predominantly Spanish-speaking children with language impairment. *Journal of Speech, Language, and Hearing Research, 41,* 1398–1412.

Robinson-Zañartu, C. (1996). Serving Native American children and families: Considering cultural variables. *Language, Speech and Hearing Services in Schools, 27*(4), 373–384.

Romaine, S. (1996). Bilingualism. In W. C. Ritchie and T. K. Bjatia (Eds.), *Handbook of second language acquisition* (pp. 571–592). San Diego, CA: Academic Press.

Roseberry-McKibbin, C. A., & Eicholtz, G. E. (1994). Serving children with limited English proficiency in the schools: A national survey. *Language, Speech and Hearing Services in Schools, 25,* 156–164.

Schiff-Myers, N. B. (1992). Considering arrested language development and language loss in the assessment of second language learners. *Language, Speech and Hearing Services in Schools, 23,* 28–33.

Tabors, P. O. (1997). *One child, two languages: A guide for preschool educators of children learning English as a second langua*ge. Baltimore, MD: Brookes.

Taylor, O. L., & Payne, K. T. (1983). Culturally valid testing: A proactive approach. *Topics in Language Disorders, 3,* 8–20.

Tomblin, J. B. (2000). Perspectives in diagnosis. In J. B. Tomblin, H. L. Morris, and D. C. Spriestersbach (Eds.), *Diagnosis in speech–language pathology* (pp. 3–34). San Diego, CA: Singular.

Toronto, A. S. (1976). Developmental assessment of Spanish grammar. *Journal of Speech and Hearing Disorders, 41,* 150–171.

Ukrainetz, T. A., Harpell, S., Walsh, C., & Coyle, C. (2000). A preliminary investigation of dynamic assessment with Native American kindergartners. *Language, Speech and Hearing Services in Schools, 31,* 142–154.

van Kleeck, A. (1994). Potential cultural bias in training parents as conversational partners with their children who have delays in language development. *American Journal of Speech-Language Pathology, 3,* 67–78.

Wolfram, W. (1983). Test interpretation and sociolinguistic differences. *Topics in Language Disorders, 3,* 21–34.

Wong-Fillmore, L. (1979). Individual differences in second language acquisition. In C. J. Fillmore, D. Kempler, and W. S.-Y. Wang (Eds.), *Individual differences in language ability and language behavior.* New York: Academic Press.

Zayas-Bazán, E., & Fernández, J. B. (1993). *Arriba: Comunicación y cultura.* Englewood Cliffs, NJ: Prentice Hall.

Zentella, A. C. (1997). *Growing up bilingual.* Malden, MA: Blackwell.

Zimmerman, I. L., Steiner, B. S., & Pond, R.E. (1993). *Preschool Language Scale-3, Spanish Edition (PLS-3 Spanish).* San Antonio, TX: Psychological Corporation.

Use of the World Wide Web for Professional Education Appropriate for Bilingual Students

Practical and Applied Sites

When students from bilingual backgrounds enter the public schools, they enter a system designed to meet the needs of an English-speaking and mainstream-culture student population (i.e., white middle class), but the system may not meet their diverse language needs (Brice-Heath, 1986; MacArthur, 1993). Students who are culturally and linguistically diverse (CLD) are often quickly enrolled full-time into general education classrooms after limited English as a second language instruction (Brice & Montgomery, 1996). Teachers and administrators with general education backgrounds may expect these transitional students from CLD backgrounds to perform well in all aspects of language including pragmatics (Cummins, 1984). The period of English as a second language (ESL) instruction may not be sufficient for students with culturally and linguistically diverse backgrounds to acquire all the necessary oral, written, and academic language skills (Collier, 1987; Cummins, 1984).

Bilingual students needing speech and language services may especially need more time to acquire the requisite English language skills for academic success (Roseberry-McKibbin, 1995). What language to use in the home and in therapy sessions is a common concern for speech–language pathologists treating students with language disorders who come from CLD backgrounds (Brice, 1994; Wong-Fillmore, 1993). Thus, a variety of issues confront school-based SLPs treating bilingual students. It is imperative that SLPs be knowledgeable about second language acquisition issues and be able to adapt existing therapy methods to meet the needs of their bilingual students (Banks, 1988).

Speech–language pathologists are serving, and will continue to serve, bilingual populations, and they still need information about serving bilingual students in therapy. The number of bilingual speech–language pathologists in the United States is currently inadequate to serve the growing bilingual school population (Kayser, 1995). One illustration is the lack of Spanish–English-speaking SLPs. In 1993, there were only 705 Hispanic certified speech–language pathologists within the American Speech-Language-Hearing Association (Kayser, 1996). Deal-Williams (personal communication, December 7, 1999) stated that as of June, 1999, there were 1,507 Hispanic certified SLPs and 16 who were dual certified in audiology. Statistics documenting the increase in the growing Hispanic population indicate that Hispanics comprise 28 million, or over 10% of the U.S. population (U.S. Department of Commerce, 1990). From estimates that 1–3% of the population needs some speech–language therapy, then it can be expected that between 280,000 and 840,000 Hispanic individuals need to be served, which means that the number of bilingual, Spanish–English-speaking SLPs is insufficient to serve the Hispanic client base in all settings, including schools. Therefore, it is imperative that both monolingual and bilingual speech–language pathologists serve students from bilingual and multicultural backgrounds.

All speech–language pathologists need training to serve bilingual populations (Roseberry-McKibbin, 1995). The working knowledge base that SLPs need about language goes beyond information obtained through general cultural exposure. Being a member of a particular cultural group does not necessarily provide one with the background and training sufficient to provide appropriate services. All SLPs need to obtain information specifically related to the population they will serve. Thus, it is critical that all SLPs (monolingual and bilingual) be informed about their client base.

School-based SLPs face four major challenges as they provide services to bilingual students: (1) identifying those in need of speech–language services, (2) serving those in need of therapy, (3) finding appropriate materials, and (4) using the appropriate materials. Regarding the first challenge, information on assessment of bilingual students is growing (Brice & Montgomery, 1996; Cheng, 1996; Crago, Eriks-Brophy, Pesco, & McAlpine, 1997; Gutierrez-Clellen, 1996; Hamayan & Damico, 1991; Kayser, 1996; Kayser, 1995; Langdon & Saenz, 1996; Quinn, 1995; Roseberry-McKibbin, 1997; Westby, 1997). Unfortunately, information on appropriate intervention materials for bilingual students lags behind assessment information (Brice & Montgomery, 1996; Cheng, 1991; Gutierrez-Clellen, 1996; Hamayan & Damico, 1991; Langdon & Saenz, 1996; Peña, Quinn, & Iglesias, 1992; Roseberry-McKibbin, 1995). Use of existing therapy materials should be expanded for bilingual students who may use a learning style of group interaction for problem solving and learning (Campbell, 1994; Kayser, 1995; Langdon, 1992; Roseberry-McKibbin, 1995). Other students may show a greater ability to cooperate, be more socially inclined, and show a greater sensitivity to interpersonal relationships (Gilbert & Gay, 1985). Hence, speech–language pathologists must supplement existing materials and methods with new methods and materials (for example, accommodating a field-dependent learning style) obtained from the Web in order to better serve the needs of the bilingual students.

Technology Use

With the advent and popularity of the Web has come a new use of computer technology. Masterson, Kuster, McComas, McGuire, Shane, Kuehn, and Zingster (1998) stated that "the internet will quickly become a tool that *will* [emphasis added] enhance professional development as a researcher, an academician, a student, a practicing speech–language pathologist or audiologist, a hearing or speech scientist, or an administrator" (1998, paragraph 3). The Web is emerging as a growing resource tool for therapy applications. The current apparent underutilization of the Web may be due to the newness of the medium and the necessary learning curve and/or the lack of sites specifically devoted to speech–language therapy.

Availability of Web materials now allows for access to new information. Hence, therapy information is available from other sources. Access to the Web for school-based SLPs is growing as many public schools have Web access. Speech–language pathologists must also overcome the learning curve associated with new technologies in order to access the published Web information. This chapter will discuss only how the information may be utilized and not the technical aspects of accessing the Web. The purpose of this chapter is to provide a review of 30 sites and links that speech–language pathologists will find useful in serving bilingual students. Some of these sites cover current research or theories on bilingual education (reviewed in this chapter under the sections "Bilingual Education Resources," "English as a Second Language Sites," and "Spanish Language Sites"), intervention suggestions and ideas for making changes in the school learning environment, and programs for direct intervention with bilingual children ("Bilingual Speech Language Pathology Sites").

Speech–language pathologists must use oversight to ensure appropriate clinical application of material gained from the Web. The information should be used as a supplement to existing training resources and not as a replacement of current materials. In addition, use of Web materials should not be seen as a substitute for professional training and courses.

It is possible for school-based SLPs to find many materials, approaches to assessment and treatment, and practical sources of information that pertain to serving bilingual students. For example, there is a great deal of information in the area of bilingualism (Anderson, 1997).

Speech-language pathologists should provide supervision and clinical direction at all times when using the sites interactively with students, that is, use of the sites in real-time therapy with students should be under the supervision of a speech–language pathologist.

These sites were selected to serve the following aims:

1. To increase the clinician's knowledge about definition of terms, educational-therapeutic approaches, or knowledge of basic second language acquisition issues.
2. To provide materials that clinicians might give, possibly as handouts, to in-service colleagues and parents concerning issues pertaining to bilingual students with possible language or learning disabilities.
3. To provide information that will assist in treatment of bilingual students with language and learning disabilities. Another application of the sites may be to supplement existing lessons.

The chapter is divided into two sections, one related to the education of bilingual students and the other relating to language and learning disabilities. Suggestions are also made as to how the information may be applied clinically.

The three criteria employed in selecting this nonexhaustive listing were (a) that the materials, approaches, and sources must be appropriate for students from bilingual backgrounds, (b) that the materials, approaches, and sources must be appropriate for students with language or learning disabilities, and (c) that the materials, approaches, and sources must be clinically relevant (i.e., not entirely theoretically based). Please remember that sites may appear and disappear; however, all attempts at finding stable sites have been made. The name of the site (in bold) and the address, a brief description, and information about how the material, approach, or source may be clinically applied are given in the listings.

Bilingual Education Resources

1. **Learning Language and Loving It: A Guide to Promoting Children's Social and Language Development in Early Childhood Settings** (http://hanen.velocet.ca/resources_2ndlang.shtml) is a site developed by the Hanen organization that is devoted to clarifying issues related to bilingualism in children. Topics and sections cover the areas of (a) simulta-

neous bilingualism, (b) sequential bilingualism, (c) normal patterns of language use in second language learners, and (d) information regarding support of second language learners. This site increases the clinicians' knowledge of basic second language acquisition issues, including definition of terms.

2. The **Internet TESL Journal** (http://www.aitech.ac.jp/~iteslj/) is a monthly electronic journal devoted to articles, research papers, lesson plans, classroom handouts, teaching ideas, and links in English as a second language. This information may address the SLP's knowledge of learning English as a second language.

3. The ERIC Clearinghouse on **Disabilities and Gifted Education for Cultural Diversity Issues in Multicultural Education** (http://www.ncrel.org/sdrs/areas/issues/educatrs/presrvce/pe3lk1.htm).   Topics covered include: (a) Initial thoughts on multicultural education, (b) Varieties of multicultural education: An introduction, (c) Research knowledge and policy issues in cultural diversity and education, (d) Academic achievement, culture, and literacy: An introduction, (e) Considerations in teaching culturally diverse children, (f) Educating language-minority children, (g) Language-minority students in school reform: The role of collaboration, (h) Communicating with culturally diverse parents of exceptional children, (i) Multicultural education for exceptional children, (j) Teaching about ethnic diversity, (k) Teaching with a multicultural perspective, (l) Working with diverse learners and school staff in a multicultural society, (m) Educating all our students: Improving education for children from culturally and linguistically diverse backgrounds, and (n) Rethinking the education of teachers of language-minority children: Developing reflective teachers for changing schools. This site increases the clinicians' knowledge of basic second language acquisition issues and may also provide information as a supplement to existing lessons (e.g., teaching with a multicultural perspective).

English as a Second Language Sites

1. The Comenius Group has a site for on-line access to relevant English language materials, services, and products. They offer a **Monthly Idiom** list (http://www.comenius.com/idioms/) with definitions. This site provides daily vocabulary words that can be used with bilingual and monolingual students receiving speech and language therapy and also accomplishes aim three.

2. The Comenius Group also offers **Fluency Through Fables** (http://www.comenius.com/fables/). This site aims to improve reading comprehension of English. This site provides daily vocabulary, syntax, reading, and comprehension materials that can be used with both bilingual and monolingual students receiving speech and language therapy; it also fulfills aim three.

3. Sperling's ESL Grammar Quiz Center (http://www.pacificnet.net/ ~sperling/quiz/#grammar). Quizzes at this site cover (a) geography, (b) grammar, (c) history, (d) idioms and slang words, (e) people, (f) reading comprehension, (g) science, (h) world culture, and (i) writing. This site provides syntactic practice (i.e., grammar exercises) that can be used with bilingual and monolingual students receiving speech and language therapy, and thus it accomplishes aim three.

4. Improving Your English on the Web (http://www.geocities.com/ rnegretti/english.htm) includes sections for ESL reading, ESL writing, ESL quizzes and TOEFL exercises, ESL listening and speaking, and Recommended English Learning Websites. This location serves criterion three by providing materials and information for therapy with bilingual and monolingual students in the form of listening comprehension.

5. Pizzaz! . . . Tongue Twisters (http://darkwing.uoregon.edu/ ~leslieob/twisters.html) provides multiple tongue twisters that may be used in articulation and phonology therapy, thus satisfying the aim of providing materials that can be used in therapy with bilingual and monolingual students. In addition, these twisters provide ample opportunities for discussion of new vocabulary items.

6. The Intercultural E-Mail Classroom Connections (http:// www.iecc.org/index.html) provides mailing lists to help teachers and classrooms link with electronic pen pals in other countries and so provides opportunities for writing and expression of ideas. It serves aim three by indirectly providing a language-experience approach to writing. The SLP may assist the students in formulating their ideas and thus also provide for opportunities for` oral language practice.

7. TOEFL On-Line (http://www.toefl.org/) is the official Website for the Test of English as a Foreign Language (TOEFL) programs and services. This site offers tutorials and practice questions for nonnative-English-speaking university students. Students can download practice guides for a small fee. This location serves aim three by providing materials and information for instruction with adult bilingual students.

8. Learning English On-Line from the Applied English Center at the University of Kansas (http://www.aec.ukans.edu/leo/index.shtml). This site links to sections on grammar, vocabulary, reading, and listening and provides SLPs with information that may assist adult English language learners, thus, achieving aim three.

9. English for Internet (http://www.study.com/) offers language classes in grammar, reading, writing, listening, and speaking. This site is offered through a teaching project at the University of California at Berkeley (Extension) English Language Program. Classes are offered for free. This location also serves aim three by providing materials and information for instruction of bilingual adult students.

10. The **University of Illinois, Urbana-Champaign Lingua Center** (http://deil.lang.uiuc.edu/index2.html) provides grammar, listening, and reading. The interactive listening page allows students to listen to radio and television broadcasts (RealAudio player is required). Students can take an exam covering the material presented in the listening activity. They may check their answers immediately and are encouraged to listen again when they give a wrong answer. This page also serves aim three by providing materials and information for instruction of bilingual adult students. Adolescent students can also benefit from the activities found here.

Spanish Language Sites

1. The **Estrellita Accelerated Beginning Spanish Reading Bilingual Education Resources on the Net** (http://www.estrellita.com/) is a collection of links, such as *Sonidos* ("Sounds"), *Sílabas* ("Syllables") and *Cuentos* ("Stories"). This site may be used in conjunction with phonemic awareness and reading lessons that SLPs and classroom teachers may address in therapy and so fulfills aim three. The monolingual therapist may need to have a bilingual, Spanish–English-speaking parent or teacher assist during visits to this site. This collaboration with the parent or aid enables the SLP to establish connections with the bilingual community.

2. The **Bahrona Center for the Study of Books in Spanish for Children and Adolescents** (http://www.csusm.edu/campus_centers/csb/index.htm) is a bilingual site devoted to the development of reading skills for bilingual and monolingual children. One of its links connects to the International Reading Association (http://www.reading.org). This site may also assist with lessons, particularly reading. Reading has been shown to be a language skill that transfers readily between the native language (L1) and English (L2) (Brice & Rivero, 1996; Carson, Carrell, Silberstein, Kroll, & Kuehn, 1990; Genesee, 1979: McLaughlin, 1987). Thus, this site serves aim three of providing information and materials for use in therapy.

Bilingual Speech–Language Pathology Sites

1. Selected Resources: Identification and Assessment of Culturally and Linguistically Diverse Students with Disabilities 1993–1996 (http://www.cec.sped.org/ericec/minibibs/eb1.htm) is a site containing abstracts of articles covering issues of assessment and treatment of CLD children. It fulfills aims one and two. It may increase the SLP's knowledge of second language issues, and it may provide materials for dissemination to other professionals.

2. ASHA's **Multicultural Issues Board Fact Sheets** (http://www.asha.org/multicultural/fact_hp.htm). The Multicultural Issues Board has gathered and put together 17 fact sheets in the following areas: Asian and Asian-American Issues, Pacific Islander Issues, Native American Issues, African American Issues, Hispanic Issues, Multicultural History and Demographic Profile of the United States, ESL/Accent Modification/SESD Issues, Regional and Social Dialects, Cultural Differences in Communication and Learning Styles, Least-Biased Assessment, Language Attitudes and Educational Policy, Bilingualism and Language Development in Multicultural Populations, Intervention with Multicultural Populations, Neurological/Fluency/Voice Disorders in Multicultural Populations, Audiological Concerns, Research on Multicultural Populations/Ethnography, and Service Delivery with Multicultural Populations. The ASHA fact sheets are a good source of second language information, which can be used as in-service materials for dissemination to other colleagues. Thus, this site achieves aims one and two.

3. ESL/Accent Modification Issues (http://www.asha.org/multicultural/fact_7.htm) covers ASHA position statement regarding this topic. It educates the SLP regarding second dialect issues, and the information can be distributed to other SLPs or professionals.

4. Providing Speech–Language Pathologists Materials and Research: Issues of Cultural and Linguistic Diversity (CLD) (http://www.asha.ucf.edu) is a site from the University of Central Florida awarded an ASHA Office of Multicultural Affairs grant. It seeks to promote cultural and linguistic diversity in speech–language pathology and audiology. This site contains the *Multicultural Electronic Journal of Communication Disorders* (MEJCD) and the "Therapy materials and diagnostic tests database." It also serves the aims of providing information on second language acquisition and providing materials for dissemination to other SLPs and colleagues.

5. The **Network on Multicultural Communication Sciences and Disorders** (http://www.utexas.edu/coc/csd/multicultural/network/home.htm)is a site from the University of Texas at Austin that provides "information and links related to universities and training programs, research and funding, and resources." This site was also funded by an ASHA Office of Multicultural Affairs grant. It serves the aims of providing information on second language acquisition and providing materials for possible in-service or dissemination to colleagues.

6. The Canadian Association of Speech Language Pathologists and Audiologists (CASLPA) Journal of Speech–Language Pathology and Audiology. **Special Issue - The Speech, Language, and Hearing Assessment of the Francophone Client: State of the Art (Vol. 21, No. 4)** (http://www.caslpa.ca/english/pubs/dec97.htm). This is a special issue on speech, language, and hearing assessment of the bilingual, French–English-speaking client, and the site provides abstracts of the articles within this issue. The articles and abstracts cover (a) The speech, language, and hearing assessment of the Francophone client: State of the art, (b) The acquisition of French as a native language: Structural and functional determinants in a crosslinguistic perspective, (c) Language development in preschool bilingual children, (d) Assessment of language and speech disorders in Francophone adults, (e) Central auditory disorders in brain-injured children and adolescents: Audiological assessments made from nonverbal tests and from French-language adaptations of verbal tests, and (f) Speech audiometry in French-speaking Quebec. This location accomplishes the first aim of increasing the SLP's knowledge of bilingual and second language issues as they pertain to speech and language disordered clients.

7. The **Center For Research in Language Bilingual Research Projects** (http://crl.ucsd.edu/bilingual/) from the University of California at San Diego investigates whether the bilingual mind contains two separate dictionaries, whether is there one highly interconnected system, and whether there is a single system with variations in the strength of within-versus between-language associations. This location also accomplishes the first aim of increasing the SLP's knowledge of bilingual and second language issues.

8. ASHA's **Intervention with Multicultural Populations Factsheet** (http://www.asha.org/multicultural/fact 13.htm) provides SLPs with a reading list of articles and chapters that cover the topics of determining the most appropriate language of intervention with speakers who are bilingual and or speak other dialects of English; cultural factors that may impact on the intervention process; and selecting culturally appropriate materials and activities. This URL meets aim one of this chapter, that is, it increases the SLP's knowledge base.

9. Taylor's book **Cross-cultural communication: An essential dimension of effective education** is available on-line (http://www.nwrel.org/cnorse/booklets/ccc/index.html#return) through The Mid-Atlantic Equity Center. Chapters include: (a) Introduction, (b) Discovering characteristics of other cultures, (c) Culture, communication, and language (d) Using cross-cultural communication to improve relationships, (e) Teaching standard English to speakers of nonstandard English dialects, (f) Communication differences, test performance, and educational placement, (g) Communication differences and discipline problems, and (h)

Summary. This on-line book attains the aim of increasing the SLP's knowledge of cross-cultural communication issues.

10. Kuster's section devoted to **Multicultural/Disability Issues** (http://www.mankato.msus.edu/dept/comdis/kuster2/basics/esl.html) is part of the larger, comprehensive Internet publication "Net connections for communication disorders and sciences" (http://www.mankato.msus.edu/dept/comdis/kuster2/welcome.html). This location provides links to other sites and thus fulfills the first aim of this chapter.

11. The Stuttering Foundation of America's notes to classroom teachers (in Spanish) about children who stutter are on the site **The Child Who Stutters in School: Recommendations for Teachers** (http://www. stuttersfa.org/br _ spnts.htm). This site accomplishes the aim of providing materials for handouts to Spanish-speaking parents (aim two).

12. The **Center for Bilingual Speech and Language Disorders** (http://www.cbsld.com/) is a private-practice operation in Miami, Florida, that provides speech and language therapy services in Spanish and English. Through its Web page, it provides definitions of a bilingual SLP and children and bilingualism (provided by ASHA). In addition, the site provides information about the Center's infant and preschool programs. The Center was awarded an ASHA grant (Bilingual/Multicultural Clinical Training in Speech and Language Pathology 2000/2001) to have SLPs intern in bilingual/multicultural clinical training. This site accomplishes aim three by providing information to SLPs for the treatment of bilingual students.

13. ASHA's **Minority/Bilingual Emphasis Programs** (http://www. asha.org/multicultural/mc _ institutions.htm#bilingemph) is a list of communication disorders programs at historically Black institutions and of programs with a bilingual emphasis. This site serves the purpose of providing information that may assist the SLP in establishing contacts and thus better serving culturally and linguistically diverse clients.

14. The **Spanish Pronunciation Guide** (http://www.cas.usf.edu/ csd _ speech _ lab/pronunciation _ guide.html) was developed by bilingual speech–language pathology students at the University of South Florida. It covers the basic consonants and phonemes of Spanish. An audio/basic ULAW Audio™ (au) plug-in is required. For Windows™ machines, the WPlany™ program is needed (ftp://ftp.ncsa.uiuc.edu/Web/Mosaic/Windows/viewers/wplny12a.zip); on Macintosh™ computers, SoundMachine™ is needed (ftp://ftp.ncsa.uiuc.edu/Mosaic/Mac/Helpers/). (Refer to Table 11.1 for a listing of applications needed to play audio, video, images, and portable documents.) This URL can be used to assist the SLP in articulation therapy or as a source of learning about Spanish sounds.

TABLE 11.1　*Applications Needed to Play Sound, Video, Image, Live Audio/Video and Portable Documents*

File Type	Windows	Macintosh
Sound		
.aiff	WPlany™	SoundMachine™
.au	WPlany™	SoundMachine™
MPEG (.mpg2)	mpgaudio™	mpegaudio™
RealAudio (.ram)	RealPlayer™	RealPlayer™
.wav	WPlany™	SoundApp™
Video		
.avi	MediaPlayer™ (built into MS Windows™)	MacZilla™
.mov	Quicktime™	Quicktime™ (built into Mac OS)
.mpg	MpegPlay™	Sparkle™
RealVideo (.ram)	RealPlayer™	RealPlayer™
Image/Graphics		
.gif	LView™	JPEGview™
Live Audio/Video		
CU-SeeMe	CU-SeeMe™	CU-SeeMe™
RealPlayer	RealPlayer™	RealPlayer™
Portable Documents		
.pdf	Adobe Acrobat Reader™	Adobe Acrobat Reader™

15. ASHA's Office of Multicultural Affairs (http://www.asha.org/multicultural/multicultural.htm#issues) (Adobe Acrobat™ . . .). This site offers some of the most frequently requested materials dealing with multicultural issues, covering the topics of . . . . (a) Clinical management of communicatively handicapped minority language populations, (b) Social dialects, and (c) Bilingual speech–language pathologists and audiologists. This location serves aims one and two of this chapter in providing more information about cultural and linguistic diversity and is also as an excellent source for dissemination materials.

General Search Engines

Because the Web is constantly changing it is expected that some of these Web sites will stay, while others will disappear. However, the chapter provides the reader with an idea of what is available. In addition, the following list of search engines should enable the reader to conduct a personal search of appropriate multicultural sites.

1. **Altavista**™ from Digital is a Web and newsgroup search engine (http://www.altavista.com/).
2. **Excite**™ provides consumers and advertisers services with extensive personalization capabilities (http://www.excite.com/).
3. **Google**™ uses text-matching techniques to find pages to aid the search (http://www.google.com/).
4. **Hotbot**™ offers a point-and-click interface, pulldown menus, and the ability to use plain English for conducting searches (http://hotbot.lycos.com/).
5. **Lycos**™ provides on-line guides to locate and filter information on the Web (http://www.lycos.com/).
6. **MegaCrawler**™ is a multiple search engine locator (http://216.22.162.11/cgi-bin/search.cgi).
7. **Netguide**™ is a daily guide to the Internet (http://www.netguide.com/).
8. **Netscape Search**™ combines search results from the Netcenter and Open Directory (http://search.netscape.com/).
9. **Yahoo**™ provides a category-based Web directory. (http://www.yahoo.com/).

Conclusions

The main advantage of using the Web to find information is the vast amount of material that is available. For little or no cost, school-based clinicians may access and collect easily obtainable information. This information is not meant to replace educational training provided through courses or continuing education. However, this material may supplement the SLP's repertoire of techniques and materials currently used (Iskowitz, 1998; Scott, 1998). Clinicians can use information about bilingual education resources as well as information about language and learning disabilities in bilingual students to increase their and others' knowledge about improving services to bilingual students in schools.

References

Anderson, R. (1997, February). Surfing the world wide web: Bilingual sites. *Communication Disorders and Sciences in Culturally and Linguistically Diverse Populations Newsletter, 3*(1), 17–18.

Banks, J. (1988). Approaches to multicultural curriculum reform. *Multicultural Leader, 1* (2), 1–2.

Brice, A. (1994). Spanish or English for language impaired Hispanic children? In D. Ripich & N. Creaghead (Eds.), *School discourse problems* (2nd ed.). San Diego: Singular Publishing.

Brice, A., & Montgomery, J. (1996). Adolescent pragmatic skills: A comparison of Latino students in ESL and speech and language programs. *Language, Speech, and Hearing Services in Schools, 27*, 68–81.

Brice, A., & Rivero, Y. (1996) Language transfer: First (L1) and second (L2) proficiency of bilingual adolescent students. *Per Linguam. The Journal for Language Teaching and Learning, 12*(2) 1–16.

Brice-Heath, S. (1986). Sociocultural contexts of language development. In D. Holt (Ed.) , *Beyond language: Social and cultural factors in schooling language minority students* (pp. 142–186). Los Angeles: Evaluation, Dissemination, and Assessment Center.

Campbell, L. R. (1994). Clinical practicum and English proficiency. In D. Scott (Ed.), *Challenges in the expansion of cultural diversity in communication sciences and disorders, Sea Island multicultural institute: Compilation of papers* (pp. 59–62). Rockville, MD:American Speech-Language-Hearing Association.

Carson, J. E., Carrell, P. L., Silberstein, S., Kroll, B., & Kuehn, P. A. (1990). Reading-writing relationships in first and second language. *TESOL Quarterly, 24*, 245–265.

Cheng, L. (1996). Enhancing communication: Toward optimal language learning for the limited English proficient student. *Language, Speech, and Hearing Services in Schools, 27*(4), 347–354.

Cheng, L. (1991). *Assessing Asian language performance.* Oceanside, CA: Academic Communication Associates.

Collier, V. (1987). Age and rate of acquisition of second language for academic purposes. *TESOL Quarterly, 21*(4), 617–641.

Crago, M., Eriks-Brophy, A., Pesco, D., & McAlpine, L. (1997). Culturally based miscommunication in the classroom. *Language, Speech, and Hearing Services in Schools, 28*(3), 245–254.

Cummins, J. (1984). *Bilingualism and special education : Issues in assessment and pedagogy.* San Diego: College-Hill Press.

Genessee, F. (1979). Acquisition of reading skills in immersion programs. *Foreign Language Annals, 1*, 71–77.

Gilbert, S., & Gay, G. (1985). Improving the success in school of poor Black children. *Phi Delta Kappan, 67*, 133–137.

Gutierrez-Clellen, V. (1996). Language diversity: Implications for assessment. In K. Cole, P. Dale, & D. Thal (Eds.), *Advances in assessment of communication and language* (pp. 29–56). Baltimore, MD: Brookes Publishing.

Hamayan, E., & Damico, J. (Eds.). (1991). *Limiting bias in the assessment of bilingual students.* Austin, TX: Pro-Ed.

Iskowitz, M. (1998). Software solutions. *Advance for Speech-Language Pathologists and Audiologists, 23* (8), 7–9.

Kayser, H. (1996). Cultural/linguistic variation in the United States and its implications for assessment and intervention in speech-language pathology: An epilogue. *Language, Speech, and Hearing Services in Schools, 27*(4), 385–386.

Kayser, H. (Ed.). (1995). *Bilingual speech-language pathology. An Hispanic focus.* San Diego, CA: Singular.

Langdon, H. (1992). *Hispanic children and adults with communication disorders.* Gaithersburg, VA: Aspen Publications.

Langdon, H., & Saenz, T. (Eds.). (1996). *Language assessment and intervention with multicultural students.* Oceanside, CA: Academic Communication Associates.

MacArthur, E. K. (1993). *Language characteristics and schooling in the United States, a changing picture: 1979 and 1989.* Washington, D.C.: National Center for Education Statistics.

Masterson, J. J., Kuster, J. M., McComas, K., McGuire, R., Shane, H., Kuehn, D., & Zingster, L. (1998). *Technology 2000: Clinical applications for speech-language pathology.* [On-line]. Available: http://www.asha.org/professionals/tech_resources/tech/tech2000/4.htm [1998, March 2].

McLaughlin, B. (1987). Reading in a second language: Studies with adult and child learners. In S. R. & H. T. Trueba (Eds.), *Becoming literate in English as a second language* (pp. 57–70). Norwood, NJ: Ablex.

Peña, E., Quinn, R., & Iglesias, A. (1992). The application of dynamic methods to language assessment: A nonbiased procedure. *The Journal of Special Education, 26*(3), 269–280.

Quinn, R. (1995). Early intervention? Qué quiere decir éso... What does that mean? In H. Kayser (Ed.), *Bilingual speech-language pathology. An Hispanic focus* (pp. 75–96). San Diego, CA: Singular.

Roseberry-McKibbin, C. (1997). Understanding Filipino families: A foundation for effective service delivery. *American Journal of Speech-Language Pathology, 6*(3), 5–14.

Roseberry-McKibbin, C. (1995). *Multicultural students with special language needs: Practical strategies for assessment and intervention.* Oceanside, CA: Academic Communication Associates.

Scott, A. (1998). Computer creations. *Advance for Speech-Language Pathologists and Audiologists, 23* (8), 10–12.

U.S. Department of Commerce. (1990). *Current population.* Washington, DC: Bureau of the Census.

Westby, C. (1997). There's more to passing than knowing the answers. *Language, Speech, and Hearing Services in Schools, 28*(3), 274–287.

Wong-Fillmore, L. (1993, January). *Educating citizens for a multicultural society: The roles, responsibilities and risks.* Presentation at the National Association for Multicultural Education, Los Angeles, CA.

Principles and Strategies in Intervention

Celeste Roseberry-McKibbin

Introduction

As the United States becomes increasingly diverse, there are greater numbers of Hispanic residents than ever before. In 1998, for example, in California there were 9,454,000 Hispanic residents. In 1998, Texas had 5,640,000 Hispanic residents while Florida had 2,080,000 residents of Hispanic origin (U.S. Bureau of the Census, 1999). It is projected that by the year 2030, there will be 63 million Hispanics in the United States (U.S. Bureau of the Census, 1996). Thus, public schools all over the country have increasing numbers of Hispanic students in their classrooms.

Classroom teachers may refer Hispanic children for assessment of possible language learning disabilities (LLD), and a major challenge for speech–language pathologists (SLPs) is to differentiate language differences from disorders in these students. SLPs do see a number of Hispanic students with genuine LLD. In a national survey of over 1,100 public school SLPs, Roseberry-McKibbin and Eicholtz (1994) found that Hispanic children were the most commonly served minority group on the clinicians' caseloads.

Speech–language pathologists face several major challenges as they seek to provide effective intervention to Hispanic students. First, Hispanic students are a very heterogeneous group (Roseberry-McKibbin & Hegde, 2000). Two major Spanish dialects in the United States are the Carribean (e.g., Puerto Rican and Cuban) dialect and the southwestern (Mexican/ Mexican American) dialect (Goldstein & Iglesias, 1996). However, there are numerous other Spanish dialects, and these can differ markedly from each other in terms of pragmatics, syntax, phonology, and morphology (Goldstein, 2000). Second, there is a lack of developmental data for Spanish speakers (Anderson, 1998), and this makes effective treatment more challenging. Third, many SLPs do not possess a foundation of knowledge about normal second language acquisition and bilingualism; this knowledge is critical in effective service delivery. Fourth, many SLPs speak only English and thus provide services in English only.

This chapter focuses on principles and strategies for effective intervention with Hispanic students. The chapter is broadly divided into two major sections. The first section summarizes important sociocultural variables that must be considered in working with Hispanic students, assuming that students should be treated as members of a family and cultural unit—not as isolated individuals (McNeilly & Coleman, 2000). The second section, which comprises the primary portion of the chapter, provides specific, practical suggestions for service delivery to Hispanic students with LLD. In this section, there is an emphasis on intervention strategies based on current research that focuses specifically on Hispanic students. Ideally, all treatment strategies should be based on research. In this chapter, a scientific basis for intervention recommendations has been utilized as much as possible.

General Principles in Working with Hispanic Families

All SLPs are aware of the overall importance of including families in intervention. However, the importance of the principle of developing a good relationship with the families of LLD Hispanic students cannot be overemphasized. Relationships are very important to Hispanic families, and the SLP's personal qualities (e.g., respectfulness toward the family, approachability, personal interest in the family) may be even more important to families than the SLP's technical qualifications (Kayser, 1998a). It is important for SLPs to have a humanistic rather than task orientation when working with Hispanic families and not to appear hurried (Brice, Roseberry-McKibbin, & Kayser, 1997). Hispanic families appreciate *simpatía,* the social script that emphasizes positive personal interactions that convey harmony in relationships and empathy for others. When families are included and made to feel comfortable, they will understand the importance of their participation in the overall intervention process. They will also usually be more satisfied with the whole intervention process (McNeilly & Coleman, 2000).

Another basic principle in working with Hispanic families is to encourage parents to speak, at home, the language in which they are most comfortable (Brice, 1993; Gutierrez-Clellen, 1999; Patterson, 1999). For most parents, this is Spanish. One of the worst disservices SLPs can do to Hispanic LLD children and their families is to tell parents with limited English to "speak only English at home." If parents provide their children with comprehensible input in Spanish, this will enhance the children's cognitive–linguistic development much more than grammatically incorrect, semantically impoverished models of English (Roseberry-McKibbin, 1997). This is especially critical with preschool children who are still gaining a foundation in their first language of Spanish (Tabors, 1997). Patterson (1999) and Brice (2000a) state that parents should also be reassured that modeling the behavior of code switching (changing languages over words, phrases, or sentences) is not detrimental to their children's language development in English or Spanish. Speech–language pathologists should emphasize to parents that being bilingual is a great asset in today's society, with bilingual adults being very attractive to employers (Roseberry-McKibbin, 1995a). Again, SLPs should encourage parents to support their children's Spanish development in the home.

Health Care and Beliefs Regarding Disabilities: Implications for Intervention

A major factor impacting health care for Hispanic students and their families is socioeconomic status. A United Nations report stated that white Americans have the highest standard of living in the world, while Hispanic Americans' ranks 35th (Sleeter, 1994). According to the U.S. Bureau of the Census (1999), in 1997 36.4% of Hispanic children lived below poverty level as compared with 15.4% of white children. A major implication of living at or below the poverty level is lack of access to health insurance.

Roseberry-McKibbin, Pena, Hall, and Smith-Stubblefield (1996) found that of 254 California migrant Hispanic families surveyed, 90% had no health insurance; these families were the "working poor" who did not have health benefits on the job and did not make enough money to purchase private health insurance. Families who have no insurance and who generally lack access to health care tend to have more children who experience untreated middle ear infections. These untreated middle ear infections (otitis media) can lead to problems with articulation, language, and auditory processing. Also, children may have dentition problems (which the family cannot afford to have treated), which preclude successful articulation therapy. Children who are sick miss more school, which negatively impacts their overall academic development and learning. It is best if SLPs have a list of local, low-cost resources for families who need health care to share with the families. Sometimes, families can also find out about health care resources from their local churches or parishes. It must be kept in mind that families' utilization of health care is somewhat related to their religious beliefs.

Many Hispanics come from Catholic backgrounds. However, some Cuban Hispanics practice the Santeria religion, a combination of Roman Catholicism and African religion (Brice, 1993). Some Hispanic families believe in folk medicine practices such as herbs, massage, and utilizing the services of spiritualists; these families might be more likely to turn to these practices than to a health care practitioner such as a SLP. A visible disability such as a cleft palate can be attributed to an external, nonmedical cause such as witchcraft. Some parents may believe that if the child has a disability, the parents are being punished for their sins (Zuniga, 1998). Other parents may accept disabilities stoically, as part of a larger divine plan that humans do not understand (Maestas & Erickson, 1992). Parents who have these types of beliefs might be less open to utilizing the services of a SLP for their child with LLD.

Speech–language pathologists can work in concert with parents and their practices; it is not necessary or appropriate to tell parents that their beliefs are "wrong." Rather, SLPs can advise the provision of therapy in addition to other forms of healing (e.g., herbs) that the family is seeking. Speech–language pathologists should also encourage the family to seek treatment for all disorders, not just visible ones.

Some families believe that "invisible" disabling conditions do not exist. It might be more difficult to persuade a family to seek intervention for an invisible disability such as a language learning disability than to accept services for a visible problem such as cerebral palsy, cleft palate, and others. This author was recently told by a Mexican mother (of a 4th grade boy with LLD) that her son was "just lazy" and did not try hard enough. The author tried, in a sensitive manner, to share that the boy was making great efforts but that his LLD was preventing him from making the expected progress in school. It is challenging for SLPs to help families see that invisible disabilities such as LLD, stuttering, and others merit intervention as much as visible disabilities.

Family Life and Practices: Implications for Intervention

Family life is a very high priority among most Hispanics. Loyalty to the immediate and extended family is strongly emphasized. Divorce is relatively uncommon in Hispanic families as compared with other ethnic groups, and children are desired and valued. Thus, SLPs must be careful to include the family in any intervention decisions and processes. However, some Hispanic families may be uncomfortable in collaborating with professionals; they may not perceive this as their role (Goldstein, 2000; Roseberry-McKibbin, 1997; Zuniga, 1998). Speech–language pathologists should sensitively convey that in mainstream U.S. culture, a team approach between professionals and families is highly desired and encouraged.

As viewed through mainstream American eyes, Hispanic children may be "babied" and indulged more than white American children (Brice, 1993; Zuniga, 1998). For example, preschoolers may be allowed to drink from baby bottles; preteens might sit on their mothers' laps (Zuniga, 1998). Hispanic mothers may still tie the shoes of their six-year-old sons and daughters. Speech–language pathologists must be careful to not judge these children as being immature or delayed. Many Hispanic parents are more relaxed about their children's development than mainstream white parents. Thus, SLPs must remember that early intervention might not seem appropriate to some Hispanic families, who do not emphasize early independence. These families may also not talk with their children in ways that mainstream white SLPs expect.

In some Hispanic homes, parents do not verbalize about ongoing events or relate actions to words (Mann & Hodson, 1994). Langdon (1992) states that some Hispanic children are not asked to foretell what they will do or to repeat facts. Adults do not ask their children for emotional evaluations or interpretations of events. However, Wong-Fillmore (1982, 1986) stated that in some Mexican homes where the family is of low socioeconomic status, eventcasting takes place. In eventcasting, a person describes an activity that is happening at the moment or that is planned for the future (Langdon, 1992). Speech–language pathologists must view each family individually to see if eventcasting and other behaviors such as verbalizing about ongoing events are taking place regularly. It is also helpful to ascertain what families believe about children's knowledge of basic concepts.

Many Hispanics do not believe that it is important for their children to know colors, numbers, or letters; rather, politeness and respect are emphasized. Children are not expected to participate in adult conversations, and children show their respect for adults by not considering themselves to be equal to the adult during interactions between adults and children. Peers are considered to be equal partners in conversation (Kayser, 1998a). Many Mexican mothers regard themselves as mothers, not teachers (Madding, 2000). In one longitudinal study of Mexican Latino mothers and their children, it was found that most mothers showed reticence toward reciprocal interactions with their children. They tended to be nonverbal or directive and less responsive than most other mothers to a child's attempt to speak or manipulate an object. When asked who would teach their children such concepts as shapes, colors, and body parts, the mothers most often responded that teachers would do that. Many mothers believed that it was not appropriate to begin reading with children until age five when they were of kindergarten age, and many did not have books in their homes (Madding, 1999). Thus, SLPs must be sensitive to these cultural differences in interaction patterns between adults and children in Hispanic families.

Because so many Hispanic families experience poverty, one can assume that in many Hispanic homes, young children do not receive the amount of language stimulation that their higher-socioeconomic-status peers do. Hart & Risley (1995), in their longitudinal study of children from homes of various income levels, found some major differences in the amount of talking that went on in the homes of poor children versus children whose families had more money. They concluded that,

> . . . to ensure that an average welfare child had a weekly amount of experience equal to that of the average child in a working-class family . . . 41 hours per week of out-of-home experience as rich in words as that in an average professional home would be required . . . by the time children are 3 years old, even intensive intervention cannot make up for the differences in the amount of such experience children have received from their parents (p. 210).

Due to cultural differences in adult–child interactions and to the presence of poverty in many Hispanic homes, SLPs need to be especially careful to be sensitive in working with parents in helpful yet nonoffensive ways. Kayser (1998a) suggests that in working with Hispanic parents, SLPs help parents understand the language expectations of mainstream society. If SLPs can sensitively convey that mainstream American schools and eventually employers have certain language expectations, Hispanic families can use this knowledge to modify their interactions with their children at home. It is a "fine line," for SLPs do not want to be insensitive or make parents uncomfortable. However, as Zuniga (1998) emphasizes, many Hispanic parents have come to the United States specifically to obtain better educational opportunities for their children. It would be a disservice to withhold from parents information about mainstream language expectations in the United States and how parents can facilitate children's language development in the home to help children meet those expectations to increase academic and vocational success. Speech–language pathologists can also work with siblings of Hispanic LLD students, training those siblings to interact in ways that enhance language skills. Speech–language pathologists can help parents learn where to find quality reading materials for their children—for example, the local library or even garage sales. Speech–language pathologists can also tell parents about local adult literacy classes that exist in their area for helping parents learn English. It is helpful to send books home with children to read or look at with their parents. If the parents do not read, children can read to them. Also, wordless books can be discussed in Spanish (Roseberry-McKibbin, 1995a).

Summary

Speech–language pathologists, before initiating intervention with Hispanic students, must be aware of and sensitive to sociocultural variables that could impact upon service delivery. It is important to consider health care and beliefs regarding disabilities, family life and practices, and the need for supporting parents' use of Spanish in the home if that is their most fluent language. When SLPs are able to be sensitive to and work with these fundamentals, intervention will be far more successful with Hispanic students with LLD.

General Service Delivery Issues

The type of service delivery model used to support LLD Hispanic students is largely determined by the resources of the particular school and district in which the student resides. Decisions about service delivery models are also made based on the philosophies of the general and special education personnel within a particular school and district.

Unfortunately, many school districts in the United States do not have bilingual regular or special education available for students. Many LLD Hispanic students are placed into all-English classrooms with no support in their primary language of Spanish (Brice & Montgomery, 1996); this is extremely detrimental to these students' overall learning and educational progress. Language loss of Spanish is a major issue for these students, especially as they get older (Kohnert, Bates, & Hernandez, 1999; Roseberry-McKibbin, 1994).

In other situations, LLD Hispanic students are placed in all-English-speaking classrooms but receive some type of support. This support includes tutors in English, Spanish, or both, as well as English as a Second Language pullout models, where children are pulled out of the classroom once to several times a week to receive additional tutoring in Spanish, English, or both. These options are not ideal for promoting the cognitive–linguistic foundation of Hispanic students with LLD. Ideally, Hispanic students with LLD would receive bilingual instruction, which would maintain and promote their Spanish skills while also helping them learn English (Brice, 2000b; Gutierrez-Clellen, 1998, 1999; Restrepo & Kruth, 2000). Many experts discuss the fact that students will learn faster and more thoroughly and experience less language loss if they learn in these ideal bilingual situations (Goldstein, 2000; Gutierrez-Clellen, 1999; Kayser, 1998b; Kiernan & Swisher, 1990; Mattes & Omark, 1991; Perrozi & Sanchez, 1992; Roseberry-McKibbin, 1995a; Saenz, 1996)

This can occur through participation in several different formats: bilingual regular education classrooms, bilingual special education classrooms, and bilingual speech–language pullout therapy (Roseberry-McKibbin, 1995a). Unhappily, these service delivery models are very infrequent due to lack of resources such as personnel and funding. Thus, many Hispanic LLD students are served through pullout therapy in English only, and they spend the rest of their time in classrooms where all the teaching is conducted in English. In these far from ideal conditions, the best many SLPs can do is work with regular education teachers to help LLD Hispanic students succeed in the general education classroom with the school curriculum.

Collaborating with Regular Education Classroom Teachers and Curriculum

Many SLPs serve students in the schools in a pullout model where students receive therapy several times a week in small groups. A typical prototype is a schedule where each student receives therapy 1/2 hour a week for 20–30 minutes in a small-group format. Although SLPs can accomplish some language intervention in this way, it is best to collaborate with classroom teachers to help students succeed within the general curriculum in the regular education classroom (Brice & Roseberry-McKibbin, 1999; Dodge, 1994, 2000; Goldstein, 2000; Pena & Valles, 1995; Seymour & Valles, 1998). O'Brien & Huffman (1998, p. 268) state that

> . . . speech–language pathologists must be even more focused on the relationship between therapy and the educational outcomes that will be defined for the students with whom they work. Speech–language pathologists must strengthen the critical collaborative/consultative model in order to ensure relevance and carryover of this therapy.

In order to strengthen and promote a collaborative approach to service for LLD Hispanic students, SLPs can share the following ideas with classroom teachers in order to increase classroom success for these students. SLPS can also use these strategies in small-group intervention formats. Ideally, SLPs can use these ideas in collaboration in the classroom as well as in small groups where targeted skills are taught directly (Pena & Valles, 1995).

Facilitating Self–Esteem

Although it is tempting for SLPs to immediately share strategies for successful teaching, it is imperative to emphasize the foundation for helping students succeed: increasing students' self-esteem and respecting them as individuals as well as members of the Hispanic culture and as speakers of Spanish (Kayser, 1996; Langdon, 1996; Midobuche, 1999). Specific suggestions for helping teachers show respect for Hispanic LLD students (Beaumont, 1992; Brice & Roseberry-McKibbin, 1999; Roseberry-McKibbin, 1995a) and thus increasing these students' self-esteem are

1. Reduce students' anxieties as much as possible. One way to do this is to not pressure beginning English learners to speak right away. Krashen (1996) discusses the silent period, a time of weeks or several months when students learning a second language do not speak but rather focus on comprehension. This is a normal second-language learning phenomenon and should be respected in the classroom (Roseberry-McKibbin, 1994).

2. Teach the entire class words, phrases, songs, and poems in Spanish. The use of Spanish in the classroom conveys an implicit appreciation of Hispanic students' culture and language (Brice & Anderson, 1999).

3. Read (or have students read) stories about Hispanic leaders and role models; these stories can be discussed and students can write essays about them.

4. Invite parents and other persons from the Hispanic community to come and speak to all students about Hispanic culture and customs and about the countries the speakers are from.

5. Label everything in the classroom (e.g., with cards) in both Spanish and English. This will enhance the second language skills of all students in the classroom.

6. Encourage students to use Spanish in the classroom. If the teacher speaks Spanish, he or she should encourage the use of complex sentences and grammatically correct sentences. Restrepo (1998) found that Spanish-speaking children with language impairments used less complex sentences than normally developing Spanish-speaking children. Restrepo, Gutierrez-Clellen, and Galliano (1999) also found that children with significant grammatical errors in expressive language had problems in both English and Spanish. It is best if Hispanic students with LLD can be encouraged to increase length, complexity, and grammaticality of their sentences.

7. Ask students to talk about their native countries and cultures.

8. Discuss the advantages of being bilingual in today's society.

9. Recruit Spanish-speaking tutors (who speak the same dialect as the students) from churches, local community organizations, and local universities. One option is to invite older Hispanic students (e.g., high school students) to work with and tutor younger Hispanic students. This has been shown in some school districts to enhance the older students' self-esteem and provide the younger students with role models.

10. Avoid stereotyping—for example, avoid showing pictures of Hispanics always living in poverty or being in rural settings.

11. Avoid disconnecting—for example, avoid discussing Hispanics only on Cinco de Mayo or presenting a unit on Hispanics without relating the unit to the general curriculum.

12. Remember that achieving academic English language skills takes much longer than achieving conversational, face-to-face English language skills (Cummins, 1992). Have realistic expectations of students' performance abilities in academic contexts that include much abstract information.

13. Help students master the "hidden rules" of school culture; students are often unfamiliar with the unspoken culture of the school and the classroom (Cheng, 1996; Damico & Hamayan, 1991). For example, students need to be taught explicitly that if they do not contribute

during class discussions, this is not considered courtesy to the teacher (as it would be in many Spanish-speaking countries), but rather is viewed negatively as passivity and disinterest.

In summary, if SLPs and classroom teachers can work collaboratively to implent some of the above ideas, the self-esteem of Hispanic LLD students will be enhanced. This enhanced self-esteem will enable these students to be more successful learners and profit more from the strategies described in the next section.

Strategies for Enhancing Learning in the Classroom

Speech–language pathologists can share, with classroom teachers, specific strategies for enhancing the learning of Hispanic students with LLD. These classroom strategies can also be used in small groups of students (Beaumont, 1992; Brice & Roseberry-McKibbin, 1999; Damico & Hamayan, 1991; Goldstein, 2000; Roseberry-McKibbin, 1995a; Roseberry-McKibbin & Hegde, 2000). The strategies include:

1. Using themes and interest units to help students integrate information.
2. Encouraging students to interact with one another regularly, not learn passively while the teacher does all the talking.
3. Facilitating more complex cognitive–linguistic skills rather than only expecting students to complete simple recall activities (Brice & Montgomery, 1996). These increasingly complex skills include helping students to analyze information critically, apply it to new contexts, explain new information in their own words, and relate new information to what they already know.
4. Asking questions to increase students' participation in the classroom learning experience. Teachers can ask students to summarize what has been said, and they can also ask students to express opinions about material. Open-ended questions allow for elaboration and expansion. Students grow cognitively when they are asked to expand on and make predictions about information that has been presented (Brice & Montgomery, 1996). For example, during the reading of a story, the teacher can ask a student what he thinks will happen to the characters at the end of the story.
5. Encouraging, acknowledging, and responding to students' attempts to share in the classroom and answer questions (Langdon, 1996; Brice, Mastin, & Perkins, 1997). Brice and Montgomery (1996), in a study of Latino adolescents, found that both general and special education Latino adolescents were not able to regulate others using language; they showed difficulty expressing themselves in the classroom and

rarely initiated class discussions. Thus, SLPs need to encourage teachers to make sure Hispanic students participate actively in classroom discussions and activities.

6. Helping students learn to take notes and write down instructions to facilitate organization and memory.
7. Helping students learn to use the dictionary. One idea for specifically guiding students in dictionary use is to help them write about their word, as shown in Figure 12.1.

Hispanic students with LLD will have their learning and academic success enhanced when SLPs and teachers can collaborate to utilize these strategies in the regular classroom setting.

Modifying Teaching Style and Delivery

Many teachers in mainstream U.S. schools have been trained specifically to teach monolingual, English-speaking students. These teachers often experience success using a certain teaching style with these students. However, many teachers have not received specific training in modifying their teaching style to accommodate second language learners. When these second language learners also have LLD, the situation becomes complicated for everyone. SLPs can share with teachers specific suggestions for modifying their teaching style and delivery of information to promote classroom success for Hispanic students with LLD.

NAME:_____

My word is:_____

I found my word on page_____

My word means:_____

_____

_____

_____

Here's a sentence using my word:_____

_____

_____

_____

FIGURE 12.1 *Dictionary Use*

In terms of teaching style and delivery, teachers can make their input more comprehensible to beginning and intermediate English learners by avoiding use of slang and idioms, avoiding frequent use of polysyllabic words, using shorter sentences, and pausing frequently to avoid cognitive–linguistic overload on students (Brice & Roseberry-McKibbin, 1999; Roseberry-McKibbin, 1995a). Teachers can also slow down their rate of speech and rephrase and restate information to facilitate comprehension of information. Many teachers state things quickly one time. It is common for students to receive many directions during a short time period and have few opportunities to ask for clarification or seek help (Brice, Mastin, & Perkins, 1997). This makes learning very difficult for Hispanic students with LLD. Teachers can contextualize instruction by simplifying directions, using nonverbal cues to facilitate comprehension, paraphrasing, and repeating what they say (Roy, Roseberry-McKibbin, Rau, Lambert, McLean, & Madding, 2000; Saenz, 1996). Teachers need to use a multimodal approach to teaching; Hispanic students with LLD learn better when there are hands-on activities and visuals to accompany auditorially presented information. Teachers can use pictures, diagrams, and maps to illustrate concepts being taught. They can utilize overheads to make auditorially presented information more redundant (Brice & Roseberry-McKibbin, 1999). Teachers can also write daily schedules on the chalk- or dry-erase board and review these schedules at the beginning of the day, thus providing students with a preparatory set for what is about to take place. Use of lead statements to start lessons can cue students about what is going to occur (Brice, Mastin, & Perkins, 1997). These approaches are very effective for Hispanic students with LLD.

In order to further support these students, teachers need to review information very frequently (Roseberry-McKibbin, 1995a). One commonly quoted statistic is that the average person forgets 95% of what is heard within 72 hours of hearing it. Hispanic students with LLD who are learning English as a second language have even more difficulty. Thus, frequent review of information will help aid students' retention. It is also important for teachers to allow extra processing time for students; the average teacher waits for only two seconds after a question is asked. Allowing second language learners to take additional time to respond to questions will help these learners process the questions and formulate appropriate responses (Langdon, 1996).

Hispanic students with LLD not only frequently have difficulty with speed of processing information, they also often have challenges processing incoming information in noisy conditions. Teachers need to maintain a classroom atmosphere that is as quiet and nondistracting as possible in order to help Hispanic LLD students learn optimally. It is helpful to seat students near the front of the classroom where they can easily see and hear the teacher.

Teachers also need to be flexible and broaden the rules for what is acceptable in classroom interaction and participation. In several classrooms studied by Westby, Dezale, Fradd, & Lee (1999), it was observed that

> Hispanic teachers permitted and even encouraged students to engage in overlapping discourse to coconstruct their understanding of the tasks. The interaction style reported in this study is similar to that reported in other investigations of classrooms with Hispanic teachers and students . . . [these studies] have commented on the mixing of social talk and the academic business at hand and on communicating a sense of concern for the well-being of children and their families . . . . Social communication was used to relate personal experiences to the academic context, and humorous comments were made that appeared designed to create a positive learning atmosphere that was conducive to student participation (p. 61).

When SLPs collaborate with classroom teachers to help them facilitate Hispanic LLD students' self-esteem and use effective teaching strategies and styles, these students will experience greater academic success. In the next section, specific intervention techniques to further enhance learning for Hispanic LLD students are discussed.

Intervention Techniques and Strategies

Teachers and SLPs are always interested in specific techniques that can be used to promote learning and academic success for Hispanic students with LLD. The following techniques and strategies can be used in regular education classrooms, bilingual education classrooms, and in small groups of students receiving speech–language therapy. The techniques and strategies fall under four broad categories: (1) second language teaching, (2) promoting prevocational skills, (3) increasing oral and written vocabulary skills, and (4) enhancing literacy skills in Hispanic students with LLD.

Second Language Teaching Techniques

Most SLPs do not have background knowledge about effective strategies for teaching a second language to students. As was previously stated, it is ideal if LLD Hispanic students can receive intervention in Spanish as well as English. However, because many SLPs speak only English, it is important for these SLPs to use second language teaching strategies that are proven to be effective with second language learners. If SLPs can combine these second language teaching strategies with familiar speech–language treatment techniques, intervention with Hispanic LLD students will be much more successful. Several popular and highly effective second language teaching strategies are described in this section.

Total Physical Response. Total Physical Response (TPR) is an excellent technique for students in the earliest stages of learning English (Terrell, 1992). It utilizes bodily movement to help form stronger associations between language and its meanings than does dealing only in the abstract. It also makes language comprehensible to beginning students because it utilizes the visual and kinesthetic as well as auditory modalities. TPR can be used to teach verbs and nouns. Several illustrations are listed next:

> **INSTRUCTOR:** "Stand up" (instructor alone stands up).
>
> **INSTRUCTOR:** "Stand up" (instructor and students stand up together).
>
> **INSTRUCTOR:** "Stand up"(only students stand up).

(More commands can be added—for example, "stand up and pick up your pencil.")

> **INSTRUCTOR:** "Touch your eyes" (instructor alone touches eyes).
>
> **INSTRUCTOR:** "Touch your eyes" (instructor and students all touch their eyes).
>
> **INSTRUCTOR:** "Touch your eyes" (only students touch their eyes)

(More body parts can be added—for example, "touch your eyes and ears.")

TPR is fun, nonthreatening, and helpful for students in the early stages of language learning.

Conversational Routines.   Many Hispanic LLD students, especially those in the early stages of learning English as a second language, need practice in daily conversational routines and patterns to enhance interaction with others. Students can practice the following and other patterns and routines in a small- or large-group circle format (Terrell, 1992).

> *Routine 1*
> **STUDENT 1:** Hello. My name is _____. What's your name?
> **STUDENT 2:** My name is _____. What's your name?
> **STUDENT 3:** My name is _____. What's your name?

(The practice continues around the circle with more students.)

> *Routine 2*
> **STUDENT 1:** Hello. How are you?
> **STUDENT 2:** Fine, thanks. And you?

STUDENT 1:   I'm doing fine, thank you.

STUDENT 3:   Hello. How are you?

STUDENT 4:   Fine, thanks. And you?

STUDENT 3:   I'm doing fine, thank you.

(The practice continues around the circle with more students.)

Students can go around the circle and practice the above routines as well as others created by the SLP, thus obtaining experience in introducing themselves to and greeting others. Because some Hispanic students, especially those with LLD, are not assertive in initiating conversations, these routines are especially important to master.

Cloze Activities.   Cloze refers to the elimination of every so many words (e.g., every 5th, 7th, or 9th word) in a context. Many English as a Second Language books have published cloze activities. SLPs can also invent their own activities. There are several goals in using cloze activities: helping students predict, derive meaning from a context, and focus on the whole passage rather than isolated segments. Cloze activities help students read in segments rather than word by word. Cloze activities can be carried out orally for nonreaders but are best done in written format for students who read and write. An example follows.

Alice called the doctor's _____ to cancel an appointment _____ had made. She didn't _____ she could make it to the appointment because _____ had come up. The secretary cancelled the _____ and asked Alice if she _____ to to make another one. Because _____ needed to have a checkup, she made _____ appointment right away. The _____ checked the schedule to see what was available.

Again, cloze activities are excellent for helping students focus on and derive meaning from whole passages.

Backwards Chaining.   Backwards chaining is a technique for building phonological awareness and for helping second language learners accurately produce multisyllabic words in their second language. For example, if a student has difficulty saying "alligator," the student can repeat the word back, beginning with the last syllable and progressing syllable by syllable to the first syllable of the word. A specific example follows:

SLP: "Let's work on the word 'alligator.' Say 'tor.'"

STUDENT: "Tor."

SLP: "Good. Now say 'tor' five times."

STUDENT: "Tor, tor, tor, tor, tor."

SLP: Now, say 'ga.'"

STUDENT: "Ga."

SLP: "Now, say 'ga' five times."

STUDENT: "Ga, ga, ga, ga, ga."

SLP: "Great! Now let's try 'gator.'"

STUDENT: "Gator."

SLP: "Say 'gator' five times."

STUDENT: "Gator, gator, gator, gator, gator."

SLP: "Let's try 'I.'"

STUDENT: "I."

SLP: "Say 'i' five times."

STUDENT: "I, i, i, i, i."

SLP: "Say 'igator.'"

STUDENT: "Igator."

SLP: "Say 'igator' five times."

STUDENT: "Igator, igator, igator, igator, igator."

SLP: "Super! Let's try "all."

STUDENT: "All."

SLP: "Say 'all' five times."

STUDENT: "All, all, all, all, all."

SLP: "Now put it all together. Say 'alligator.'

STUDENT: "Alligator."

SLP: "Say 'alligator' five times."

STUDENT: "Alligator, alligator, alligator, alligator, alligator."

It is speculated that backwards chaining is so successful because if a student has been saying a word incorrectly for a long time, backwards chaining "breaks the cycle," so to speak, and gives the student a new and different framework for correct production.

Prevocational Activities and Intervention Strategies

When serving Hispanic LLD children, SLPs may not think about prevocational language goals and objectives. However, it is important to begin preparing children, starting at a young age, with some of the foundational skills they will need to eventually enter the job market. Foundational skills can be taught to younger students, while more specific skills can be taught to older students. With all students, SLPs need to address pragmatic skills that will be expected by employers and colleagues in the workplace.

Younger Students.   SLPs can engage in therapy activities that will help promote the following prevocational survival skills in younger Hispanic LLD students:

Personal Information
1. State first and last name.
2. State address and phone number.
3. State full date of birth.
4. State parents' or guardians' full names.

Time Concepts
1. State days of the week in order.
2. State months of the year in order.
3. Identify the current day and date.
4. Tell time to the hour on a traditional (not digital) clock.
5. Tell time to the half-hour on a traditional (not digital) clock.

Money
1. Label coins by name.
2. Express values of coins (e.g., "a quarter is worth 25 cents").
3. Label bills by name (e.g., "that's a $20 bill").

Survival and Safety
1. Verbally define the term *stranger.*
2. Describe at least two appropriate courses of action to take if a stranger approaches.
3. Demonstrate (using a fake telephone) how to dial 911.
4. Identify and describe circumstances when dialing 911 is appropriate.
5. Read common safety words (e.g., *fire, police, danger, caution*) and generally describe what they mean.
6. Verbally define the meaning of safety symbols (e.g., a skull and cross-bones).

If SLPs can help young Hispanic LLD students achieve these skills, the students will have a good foundation for acquiring more sophisticated prevocational skills as they get older.

Older Students.   Hispanic LLD students in grades 7–12 need to be preparing for vocations. SLPs should focus on increasing overall language skills that help students prepare to enter the job market. Following are some practical prevocational activities that SLPs can engage in with LLD Hispanic adolescents to help prepare them for the workplace:

1. Go through newspaper advertisements as an excellent activity for older students to increase their reading skills as well as building their knowledge about available jobs.
2. Require the student to go to three establishments and ask for job applications. Help with filling out actual job applications to assist older Hispanic students do a complete and acceptable job.
3. Conduct and videotape mock interviews; play the tapes back and analyze them with the students.
4. Help the student complete an inventory of strengths and weaknesses.
5. Require the student to create a job folder with a social security card, birth certificate, and other important documents.

One of the greatest services SLPs can provide for LLD Hispanic adolescents is to engage in some of the above activities to help the students prepare for the workplace. SLPs also need to address pragmatic skills that these students will need for vocational success.

Pragmatic Language Skills.   There is little research regarding the nonverbal skills of Hispanic students (Brice & Montgomery, 1996; Roseberry-McKibbin & Brice, 1999). However, it is well known that many Hispanic students have pragmatic language skills that differ in some ways from those of monolingual, mainstream, European American English-speaking students (Brice & Montgomery, 1996; Kayser, 1998a; Roseberry-McKibbin, 1995a; Zuniga, 1998). For example, as a sign of respect, many Hispanic children do not make eye contact with or speak much with authority figures.

To prepare students for the job market, it is imperative that SLPs gently and sensitively help these students to become bicultural in their pragmatics of language. That is, Hispanic students with LLD might use certain strategies, such as not making eye contact with unfamiliar adults, that are successful within their families and neighborhoods. However, in job interviews, lack of eye contact with the interviewer could cost a student the opportunity for a job. Thus, it is recommended that SLPs talk with Hispanic LLD students about "home" rules and "school and job" rules for social interaction skills. SLPs should emphasize that both sets of rules are legitimate and valid but that the sets of rules should be used appropriately depending on the context. Objectives for increasing mainstream pragmatic skills as expected in the workplace include helping the student to

1. Use appropriate eye contact.
2. Use appropriate body language.

3. Use proper introduction techniques.
4. Use an appropriate volume and rate of speech.
5. Use social amenities such as "excuse me" and "thank you."
6. Use facial expressions and head movements to show interest in the listener.
7. Initiate conversations appropriately.
8. Take conversational turns appropriately.
9. Shift topic appropriately by announcing topic shifts (e.g., by saying things such as "that makes me think of X. . .").
10. End conversations appropriately (e.g., by saying things like "I have to go now, but it was nice talking with you").
11. Take into account other people's viewpoints during conversations.
12. Make polite requests by saying "please" and asking questions instead of giving commands or making demands.
13. Accept compliments appropriately by saying "thank you."
14. Apologize appropriately when necessary.
15. Demonstrate appropriate telephone skills.
16. Request a clarification when information is not understood.

In summary, SLPs need to always bear in mind that eventually their Hispanic LLD students will be looking for jobs and striving to succeed in the workplace. Through addressing the areas described above, SLPs can help Hispanic LLD students prepare to succeed vocationally. Another area SLPs can focus on to help these students experience academic, social, and vocational success is to help the students build their vocabularies.

Increasing Vocabulary Skills: General Principles

When speech pathologists work with LLD Hispanic students, it is difficult to know "where to begin." The students have many needs, all of which seem urgent. Research and clinical experience indicate that one of the most pressing needs for Hispanic students with LLD is to learn vocabulary. The students can communicate with listeners if they have the appropriate vocabulary. With the appropriate vocabulary, these students can make meaning known to listeners even if there are grammatical errors. Consider the student who says, "I hungry—please need snack." The words "I, hungry, snack" are enough to tell listeners what they need to know to meet the student's needs although the sentence contains grammatical errors.

It is best if SLPs can teach common English words or concepts that children are already familiar with in Spanish, because this will promote faster learning (Kayser, 1998). It is important to teach students how to use formal word definitions, because this may facilitate students' performance in literacy activities. Dictionaries can be useful for this purpose (Gutierrez-Clellen & DeCurtis, 1999). Also, SLPs must remember that many Hispanic students have richer L1 vocabularies in some categories and richer L2 vocabularies in other categories (Gutierrez-Clellen, Restrepo, Bedore, Pena, & Anderson, 2000). For example, many Hispanic children will know school vocabulary in English but label home items more proficiently in Spanish.

Speech–language pathologists can apply these principles as they utilize the Thematic Redundance Approach, described in detail in the following section. The Thematic Redundance Approach is a vocabulary training paradigm that can be used to enhance the vocabulary skills of Hispanic LLD students.

Thematic Redundance Approach.   It was previously emphasized that although it is ideal for Hispanic LLD students to learn vocabulary initially in their primary language and then in English, the reality is that most SLPs are monolingual English speakers and do not have access to interpreters. Thus, SLPs end up teaching English vocabulary to students. Hispanic LLD students face two major hurdles in learning English vocabulary. First, English is a second or even a third language. Second, the LLD prevents these students from learning new words or concepts after only one or two presentations of the words or concepts. This difficulty with "fast mapping" is a major hurdle for Hispanic students with LLD. Because of this, these students need a great deal of redundance when new concepts/vocabulary items are presented. It is not enough to present new vocabulary words once or twice and expect mastery. Hispanic students with LLD need to have new words/concepts presented to them repeatedly in order for true learning and retention to take place.

In addition to redundance of presentation, Hispanic students with LLD also need to learn words in different contexts through different modalities. Consider the 4th grader who sees a picture of an apple. The speech pathologist trains the student to look at the picture and label it orally "apple." The speech pathologist then moves on to the next food vocabulary item. The difficulty with this typical teaching scenario is that the student will not retain the concept of "apple" given one or two exposures to it through merely seeing a picture and giving a verbal label. This student, to truly learn "apple" and remember it, must receive numerous presentations of the word in different situations through different modalities: visual, verbal, auditory, and kinesthetic. Ideally, students should see pictures, talk about, listen to, read about, and write about new vocabulary words.

One approach to this situation is Teaching Vocabulary through Thematic Redundance (Roseberry-McKibbin, 2001). Existing research documents the success of using themes to teach students (Beaumont, 1992; Brice & Roseberry-McKibbin, 1999; Goldstein, 2000; Hamayan & Damico, 1990). When SLPs use themes to teach vocabulary in a redundant manner, students are better able to learn and retain the words presented to them. In the Thematic Redundance Approach, students see pictures of target vocabulary words (visual), label the pictures verbally (verbal, auditory), see printed words (visual), orally define and discuss words (verbal and auditory), hear definitions and stories about words (auditory), write sentences using words (kinesthetic), and read stories using the words (visual, verbal, auditory). Words are presented numerous times in each thematic area (e.g., food, clothing) in order to ensure adequate redundance of the words. Clinicians can create activities and materials such as stories, word lists, games, and pictures to present multiple exemplars of each word.

Students begin learning new vocabulary words receptively and then move hierarchically on to expressive activities. Literature in second language acquisition documents that this is the ideal progression for learning vocabulary in a second language. Speech pathologists need to be able to document student success in learning new words. There must be a way to measure student learning quantitatively so that teachers, parents, insurance companies, IEP teams, and other involved parties will be able to assess students' progress. The Thematic Redundance teaching method provides short-term objectives as well as pre- and posttesting opportunities to assess learning success. SLPs can use these short-term objectives/benchmarks directly on individualized education plans of students. An example of teaching food items follows (adapted with permission from Roseberry-McKibbin, 2001).

Vocabulary Target: Food Items
Annual Goal
Student will demonstrate increased receptive and expressive vocabulary skills.

Short-Term Objectives/Benchmarks
Objective 1: When the SLP verbally gives names of food items, student will point to pictures of these items with 80% accuracy.

Example: **SLP:**   "Jose, point to APPLE." "Point to SANDWICH."

          STUDENT: Points to named picture.

Objective 2: When the SLP holds up a picture and says "Is this a(n) _____?" the student will verbally or nonverbally indicate yes or no with 80% accuracy.

Example: **SLP:**   (holds up a picture of milk): "Mazar, is this cheese?"

          STUDENT: No (says verbally or shakes head no).

          SLP (holds up a picture of ice cream): "Rebecca, is this ice cream?"

          STUDENT: Yes (says verbally or shakes head yes).

Objective 3: When the SLP gives a one or two sentence verbal description of a target word/concept and gives the student two choices of answers, the student will verbally supply the correct answer.

Example: **SLP:**   "Listen, Phong. This is purple and it is a fruit. It comes in bunches and is sweet. Is it GRAPES or CHERRIES?"

       STUDENT: "Grapes."

Objective 4: When shown pictures of food vocabulary words, the student will give verbal one-word labels with 80% accuracy.

Example: **SLP**   (shows picture of a tomato): "Samuel, what's this?"

       STUDENT: "Tomato."

Objective 5: When asked to verbally list three to five items in a given category, the student will do so with 80% accuracy.

Example: **SLP:**   "Rodrigo, tell me the names of four different foods."

       STUDENT: "Grapes, cheese, ice cream, orange."

Objective 6: When asked to define a target vocabulary word, the student will give a five +-word verbal description with 80% accuracy.

Example: **SLP:**   Tran, what is a SANDWICH?"

       STUDENT: "It has two slices of bread and something in the middle."

Objective 7: When given a target vocabulary food word, the student will use the word in a sentence with 80% accuracy.

Example: **SLP:**   "Maria, please use the word 'carrot' in a sentence."

       STUDENT: "A carrot is orange and it's a vegetable."

For more advanced students (written language):

Objective 8: When presented with a paragraph or word list containing the target vocabulary food word, the student will find and read the word out loud with 80% accuracy.

Example: **SLP:**   "Ginny, look at this story. Please find the word 'potato,' and read the word to me after you find it."

       STUDENT: (reads over story): "Potato" (reads word aloud).

Objective 9: When given a target vocabulary food word, the student will write a sentence containing the word.

Example: **SLP:** "Estera, please write the word 'butter' in a sentence.

STUDENT: Writes a sentence containing the word "butter."

Objective 10: When asked to spell a target word, the student will spell the word out loud with 80% accuracy.

Example: **SLP:** "Jaime, please spell the word 'hamburger.'"

STUDENT: Spells the word out loud.

A pressing need for Hispanic students with LLD is to increase their oral and written vocabularies. Using the preceding suggestions, SLPs can help students meet this goal. Increasing students' vocabularies will greatly assist these students in acquiring literacy skills.

Enhancing Literacy Skills in Hispanic Students with LLD

Many SLPs see themselves as having a role in facilitating literacy skills in students who are LLD; however, other SLPs do not. In one recent survey of professionals who worked with LLD Hispanic children, it was found that many SLPs did not consider themselves as playing an important role in fostering emergent literacy skills in these children (Ferruolo, Gonzales, Sireci, Adrianopoulos, & Boscardin, 1999). Ferruolo et al. recommended that SLPs change this attitude and consequent clinical practices because SLPs do play a critical role in facilitating literacy skills in students with LLD (Paul, 1995; Goldsworthy, 1996). The motivation of SLPs to work with facilitating literacy skills in Hispanic LLD students can be heightened by considering the uses of literacy in society. Literacy is needed for survival, employment, learning, political empowerment, personal relationships, pleasure and creativity, and to empower the mind (Baker, 1996).

General Literacy-Building Strategies. General literacy strategies SLPs and teachers can use with Hispanic LLD students include creating a literate class/therapy room environment, with many examples of print available, and encouraging collaborative learning where students work cooperatively on projects. Another useful strategy is to use predictable books, especially big ones with large print, where students are increasingly encouraged to fill in words and guess what is next. Reading aloud daily to students, while an obvious strategy, is a successful one that is frequently overlooked by SLPs. There is strong evidence that reading to children builds their language and literacy competence. When students hear stories read aloud, they hear fluent models of language production, which helps them acquire the grammar and vocabulary of printed English (Baker, 1996; Krashen, 1996). For some students who dislike reading because it is so difficult for them, being read to stimulates their interest in reading.

Other general ideas for increasing literacy in Hispanic LLD students include:

1. Writing captions for pictures or comics; this generates a great deal of language and allows students to be creative.
2. Journaling in English and/or Spanish, which helps students increase writing skills as well as express themselves.
3. Writing stories in English and/or Spanish, which is an excellent tool for developing narrative skills as well as overall written language skills. These stories can be handwritten or typed on a computer and printed out. Students can draw pictures to illustrate their stories. They can even make their own books. As a variation on this, students can shoot pictures and then write stories about the pictures they took.
4. Checking out library books, an excellent activity to develop students' knowledge of how to use libraries as well as increase their overall reading skills. Many students with limited English proficiency are unaware of what resources are available to them; encouraging library use increases students' awareness of what is available (Krashen, 1996).
5. Writing letters to pen pals or friends, which increases students' writing skills and encourages them to communicate in print. In one school district in Georgia, Hispanic students have pen pals in Mexico with whom they communicate via letter and e-mail.
6. Making family trees, which encourages verbal and written communication as well as increasing students' self-esteem and pride in their culture and heritage.
7. Preparing a newspaper, an excellent activity for helping students develop oral and written language skills. It also encourages interaction and cooperation with other students.
8. Learning to sight-read high-frequency words, which will greatly improve students' reading fluency. A list of high-frequency words in English is provided by Peregoy and Boyle, 1997 (p. 172). If students can learn to sight-read these words, reading will become much easier and therefore more informative and enjoyable.

As well as using general strategies for increasing literacy, SLPs can also specifically target three major skill areas that are critical to literacy success: (1) phonological awareness, (2) development of narrative skills, and (3) use of the preview-view-review approach to reading.

Increasing Phonological Awareness.   In order to build literacy skills, Hispanic LLD students fundamentally need to increase their phonological awareness skills. Phonological awareness skills are foundational for reading success, and thus clinicians who work with LLD Hispanic students should work to build a strong foundation of phonological awareness in these students. There are many excellent publications with detailed programs and practical suggestions for how to build phonological awareness skills (e.g., Goldsworthy, 1996; Robertson & Salter, 1997).

Following is a streamlined, practical hierarchy of objectives/benchmarks for SLPs to use to build phonological awareness skills in LLD Hispanic students (adapted with permission from Roseberry-McKibbin, 2001). These objectives are derived from the hierarchy explained in detail in Goldsworthy (1996) for increasing phonological awareness skills. Goldsworthy discusses three basic program levels (and describes numerous treatment activities within these levels) to build phonological awareness skills in students:

Level 1: increase word awareness by dividing sentences into words
Level 2: increase syllable awareness by dividing words into syllables
Level 3: increase sound awareness by dividing words into sounds

The following objectives/benchmarks can be used by SLPs when writing individualized education plans for Hispanic students with LLD.

Annual Goal
The student will demonstrate increased phonological awareness skills.

Short-Term Objectives/Benchmarks
Objective 1: With 80% accuracy, the student will count the number of words in a sentence that is prewritten or that s/he has written.

Example: **SLP:**   "Look, Guadalupe. Here is a sentence in our story. Count how many words are in that sentence."

STUDENT: Counts the number of words in the sentence.

Example: **SLP:**   "Jose, you wrote a good sentence using the word 'tomato.' Please count how many words are in your sentence."

STUDENT: Counts the number of words in the sentence.

Objective 2: When given a target vocabulary word, the student will identify the number of syllables in that word with 80% accuracy.

Example: **SLP:**   "Gustavo, how many syllables are in the word 'hamburger'?"

STUDENT: "Three."

Objective 3: When given a target vocabulary word, the student will identify the number of sounds in that word with 80% accuracy.

Example: **SLP:** "Maria, how many sounds are in the word 'butter'?"

STUDENT: "Four."

Objective 4: When the student hears a word that rhymes with a target vocabulary word, the student will identify that target word verbally or nonverbally with 80% accuracy.

Example: **SLP:** "Antonia, color the picture that rhymes with 'tease.'"

STUDENT: Colors the picture of the cheese.

Example: **SLP:** "Favio, what food rhymes with 'leg'?"

STUDENT: "Egg."

Objective 5: When the student hears the speech pathologist say a target word phoneme by phoneme, that student will state the whole word with 80% accuracy to demonstrate sound blending skills.

Example: **SLP:** "Tony, what word is this? C-a-ke."

STUDENT: "Cake."

Objective 6: When given a target vocabulary word, the student will identify the first sound in that word upon request with 80% accuracy.

Example: **SLP:** "Listen, Adriana. 'Hamburger.' What's the first sound in that word?"

STUDENT: "h"

Objective 7: When given a target vocabulary word, the student will identify the last sound in that word upon request with 80% accuracy.

Example: **SLP:** "Listen, Renee. 'Hamburger.' What's the last sound in that word?"

STUDENT: "r"

When SLPs develop foundational phonological awareness skills in Hispanic LLD students, achieving overall literacy skills will be greatly facilitated. A next important step in building literacy is to develop students' narrative skills.

Developing Narrative Skills.   Narrative skills underlie literacy, and it is extremely important for SLPs to help Hispanic LLD students develop a strong foundation of narrative skills so that reading and writing will be facilitated. Hispanic students may have narrative or storytelling rules that differ from those expected by mainstream, English-speaking, U.S. classrooms (Gutierrez-Clellen, 1999). Thus, to help Hispanic LLD students succeed in mainstream classrooms, it is imperative to help them develop the narrative skills that are consistent with mainstream school expectations.

General Suggestions.   Recent research (Brito, Perez, Bliss, & McCabe, 1999) found that Spanish-speaking children with language impairments, as compared with those whose language was developing normally, produced narratives that were characterized by a reduced number of evaluation statements. Implications of this study included the recommendation that SLPs may want to elicit more evaluative statements from LLD Hispanic children to help their narratives sound more personal and less unemotional.

Gutierrez-Clellen (1998) conducted a study of narrative performance of normally developing Spanish-speaking children of Mexican descent. One of her findings was that the task of retelling a story based on a short, silent movie elicited more complex language than the task of retelling a story based on a wordless book. Thus, SLPs and teachers might use movies as well as books to help promote development of Hispanic children's narrative skills.

It is important to ask students higher-order questions to facilitate narrative development as well as overall cognitive–linguistic skills. Thus, instead of just asking children for basic and general facts about a story, SLPs and teachers can challenge children to provide precise and accurate story information as well as to extend information (Goldstein, 2000; Pena & Valles, 1995). If children provide only partial information, SLPs can scaffold for the children until they provide specific answers. Also, as mentioned earlier, students can be asked to predict what will happen as well as give opinions and evaluative statements about the stories they read and hear. In order to help Hispanic LLD students internalize a paradigm for telling stories in a way that is consistent with mainstream school expectations, SLPs can use the following story guide described by Larson and McKinley (1995), who suggest the following specific story elements be used as a guide for narrators:

Beginning
Setting
main characters
location of story
time of story (when does it take place?)

Middle
Theme
What is the main idea of the story?

Events
What happens to the characters in the story?

Goals and Motives of Characters
What are the story characters attempting to do?
Why are the characters trying to do these things?

Reactions of Characters
How do the characters feel?
What are their plans?

End
What happens at the end of the story?
What lessons were learned from the story?

SLPs can make a chart for the therapy room with these elements written on the chart as a visual reminder to students. During narrative activities, the chart can be referred to in order to help students learn and retain story elements. Internalizing story elements will greatly help Hispanic LLD students improve their overall reading skills. These reading skills can be further enhanced by use of the preview-view-review approach.

Preview-View-Review Approach.   Reading is very important for Hispanic students who are learning English as a second language. Reading extensively contributes not only to improved reading ability but also to overall proficiency, which includes speaking and writing. However, Hispanic students with LLD have difficulty with reading and thus with academic subjects. They face three challenges: (1) there may be little home literacy experience in Spanish or English (Madding, 2000; Roseberry-McKibbin, 1995b), (2) academic materials are usually in their second language of English, and (3) their language-learning disability makes academic learning intrinsically difficult.

Speech pathologists often believe that they have to use special programs to help these students make literacy gains. In fact, SLPs can work collaboratively with the classroom teachers by using classroom textbooks, class notes, etc. and applying the following strategies of the Preview-View-Review (PVR) approach. The PVR approach is based on the premise that students need to use strategies to learn content area information in authentic situations that focus on meaning. Following is a description of the PVR approach that can help Hispanic LLD students increase their skills in reading class notes and books. This will facilitate their success in academic subjects. The suggestions can be modified and given to tutors as needed (adapted with permission from Roseberry-McKibbin, 1995a).

Preview
1. Help the student get an overview of the entire chapter by:
   - reading the chapter title
   - reading the introductory paragraph or section
   - looking at headings and subdivisions
   - examining the maps, illustrations, graphs, charts, pictures, and other visuals
   - identifying words in boldface and italics
2. Read (or have the student read) the main idea sentence of key paragraphs to understand and highlight the chapter's general concepts.
3. Highlight key vocabulary words and make sure the student understands these words. Have the student make a dictionary of new words learned.
4. Read the concluding summary or paragraph.

View
1. Read the text aloud and have the student follow along silently. Sometimes it is helpful for the student to put a finger under the words as you read.
2. At natural stopping points, ask students to explain in their own words what was just read. If students are working with a primary language tutor or clinician, then the information may be discussed in the primary language.
3. Help the student organize and outline readings from textbooks.
4. Review class notes with students, and have them explain them in their own words. Make sure they understand the concepts that were taught in class.
5. Scaffold for the student if the student cannot answer a question. For instance, if the student cannot answer the question "How many states are in the United States of America?" you ask an either/or question such as "Are there 45 or 50 states?"
6. Help students use context to enhance comprehension of material. For example, if students encounter a word they doesn't understand, ask them to keep reading and then guess the meaning of the word from the context.
7. Help students visualize what they are reading. This is especially important if there are no pictures or illustrations accompanying the text. Before starting to read, remind the student to "make pictures in your mind about what we read." For example, if the student is reading

about a certain geographic area, you can say, "Tell me what you think that looks like" or "Make a picture in your mind about that. What does it look like to you?" Students can even draw pictures that illustrate text.

Review

1. Help students look over chapter subdivisons and headings again to remind themselves of main ideas and themes
2. Ask questions about the content of the chapter. These questions can be
   - True–false questions
   - Either/or questions
   - General comprehension questions
3. Help students answer questions at the end of the chapter. This can be done orally or in writing. If computers are available, students can answer questions on the computer.
4. Have students summarize the chapter in their own words. This can also be done orally or in writing. If writing is used, a computer can be very helpful. Students can input the main points of the chapter, and if something was forgotten and omitted or put out of sequence, this can easily be changed. The student's final summary of the chapter can be printed out, and the student can keep it for review.
5. Ask students for their opinions of what was read. For instance, students can be asked:
   - What did you think were the most interesting things in the chapter?
   - Was there anything you disagreed with? Why?
   - What were the most important things in the chapter?
6. Ask the student if there are any questions about the chapter. For example, you can say, "Was there anything you didn't understand?" or "Do you have any questions about the chapter?"
7. Help the student make up possible test questions and then answer them. If there is a small group of students, they can exchange questions for practice. Readers can reproduce the following summary of the strategies for students so the students will have a handy, quick guide to remind them of the essentials of the PVR approach.

Super-Power Strategies For Better Reading
Before I read:
Look at title, headings, pictures.
Think about main ideas, vocabulary words.

While I read
Picture things in my mind.
Ask myself questions about what I just read.
Use the context to understand what things mean.

After I read:
Look at titles, headings, pictures again.
Summarize what I just read in my own words.
Ask and answer questions about what I just read.

Professionals can use the preview-view-review technique with class-room materials as well as specialty materials. When classroom materials are used, Hispanic LLD students will learn curriculum content while they also apply strategies for becoming more effective learners. Ideally, students will learn to use the strategies independently to assist themselves in learning content-area information.

Best Practices

As SLPs across the United States serve increasing numbers of Hispanic students, it is important to employ best practices when serving these students. Best practices involve the following strategies:

1. Begin with a foundation of knowledge about and sensitivity to socio-cultural variables that impact on therapy. These variables include the use of Spanish in the home, health care and beliefs regarding disabilities, and family life and practices that may impact intervention. With a foundation of knowledge about these variables, SLPs can successfully work with Hispanic students in intervention.

2. Best practices in intervention also include collaborating with regular education teachers and curriculum. Speech–language pathologists can share effective strategies, such as using themes and interest units, asking questions effectively, and facilitating higher-order, critical thinking skills. Classroom teachers also benefit when speech–language pathologists share suggestions for modifying teaching style and manner of delivery to enhance learning for Hispanic LLD students in the classroom. Best practices in this area include frequently reviewing information, utilizing a multimodal approach to teaching content information, and being flexible and broadening the rules for classroom interaction.

3. Best practices in actual intervention techniques include use of second language teaching strategies, teaching prevocational skills, increasing vocabulary skills, and enhancing literacy skills in Hispanic students with LLD. Successful second language teaching strategies, such as total physical response, help support English language learning for Hispanic LLD students. These students benefit greatly from learning prevocational skills that will eventually help them become a productive part of the U.S. workforce. It is also critical to foster vocabulary and literacy skills.

Employing best practices with Hispanic students with LLD is a multifaceted endeavor requiring a commitment to working with families, students as individuals, and school team members to foster success for the students. Hispanic students are a rapidly growing and important part of our nation's future, and they need and deserve the very best services that SLPs have to offer.

References

Anderson, R.T. (1998). The development of grammatical case distinctions in the use of personal pronouns by Spanish-speaking preschoolers. *Journal of Speech-Language-Hearing Research, 41*(2), 394–406.

Baker, C. (1996). *Foundations of bilingual education and bilingualism* (2nd ed.). Australia: Multilingual Matters.

Beaumont, C. (1992). Language intervention strategies for Hispanic LLD students. In H. W. Langdon with L. L. Cheng, *Hispanic children and adults with communication disorders* (pp. 272–342). Gaithersburg, MD: Aspen.

Brice, A. (2000a). Code switching and code mixing in the ESL classroom: A study of pragmatic and syntactic features. Advances in speech–language pathology. *Journal of the Speech Pathology Association of Australia, 20*(1), 19–28.

Brice, A. (2000b). *A comparison of language use by a bilingual first-grade teacher and a bilingual speech–language clinician: A case study of their impact on bilingual learners.* Manuscript submitted for publication.

Brice, A. (1993). *Understanding the Cuban refugee.* San Diego, CA: Los Amigos Research Associates.

Brice, A., & Anderson, R. (1999). Code mixing in a young bilingual child. *Communication Disorders Quarterly, 21*(1), 17–22.

Brice, A., Mastin, M., & Perkins, C. (1997). English, Spanish, and code switching use in the ESL classroom: An ethnographic study. *Journal of Children's Communication Development,19*(2), 11–20.

Brice, A., & Montgomery, J. (1996). Adolescent pragmatic skills: A comparison of Latino students in English as a Second Language and speech and language programs. *Language, Speech, and Hearing Services in Schools, 27*(1), 68–81.

Brice, A., & Roseberry-McKibbin, C. (1999). Turning frustration into success for English language learners. *Educational Leadership, 56*(7), 53–55.

Brice, A., Roseberry-McKibbin, C., & Kayser, H. (1997, November). *Special language needs of linguistically and culturally diverse students.* Paper presented at the American Speech-Language-Hearing Association Annual Convention, Boston, MA.

Brito, L., Perez, X., Bliss, L., & McCabe, A. (1999). *The narratives of school-aged Spanish speaking children.* Paper presented at the national convention of the American Speech-Language-Hearing Association, San Francisco, CA.

Cheng, L. L. (1996). Enhancing communication: Toward optimal language learning for limited English proficient students. *Language, Speech, and Hearing Services in Schools, 27*(4), 347–354.

Cummins, J. (1992). The role of primary language development in promoting educational success for language minority students. In D. P. Dolson (Ed.), *Schooling and language minority students: A theoretical framework* (pp. 3–50). Los Angeles: California State University, Los Angeles.

Damico, J. S., & Hamayan, E. V. (1991). *Multicultural language intervention: Addressing cultural and linguistic diversity.* Buffalo, NY: EDUCOM Associates.

Dodge, E. P. (2000). *The survival guide for school-based speech–language pathologists.* San Diego: Singular Publishing Group.

Dodge, E. P. (1994). *CommunicationLab1.* East Moline, IL: LinguiSystems.

Ferruolo, A. C., Gonzales, M. D., Sireci, S. G., Adrianopoulos, M., & Boscardin, M. L. (1999). *Techniques used to foster emergent literacy skills in Hispanic children.* Paper presented at the national convention of the American Speech-Language-Hearing Association, San Francisco, CA.

Goldstein, B. (2000). *Cultural and linguistic diversity resource guide for speech–language pathologists.* San Diego, CA: Singular Publishing Group (Thomson Learning).

Goldstein, B., & Iglesias, A. (1996). Phonological patterns in normally-developing Spanish-speaking 3- and 4-year olds. *Language, Speech, and Hearing Services in Schools, 27*(1), 82–90.

Goldsworthy, C.L. (1996). *Developmental reading disabilities: A language based treatment approach.* San Diego, CA: Singular Publishing Group.

Gutierrez-Clellen, V. F. (1999). Language choice in intervention with bilingual children. *American Journal of Speech–Language Pathology, 8*(4), 291–302.

Gutierrez-Clellen, V. F. (1998). Syntactic skills of Spanish-speaking children with low school achievement. *Language, Speech, and Hearing Services in Schools, 29*(4), 207–215.

Gutierrez-Clellen, V. F., & DeCurtis, L. (1999). Word definition skills in Spanish-speaking children with language impairment. *Communication Disorders Quarterly, 21*(1), 23–31.

Gutierrez-Clellen, V. F., Restrepo, M. A., Bedore, L., Pena, E., & Anderson, A. (2000). Language sample analysis in Spanish-speaking children: Methodological considerations. *Language, Speech, and Hearing Services in Schools, 31*(1), 88–98.

Hamayan, E. V. & Damico, J. S. (Eds.) (1991). *Limiting bias in the assessment of bilingual students.* Austin, TX: PKO-Ed.

Hart, B., & Risley, T. R. (1995). *Meaningful differences in the everyday experience of young American children.* Baltimore, MD: Paul H. Brookes Publishing.

Kayser, H. (1998a). *Assessment and intervention resource for Hispanic children.* San Diego: Singular Publishing Group.

Kayser, H. (1998b). Hispanic cultures and languages. In D. E. Battle (Ed.), *Communication disorders in multicultural populations* (2nd ed.) (pp. 157–196). Newton, MA: Butterworth-Heinemann.

Kayser, H. (1996). Cultural/linguistic variation in the United States and its implications for assessment and intervention in speech–language pathology: An epilogue. *Language, Speech, and Hearing Services in Schools, 27*(4), 385–387.

Kiernan, B., & Swisher, L. (1990). The initial learning of novel English words: Two single-subject experiments with minority-language children. *Journal of Speech and Hearing Research, 33*(4), 707–716.

Kohnert, K. J., Bates, E., & Hernandez, A. E. (1999). Balancing bilinguals: Lexical-semantic production and cognitive processing in children learning Spanish and English. *Journal of Speech-Language-Hearing Research, 42*(6), 1400–1413.

Krashen, S. D. (1996). *Every person a reader: An alternative to the California task force report on reading.* Culver City, CA: Language Education Associates.

Langdon, H. W. (1996). English language learning by immigrant Spanish speakers: A United States perspective. *Topics in Language Disorders, 16*(4), 38–53. Gaithersburg, MD: Aspen.

Langdon, H. W., with Cheng, L. L. (1992). *Hispanic children and adults with communication disorders.* Gaithersburg, MD: Aspen.

Larson, V. L., & McKinley, N. (1995). *Language disorders in older students: Preadolescents and adolescents.* Eau Claire, WI: Thinking Publications.

Madding, C. C. (2000). Maintaining focus on cultural competence in early intervention services to linguistically and culturally diverse families. *Infant-Toddler Intervention: The Transdisciplinary Journal, 10*(1), 9–18.

Madding, C. (1999). Mamá é hijo: The Latino mother-infant dyad. *Multicultural Electronic Journal of Communication Disorders,1*(2). [On-line]. Available: http://www.asha.ucf.edu/madding3.html.

Maestas, A. G., & Erickson, J. G. (1992). Mexican immigrant mothers' beliefs about disabilities. *American Journal of Speech–Language Pathology, 1(*4), 5–10.

Mann, D. M., & Hodson, B. (1994). Spanish-speaking children's phonologies: Assessment and remediation of disorders. In H. Kayser (Ed.), *Seminars in speech and language: Communicative impairments and bilingualism* (pp. 137–148). New York: Thieme Medical Publishers.

Mattes, L. J., & Omark, D. R. (1991). *Speech and language assessment for the bilingual handicapped* (2nd ed.). Oceanside, CA: Academic Communication Associates.

McNeilly, L., & Coleman, T. J. (2000). Early intervention: Working with children within the context of their families and communities. In T. J. Coleman (Ed.), *Clinical management of communication disorders in culturally diverse children* (pp. 77–100). Needham Heights, MA: Allyn & Bacon.

Midobuche, E. (1999). Respect in the classroom: Reflections of a Mexican-American educator. *Educational Leadership, 56*(7), 80–82.

O'Brien, M. A., & Huffman, N. P. (1998). Impact of managed care in the schools. *Language, Speech, and Hearing Services in Schools, 29*(4), 263–269.

Patterson, J. L. (1999). What bilingual toddlers hear and say: Language input and word combinations. *Communication Disorders Quarterly, 21*(1), 32–38.

Paul, R. (1995). *Language disorders from infancy through adolescence: Assessment and intervention.* St. Louis, MO: Mosby-Year Book.

Peña, E. D., & Valles, L. (1995). Language assessment and instructional programming for linguistically different learners: Proactive classroom processes. In H. Kayser (Ed.), *Bilingual speech–language pathology: An Hispanic focus* (pp. 129–152). San Diego: Singular Publishing Group.

Peregoy, S. F., & Boyle, O. F. (1997). *Reading, writing, and learning in ESL: A resource book for K–12 teachers.* White Plains, NY: Longman Publishers USA.

Perrozi, J. A., & Sanchez, C. M. L. (1992). The effect of instruction in L1 on receptive acquisition of L2 for bilingual children with language delay. *Language, Speech, and Hearing Services in Schools, 23*, 348–352.

Restrepo, A. (1998). Identifiers of predominantly Spanish-speaking children with language impairment. *Journal of Speech-Language-Hearing Research, 41*(6), 1398–1411.

Restrepo, A., Gutierrez-Clellen, V. F., & Galliano, R. I. (1999). *MLU analyses comparisons with Spanish-speaking children in the Southeast United States.* Paper presented at the National Convention of the American Speech-Language-Hearing Association, San Francisco, CA.

Restrepo, M. A., & Kruth, K. (2000). Grammatical characteristics of a Spanish-English bilingual child with specific language impairment. *Communication Disorders Quarterly, 21*(2), 66–76.

Robertson, C., & Salter, W. (1997). *The phonological awareness book (intermediate).* East Moline, IL: LinguiSystems.

Roseberry-McKibbin, C. (2001). *The source for bilingual language disorders.* East Moline, IL: LinguiSystems.

Roseberry-McKibbin, C. (1997). Working with culturally and linguistically diverse clients. In K. G. Shipley, *Interviewing and counseling in communicative disorders* (2nd ed.) (pp. 151–173). Needham Heights, MA: Allyn & Bacon.

Roseberry-McKibbin, C. (1995a). *Multicultural students with special language needs: Practical strategies for assessment and intervention.* Oceanside, CA: Academic Communication Associates.

Roseberry-McKibbin, C. (1995b). Distinguishing language differences from language disorders in linguistically and culturally diverse students. *National Association for Multicultural Education, 2*(4), 12–22.

Roseberry-McKibbin, C. (1994). Assessment and intervention for children with limited English proficiency and language disorders. *American Journal of Speech–Language Pathology, 3*(3), 77–88.

Roseberry-McKibbin, C., & Brice, A. (1999). The perception of vocal cues of emotion by Spanish-Speaking Limited English Proficient children. *Journal of Children's Communication Development, 20*(2), 19–25.

Roseberry-McKibbin, C. A., & Eicholtz, G. E. (1994). Serving children with limited English proficiency in schools: A national survey. *Language, Speech, and Hearing Services in Schools, 25*(3), 156–164.

Roseberry-McKibbin, C., & Hegde, M. N. (2000). *Advanced review of speech–language pathology: Preparation for NESPA and comprehensive examination.* Austin, TX: Pro-Ed.

Roseberry-McKibbin, C., Pena, A., Hall, M., & Smith-Stubblefield, S. (1996). *Health care considerations in serving children from migrant Hispanic families.* Paper presented at the Annual Convention of the American Speech-Language-Hearing Association, Seattle, WA.

Roy, M. B., Roseberry-McKibbin, C., Rau, C. L., Lamberth, E., McLean, K., & Madding, C. C. (2000). *Beyond linguistic barriers: Practical strategies for intervention with ESL students.* Short course presented at the Annual Convention of the California Speech and Hearing Association, San Diego, CA.

Saenz, T. I., with Huer, M. B. (1996). Intervention for bilingual/bicultural students with speech–language disorders. In H. W. Langdon and T. I. Saenz (Eds.), *Language assessment and intervention with multicultural students: A guide for speech-language-hearing professionals* (pp. 93–98). Oceanside, CA: Academic Communication Associates.

Seymour, H. N., & Valles, L. (1998). Language intervention for linguistically different learners. In C. M. Seymour & E. H. Nober (Eds.), *Introduction to communication disorders: A multicultural approach* (pp. 89–109). Newton, MA: Butterworth-Heinemann.

Sleeter, C. (1994). White racism. *National Association for Multicultural Education, 1*(4), 5–8.

Tabors, P.O. (1997). *One child, two languages: A guide for preschool educators of children learning English as a second language.* Baltimore, MD: Paul H. Brookes Publishing.

Terrell, T. (1992). The natural approach in bilingual education. In D. P. Dolson (Ed.), *Schooling and language minority students: A theoretical framework* (pp. 117–146). Los Angeles: California State University, Los Angeles.

U.S. Bureau of the Census (1999). *Statistical abstract of the United States, 1999* (119th ed.). Washington, DC: U.S. Department of Commerce.

U.S. Bureau of the Census (1996). *Statistical abstract of the United States, 1996* (112th ed.). Washington, DC: U.S. Department of Commerce.

Westby, C., Dezale, J., Fradd, S. F., & Lee, O. (1999). Learning to do science: Influences of culture and language. *Communication Disorders Quarterly, 21*(1), 50–63.

Wong-Fillmore, L. (1986). Research currents: Equity or excellence? *Language Arts, 63*(5), 473–481.

Wong-Fillmore, L. (1982). Minority students and school participation: What kind of English is needed? *Journal of Education, 164,* 143–156.

Zuniga, M.E. (1998). Families with Latino roots. In E. W. Lynch & M. J. Hanson (Eds.), *Developing cross-cultural competence: A guide for working with children and their families* (pp. 209–250). Baltimore, MD: Paul H. Brookes Publishing.

INDEX

234